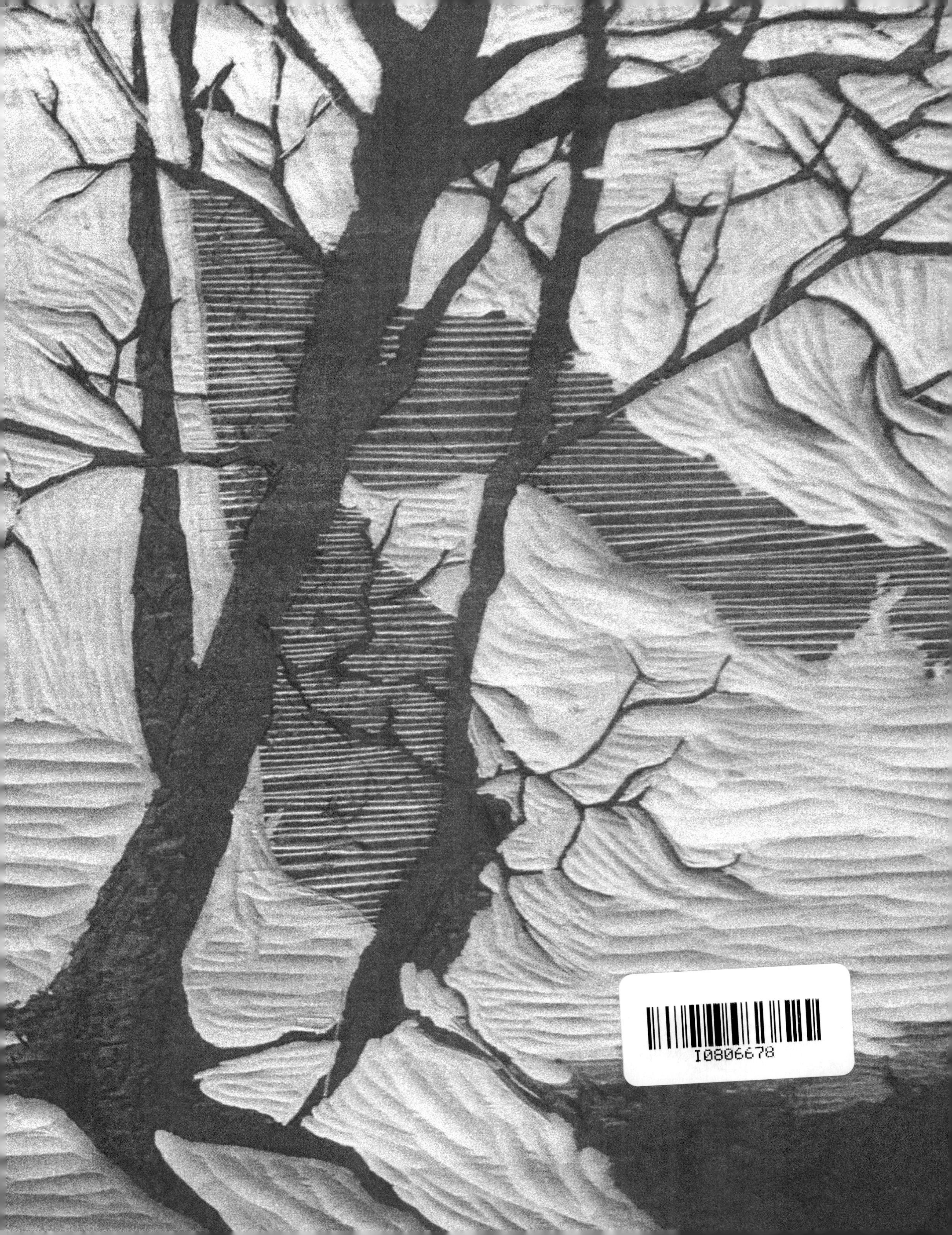

POPLAR CULTURE

the celebration *of* Esherick's tree

Edited by Paul Eisenhauer

Schiffer Publishing Ltd
4880 Lower Valley Road • Atglen, PA 19310

This book is published on the occasion of the exhibition ***Poplar Culture: The Celebration of a Tree***, curated by Paul Eisenhauer, organized by the Wharton Esherick Museum, and held at Historic Yellow Springs/Chester Springs Studio in Chester Springs, Pennsylvania, May 20 through June 10, 2012.

The exhibition and catalog were made possible, in part, by the support of the David A. and Helen P. Horn Charitable Trust, Schiffer Publishing Ltd., Hearne Hardwoods, Paoli Print, Samuel T. Freeman & Company, Moderne Gallery, and Rago Arts and Auction.

For information on the Wharton Esherick Museum, visit www.whartonesherickmuseum.org

Front Cover: James McNabb
Back Cover: Jack Larimore
Endsheet: Aurora McFee

Library of Congress Control Number: 2012937077

Type set in Ariel BT

ISBN: 978-0-7643-4208-0
Printed in the United States

Schiffer Books are available at special discounts for bulk purchases for sales promotions or premiums. Special editions, including personalized covers, corporate imprints, and excerpts can be created in large quantities for special needs. For more information contact the publisher:

Published by Schiffer Publishing Ltd.
4880 Lower Valley Road
Atglen, PA 19310
Phone: (610) 593-1777; Fax: (610) 593-2002
E-mail: Info@schifferbooks.com

For the largest selection of fine reference books on this and related subjects, please visit our website at
www.schifferbooks.com
We are always looking for people to write books on new and related subjects. If you have an idea for a book, please contact us at
proposals@schifferbooks.com

This book may be purchased from the publisher.
Please try your bookstore first.
You may write for a free catalog.

In Europe, Schiffer books are distributed by
Bushwood Books
6 Marksbury Ave.
Kew Gardens
Surrey TW9 4JF England
Phone: 44 (0) 20 8392 8585; Fax: 44 (0) 20 8392 9876
E-mail: info@bushwoodbooks.co.uk
Website: www.bushwoodbooks.co.uk

CONTENTS

FOREWORD ONE

Laurence Liss
Board President
Wharton Esherick Museum
Paoli, Pennsylvania

Challenge, inspiration and collaboration run throughout Wharton Esherick's life, and *Poplar Culture: The Celebration of a Tree,* curated by Paul Eisenhauer, reflects that pattern. Esherick faced many challenges in his life, but he survived them with his humor and vision intact. Indeed, from the challenges he produced great art.

At the Museum, we faced the challenge of removing a landmark tree. Following Wharton's lead, we decided to turn our misfortune into art. So we challenged artists to produce art from this tulip poplar tree. Poplar is the least sexy of woods – plain, bland in color, lacking the rich tones or exciting figure of more popular furniture woods. Of course, the artists rose to the challenge, as the content of *Poplar Culture* will attest.

Part of the Wharton Esherick Museum's mission is to inspire. When you spend time in this world that Wharton created, you feel his inspiration, and it is contagious. The participants in this show are among the generations of woodworkers, artists, and craftsmen who have been inspired by Esherick's vision, his lifestyle, and his work. Their work here shows that they clearly found inspiration in our challenge to them. We, in turn, were inspired by their enthusiasm for the project and by their generosity.

Esherick often said that the wood would tell him what to do – his work resulted from the conversation between his ideas and the wood. He produced the work in cooperation with his workmen, John Schmidt, Bill MacIntyre, and Horace Hartshaw. It was John Schmidt's skill in joinery that allowed Esherick to first realize his ideas of functional sculptural furniture.

We, too, depended on the cooperation of many to make this exhibition happen. The artists worked with our curator, Paul Eisenhauer, to make this show and book possible. We were also happy to be able to cooperate with our neighbor, Historic Yellow Springs/Chester Springs Studio, to stage this event. Their able and cooperative staff and beautiful galleries allowed us to present a show that could never have occurred in our limited gallery space.

Our thanks are extended to the artists, the folks at Historic Yellow Springs, and to the donors and sponsors of this exciting event.

FOREWORD TWO

Mark R. Ashton
President
Historic Yellow Springs
Chester Springs, Pennsylvania

In these challenging times for all cultural organizations, I have been preaching to fellow board members the benefits of collaboration between organizations whose mission is to preserve and celebrate art in all of its forms. Thus it was a special day when the leadership of the Wharton Esherick Museum reached out to Historic Yellow Springs with the novel idea of taking the small tragedy of a lost tree and converting it into the opportunity that is today *Poplar Culture*. It fits perfectly with the essence of Esherick-style woodworking: man taking the beauty that nature affords us to another level.

It is fitting that this event comes to our 142 acres of preserved woodland. We are blessed with the exhibition space that WEM lacks, and we hope that this will be the beginning of a long and productive collaboration between our students who paint and sculpt and the woodworker who does much the same with another medium. At an art faculty meeting last winter, one of our teachers brought up the subject of how this electronic age has taken us away from the satisfaction that comes from working material by hand. The statement resonated with me because, while I work by day as an attorney, I have taken solace at the end of the day in hand-sanding and finishing wood projects of my own. My hope is that this exhibition will inspire others to take up the chisel, the saw and the plane with a view toward celebrating a craft that has been a hallmark of this region's history for more than three centuries.

It is indeed a thrill to be a co-host to this special event.

ACKNOWLEDGMENTS

A project like this requires the work of many people. The generosity of everyone has made this an especially rewarding project. An acknowledgment here cannot convey the gratitude that I feel to everyone who helped make this exhibition and catalog a reality.

Friends volunteered countless hours of help to make this happen. Ray Kelso, George Manns, Ben Manns, Bob Zrebiec, Jesse Eisenhauer, and Bruce Haines helped move the logs from the bottom of the hill. Rick and David Vegso loaded the logs on the truck, and Rick drove them to Hearne Hardwoods in Oxford, Pennsylvania, where Rick Hearne had them milled and kiln dried. Gay Marshall and Cynthia Latham chaired the committee that put together the opening reception and organized the publicity for the show. Linda Dyke, James Mario, Johnathan Ericson, and Judy Kargher made up the rest of the committee. Bruce and Marta Simons, Nicole Riegl, and Janet Levy also provided logistical support. Lisa Lapp did a brilliant job of editing.

Paoli Print donated invitations to the event. Schiffer Publishing donated copies of the catalog to the artists and the Museum. Hearne Hardwoods donated the milling and drying of the wood.

Special thanks go to my co-workers at the Wharton Esherick Museum, Lauren Otero and Laura Heemer, who not only assisted the organizing committee in their work, proofread and edited this book, but also freed me from many Museum tasks so that I could concentrate on the exhibition. The exhibition would not have been possible without the support of the Wharton Esherick Museum's Board of Directors. Mansfield and Ruth Bascom have been an inspiration to me, as well as being a wonderful source of information.

Support from the David A. and Helen P. Horn Charitable Trust, Samuel T. Freeman and Company, Moderne Gallery, and Rago Art and Auction helped make this show possible.

My deepest gratitude goes to the 40+ artists whose work is depicted in these pages. All gave generously and eagerly to the project. They were also gracious in dealing with changing deadlines and demands, and with my errors as this process evolved in an organic way. The artists' stories of how Esherick and/or the Museum inspired and influenced them added a level of depth and meaning to this project that transcends the usual art exhibition and made it a joyous process. I think you will see that meaning and joy in the work contained here.

POPLAR CULTURE: GENESIS OF AN EXHIBITION

Paul Eisenhauer

People have coined the term "witness trees" to describe trees whose location has made them part of the history unfolding around them; they "bear witness" to important past events. The tulip poplar (*Liriodendron tulipifera*) that provided the wood for this project is one such tree. It witnessed the development of the genius of Wharton Esherick, modernist sculptor and acknowledged father of the American studio furniture movement. Theodore Dreiser, Sherwood Anderson, Jasper Deeter, George Rochberg, Sam Maloof, Wendell Castle, and other friends and clients of Esherick's passed beneath its branches.

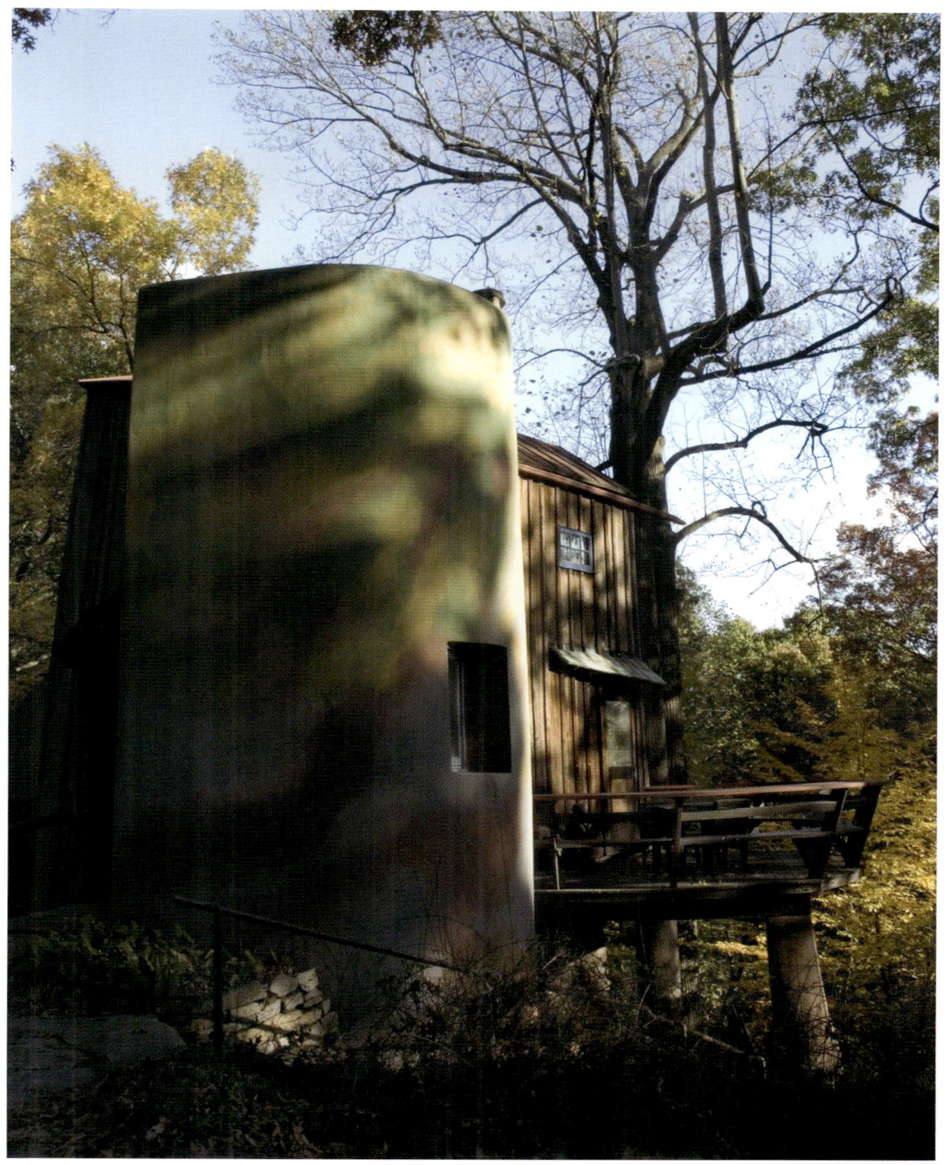

The distorted top of the poplar tree is clearly visible in this photograph of the studio from the west. *Photo by James Mario.*

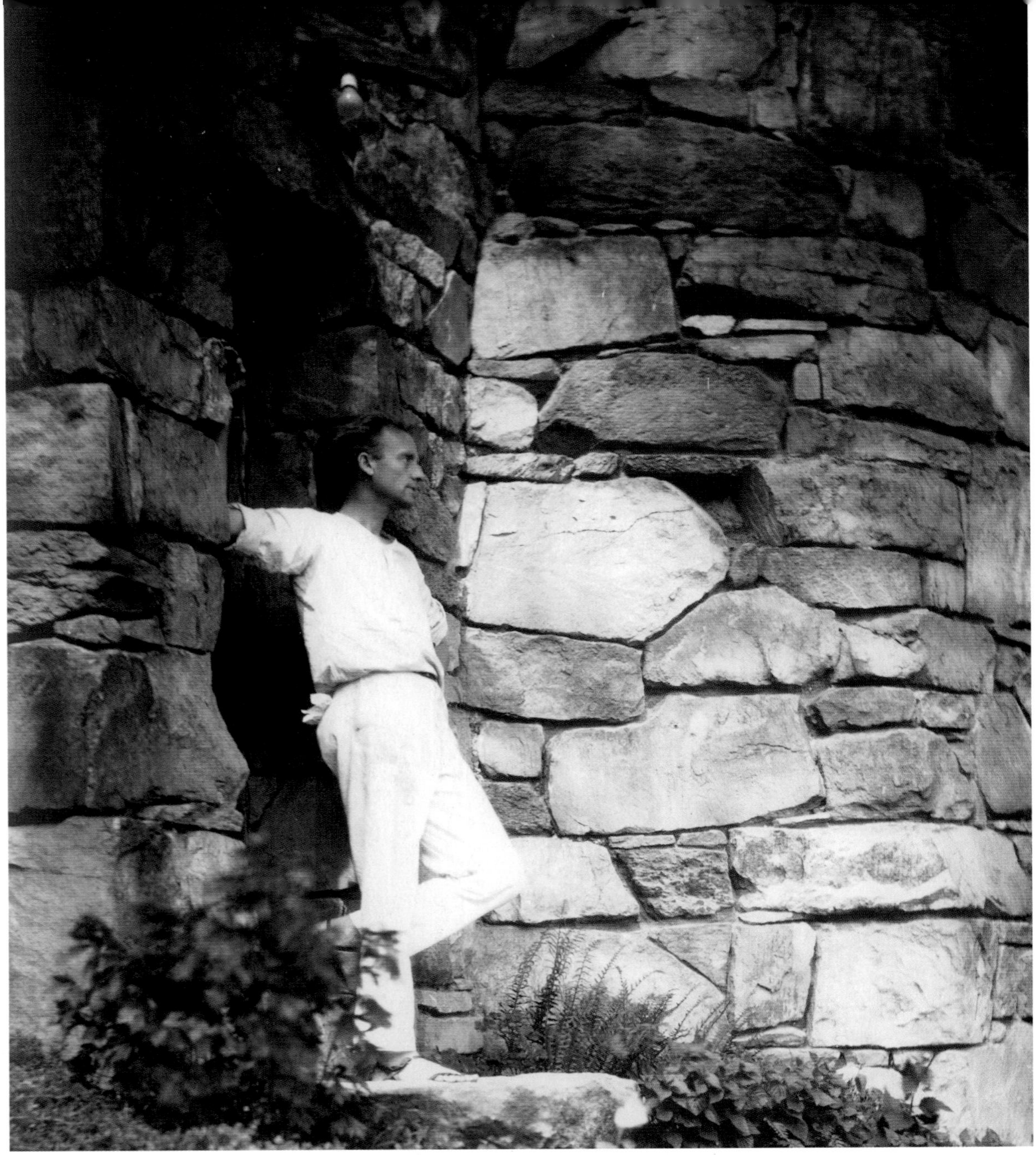

Wharton Esherick standing outside his studio, ca. 1930. From this position he would have been staring directly at the poplar tree. *Photo by Emil Luks.*

In 1926, Wharton Esherick decided to build a studio for sculpting that was large enough to hold his ideas and far enough from the family homestead that his children would not be underfoot while he worked. He chose a spot on the hillside above his family's small farm, beneath a giant leaning oak tree, in a clearing where the previous owner grew corn. His building plans were informed by the ideas of Frank Lloyd Wright, Rudolph Steiner, and the vernacular architecture of the region. The building process, however, was completely organic, growing from Esherick's ideas, Bert Kulp's and John Schmidt's skills, and the materials they had available. His work crew would arrive at the building site each morning not knowing what the day would bring until Wharton would direct them in that day's tasks.

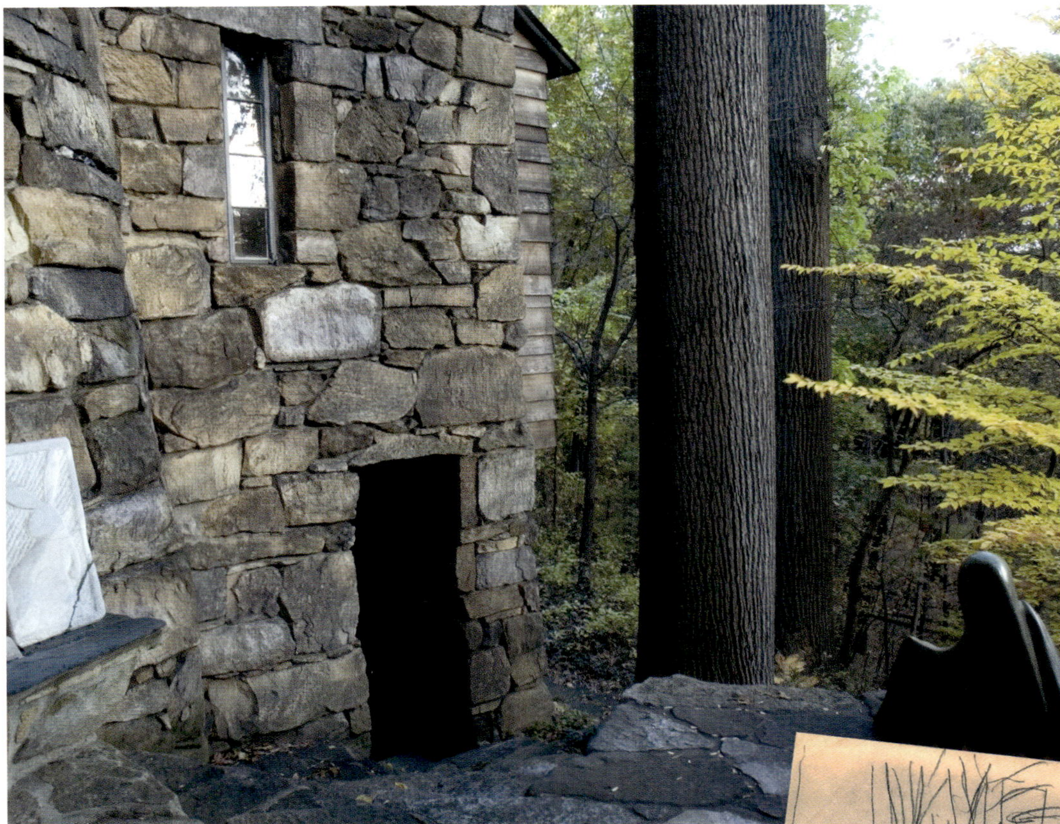

Poplar tree and studio basement door. *Photo by James Mario.*

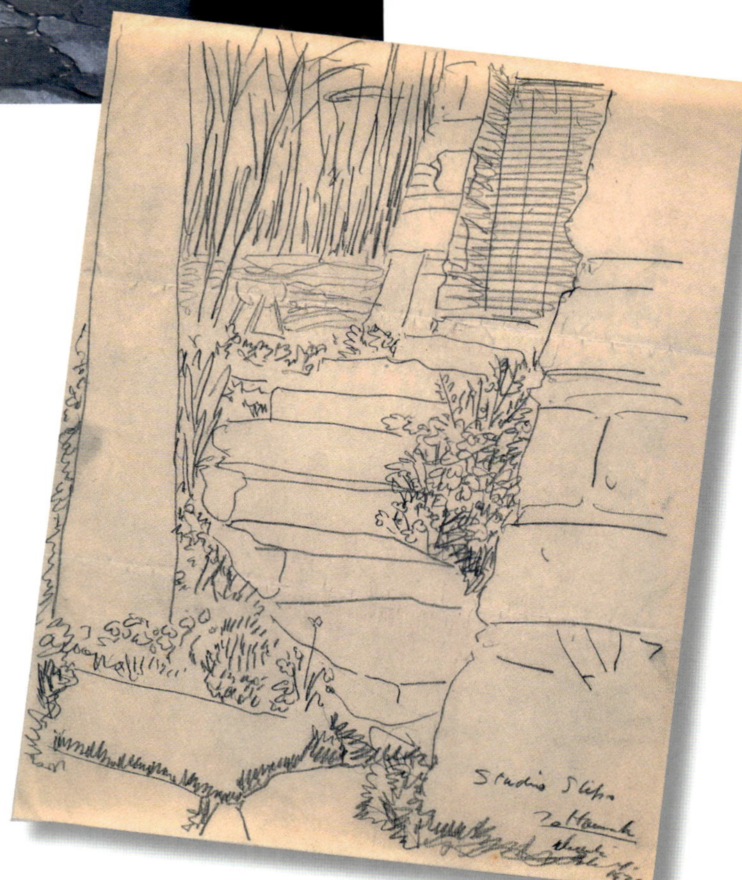

The dimensions of Esherick's studio were determined by the timbers he salvaged from an old mill in the valley. He situated it in relation to two large tulip poplar trees that stood about 15 feet apart on the hillside. He told his workmen who were digging the foundation to "Just start here, head for that tulip tree, and turn when I tell you."[1] When they reached the roots of the tree, he had them dig north and then west again. That northern wall held his basement door while the western extension held the front door to the studio. A stone stair curved around the east side of the tree connecting the two doors.

Esherick's drawing of the studio door and steps, showing the tree, 1931. *Drawing courtesy of Mark Sfirri.*

Poplars grow tall and fast, so even though they were large when Esherick began work, each was not much older than Esherick himself.[2] Old photographs show the poplar tree already straight and clear, with the lowest branches reaching out over the roof of the studio. The tree showered the studio with its spent flowers in the spring, shaded it in the summer, and dropped its yellow leaves outside Wharton's basement door in the fall, always threatening to clog the drain pipe that protected the basement from water running down the steps.

The poplar tree grew with Wharton, the subtle spiraling of the patterns on its bark undoubtedly affecting the forms he produced in the studio. When he built the wooden addition to the studio in 1940, the poplar tree filled the center of the dining room's picture window. Its majestic presence was inescapable.

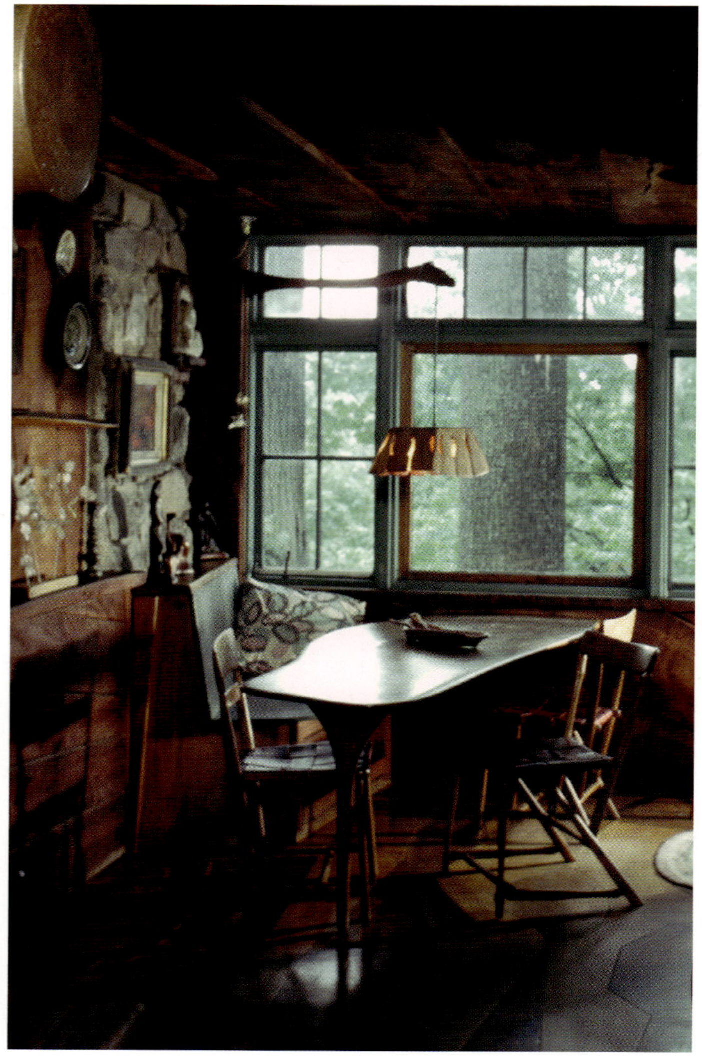

Esherick's dining room window. *Photo courtesy of the Wharton Esherick Estate.*

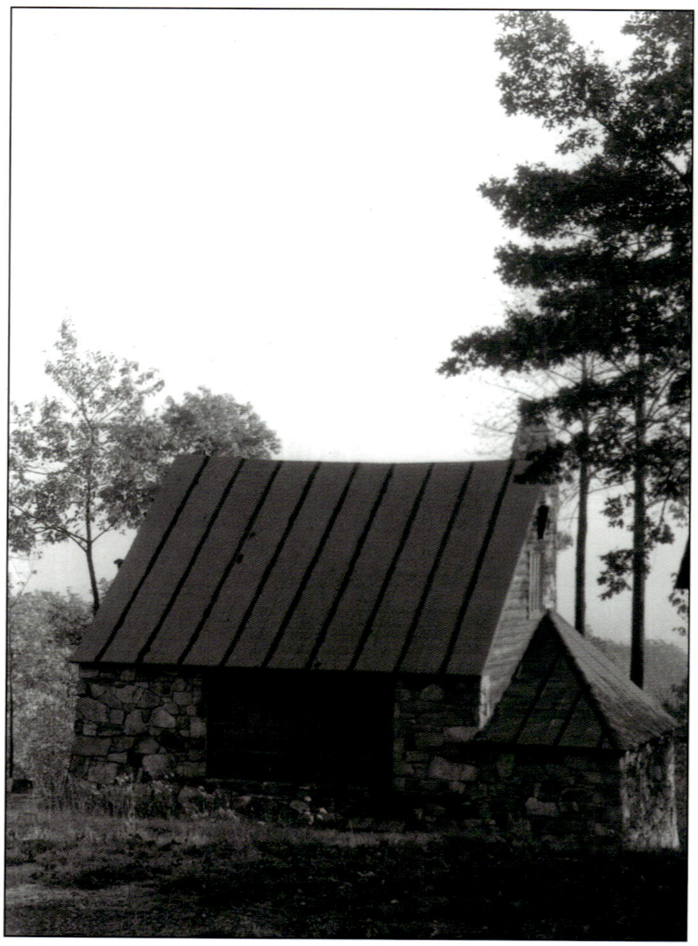

The studio, ca. 1930, showing the two poplars. The show poplar is to the right. *Photo courtesy of the Wharton Esherick Estate.*

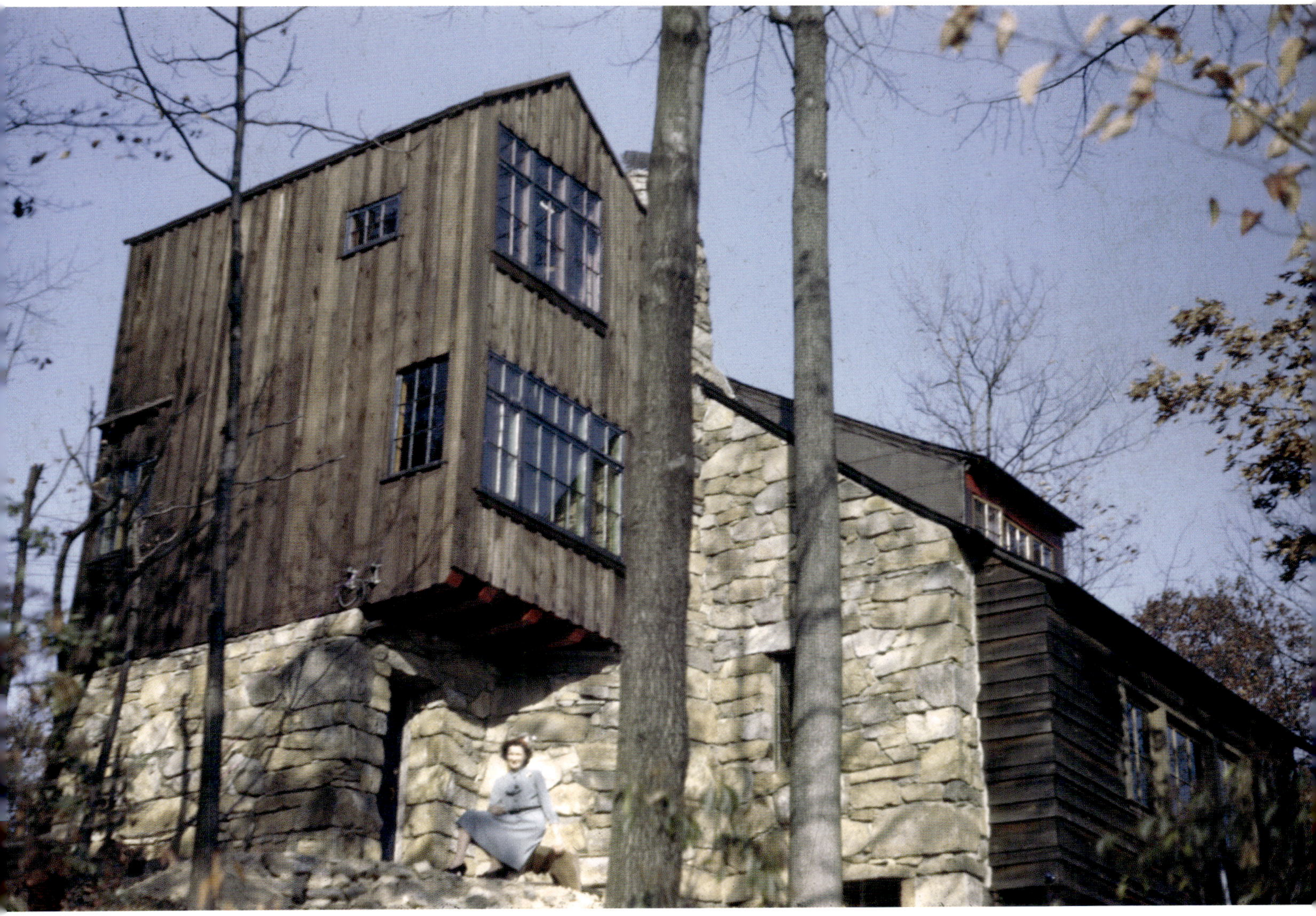

The studio ca. 1950, before the deck and silo. *Photo courtesy of the Wharton Esherick Estate.*

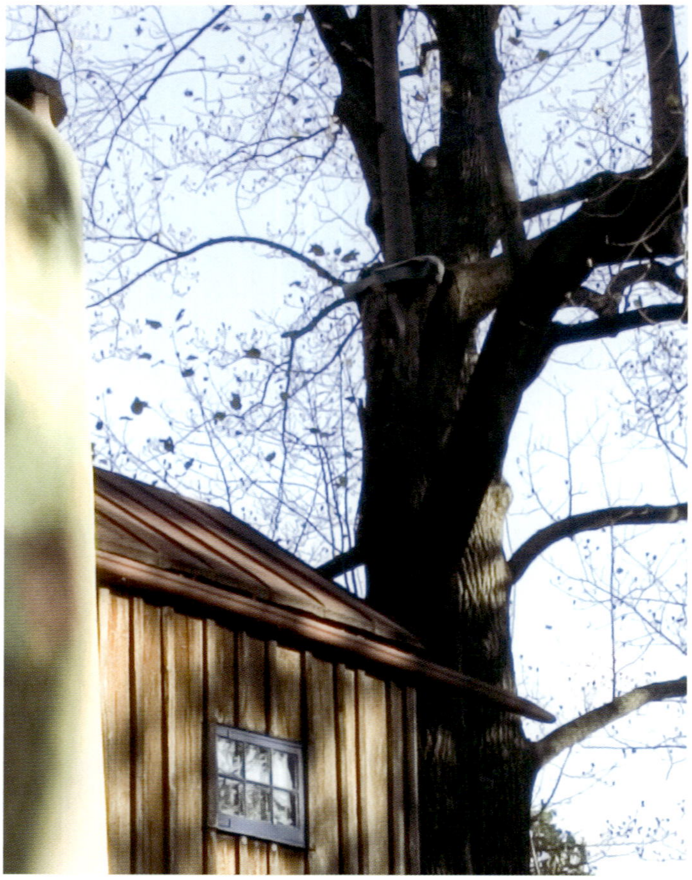

The poplar tree with its copper cap.
Photo by James Mario.

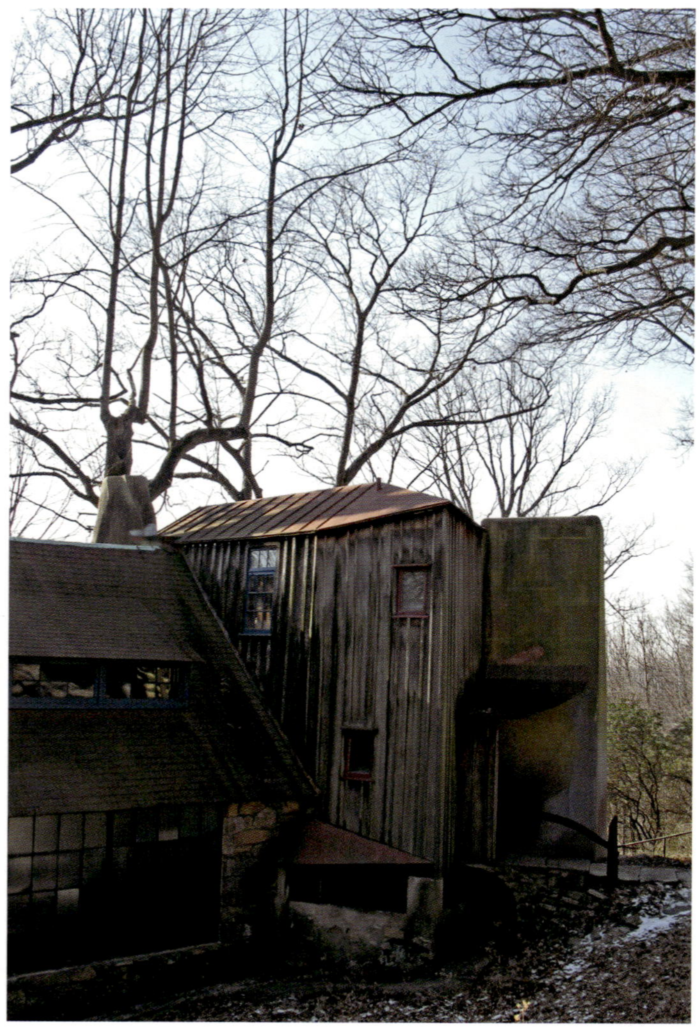

The studio with the mangled crown of tree rising behind.
Photo by Paul Eisenhauer.

In the late 1970s, the tree was struck by lightning. The damaged trunk was trimmed by arborists and its crown covered by a copper cap to keep water from draining into the center of the tree. New growth, like young saplings, quickly sprang from the old, pruned limbs. These branches grew straight and tall for 30 more years, giving the tree an odd profile that was visible over the top of the studio. Visitors would often ask what had happened to the tree and wonder whether the copper cap was a seat on top of the trunk. Its new, curious form helped define the environment of the studio for visitors.

Over time, the wood beneath the copper cap rotted, while the new branches grew taller, wider and heavier. In July 2009, the top four feet of the trunk's core fell, just missing the studio roof and landing on the basement steps. All the weight of the new growth was now supported by this hollow top with a rotting center. We knew it was time for the tree to come down.

However, a tree with such significance to the landscape and the studio could not just be taken down and abandoned. Following Wharton's lead, we decided to make something beautiful out of the problem that faced us. At the suggestion of board member Albert LeCoff, the decision was made to honor the tree by making art from its wood, and using the art to benefit the Museum.

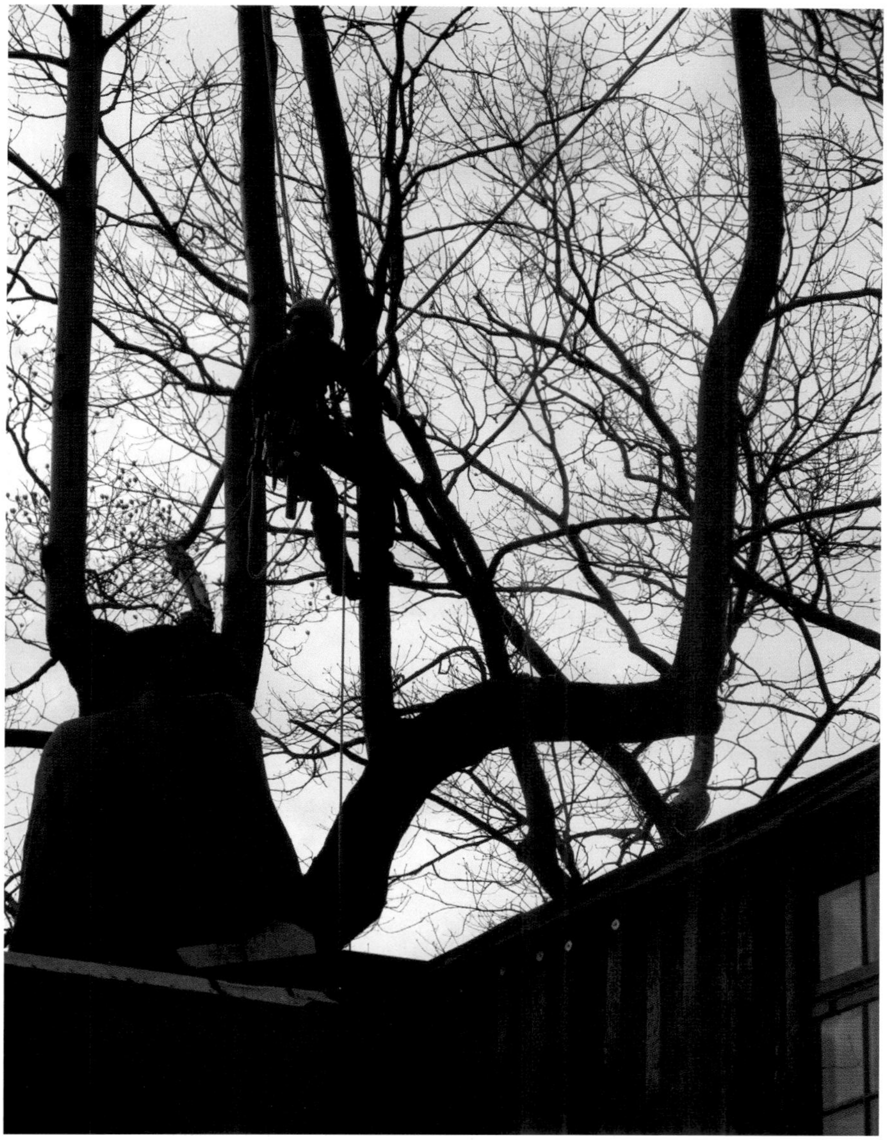

Arborist removing branches from the poplar tree. *Photo by Paul Eisenhauer.*

In January 2010, arborists came to cut down the tree. Suspended from ropes attached to the surrounding trees, they started pruning the branches at the top, carefully dropping the smaller ones and lowering the larger ones to the ground with ropes. The close proximity of the studio demanded such care. Some artists came out that day to watch the tree come down and to select specific pieces. The arborist did their best to cut the pieces as requested. The larger branch wood was cut into 3 to 4 foot long pieces and stacked in the woodshed. Woodturners, who often prefer green wood, took these sections over the next few months. The smaller branches were chipped, and the chips given to ceramicists to make wood-ash glaze.

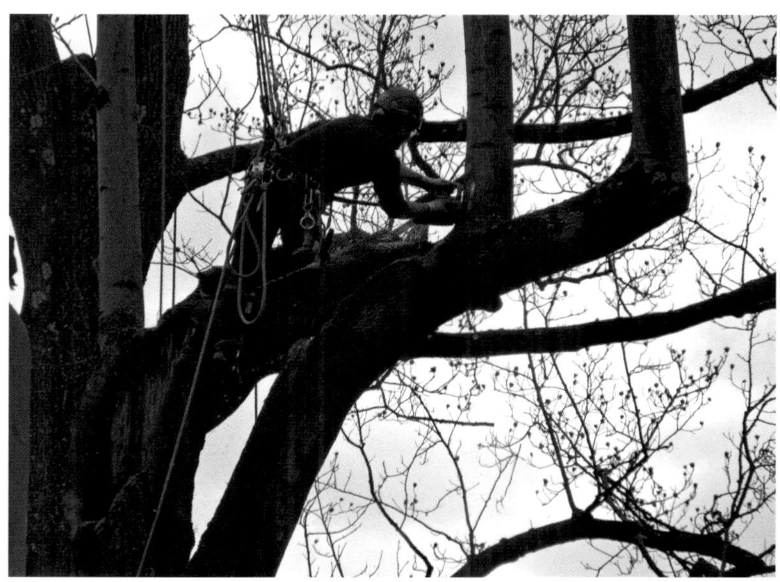

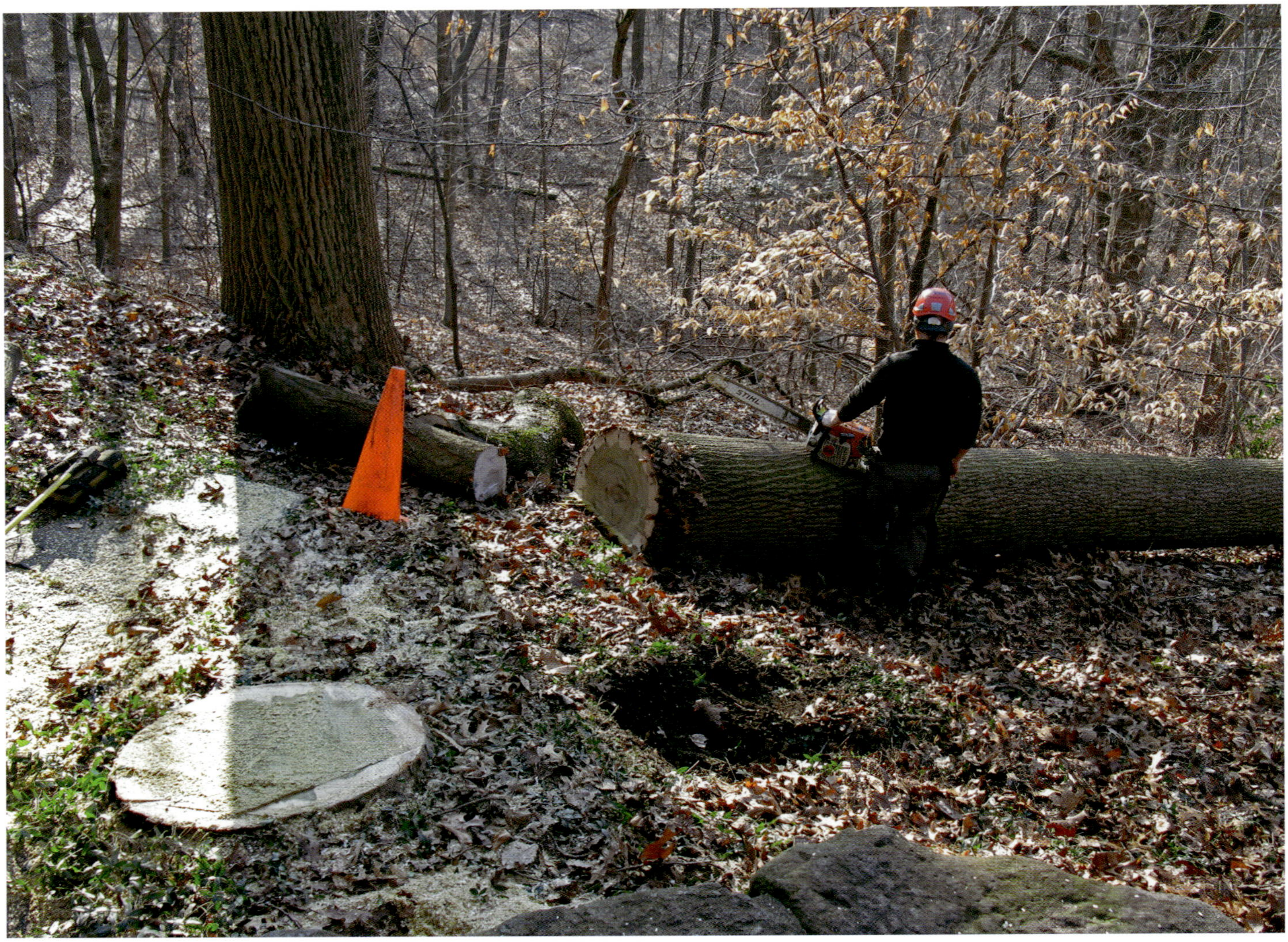

The stump and the trunk. *Photo by Paul Eisenhauer.*

It took a full day to remove all the branches, while the 40-foot long trunk was felled the next morning and cut into 8-foot sections. We wanted to mill most of these pieces into lumber for furniture makers, and leave some sections for artists who wanted to work with large pieces of trunk. We now faced the problem of moving these logs to a place where they could either be loaded onto a truck or picked up by the artists. With a diameter of 32 inches, the eight foot logs each weighed more than a ton. The Studio stood between the logs and the driveway, effectively blocking access to machinery that could move the logs. The only alternative was to roll them down the steep hill, where the abandoned roadbed of Ashenfelter Road could facilitate moving the logs to a truck.

One week later a fierce windstorm, blowing from the south, brought down trees throughout the region, including a large oak to the west of the 1956 workshop building. Despite our sadness at the tree's demise, we all felt relief that we had taken the poplar down before that storm. The high winds could have easily brought the unstable top down onto the studio.

Nature interrupted our plans to move the logs. In February we experienced the first of two back-to-back blizzards that dumped more than 30 inches of snow in the region. Any plans to move the logs would have to wait for the spring thaw.

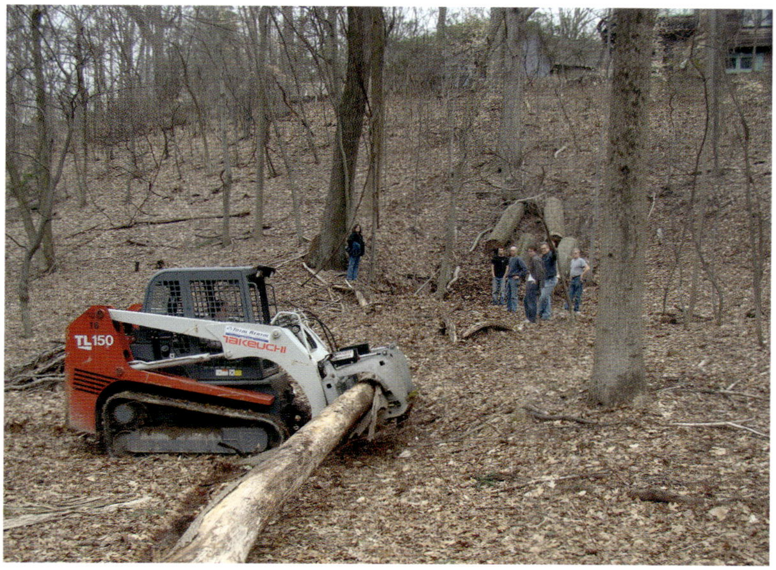

By late March 2010, the snow had melted and the ground dried enough for us to bring in the equipment to move the logs. We rented a Bobcat with a logging claw on the front, and George Manns proved adept at maneuvering it through the trees. Ray Kelso brought the logging chains that had once belonged to Ed Ray, Wharton's wood supplier, and they were used to drag the logs from the foot of the hill to the roadbed. The Bobcat carried them to the paved road, where they could be loaded onto a truck. Neighbor Rick Vegso brought some of the logs up to the Museum's parking circle and hauled the rest to Hearne Hardwood in Oxford, Pennsylvania, where they were milled into boards and kiln-dried. All of this labor was donated to the Museum.

George Manns clears fallen trees from the base of the hill behind the studio in preparation for moving the poplar logs. *Photo by Bob Zrebiec.*

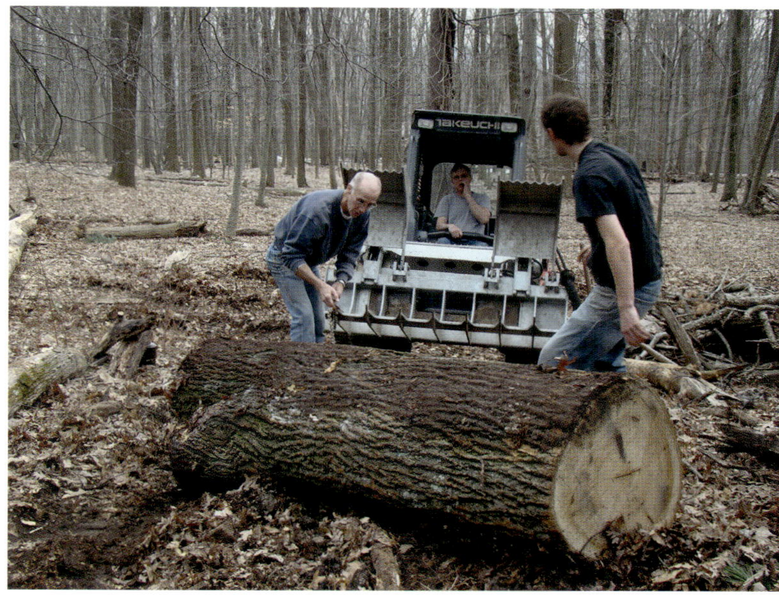

Ray Kelso (left), and Ben Manns (right) hook a log to the Bobcat driven by George Manns. *Photo by Bob Zrebiec.*

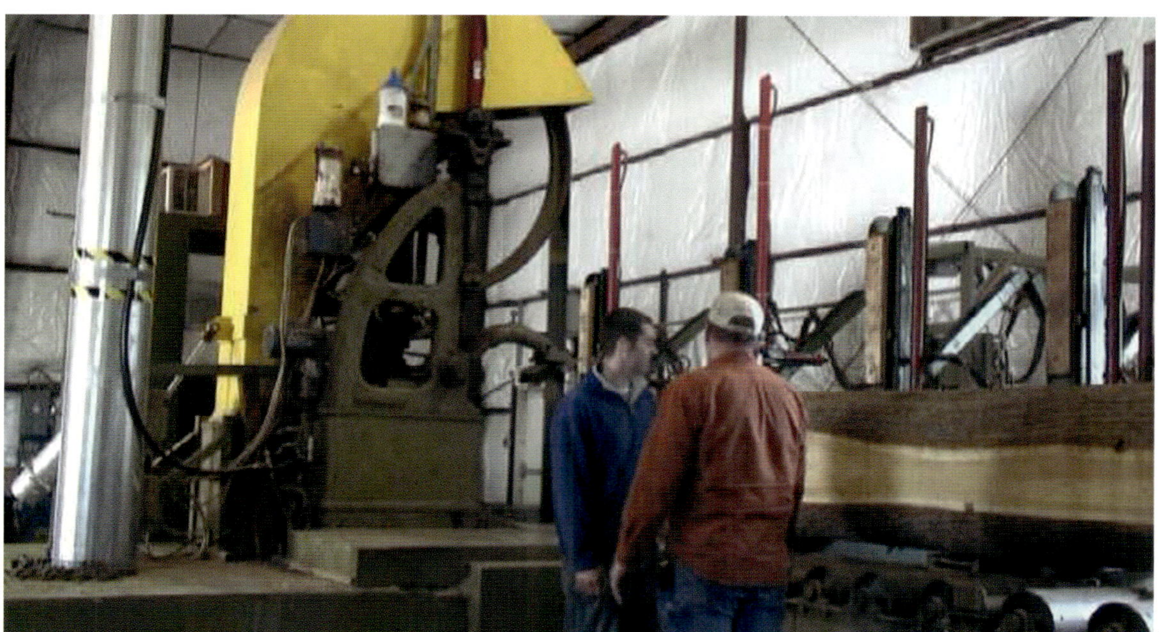

A log is cut using Hearne Hardwoods' 67" bandsaw. *Photo by Paul Eisenhauer.*

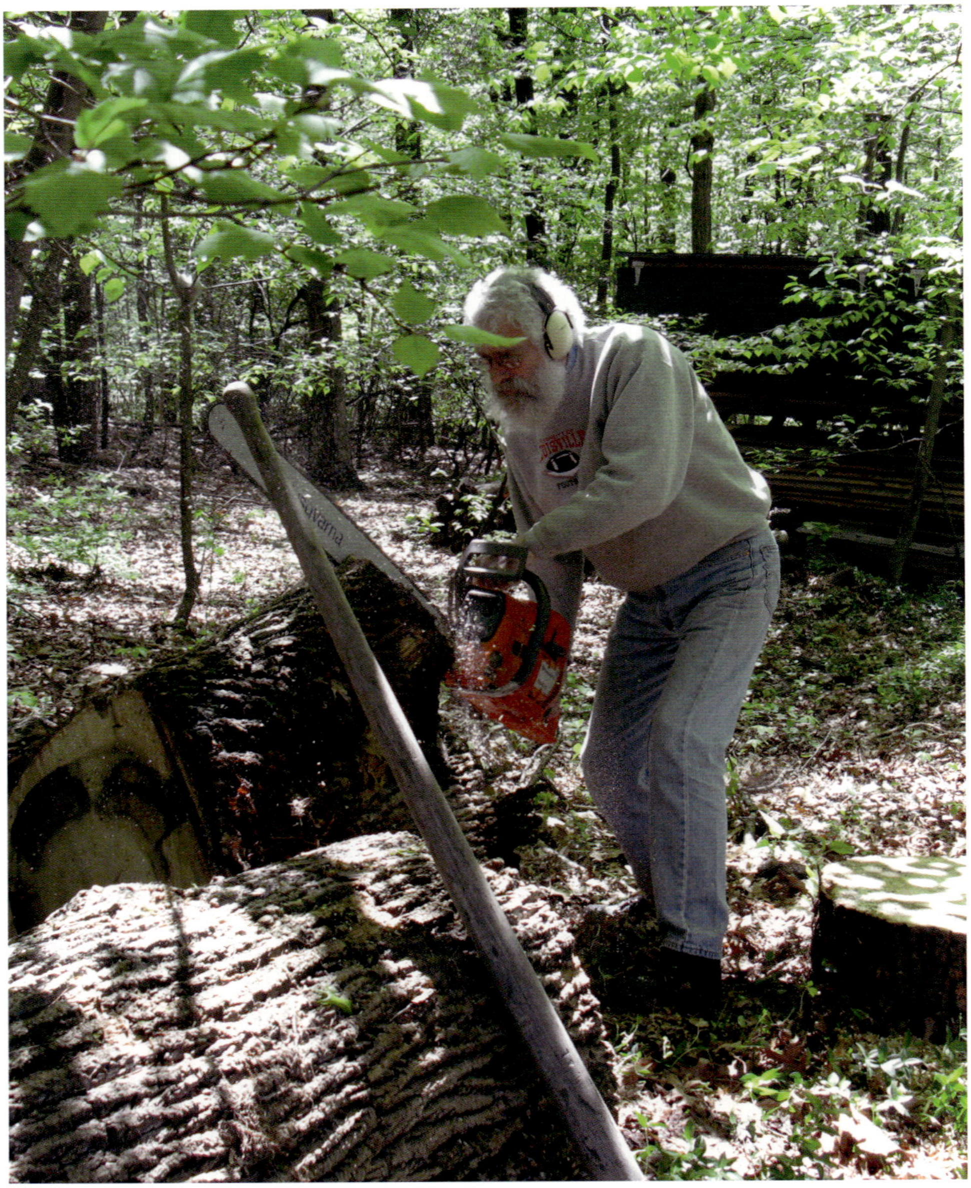

David Ellsworth cuts a piece of the trunk. *Photo by Paul Eisenhauer.*

We spread the word about the project and artists and woodworkers quickly responded. We had two goals in mind in selecting and inviting artists to participate. As Wharton was an artist who drew inspiration from a broad variety of arts and produced an eclectic body of work, our first goal was to create as diverse a show as possible – to show the vast range of objects that a single tree could produce.

Because Esherick has influenced and inspired hobbyists and professionals alike, we wanted all types of artists in the show. We made sure that established artists, emerging artists, and students beginning their careers were included. The enthusiasm with which the artists responded was both exciting and moving. All were thrilled by the opportunity. Many spoke of the impact that Esherick's work had on them and their work, while others expressed their appreciation for the Museum and the inspiration it provides.

The artists were not given direction on what to make, but were told to "honor the tree" in what they produced. They were also told to use only the poplar, not to decorate it with flashier woods. They could paint it, as poplar takes paint well, or leave it natural. The restriction was meant as a challenge: the tulip poplar generally does not get much respect from woodworkers. It is one of the softer hardwoods, with unpredictable coloration. It can range from a lovely cream color to a dark brown-black, with green, purple and brown streaks. The variegated colors make it hard to match boards for a pleasing finished piece. Usually poplar is used in drawer backs and sides, and on the back of case pieces – all places where it is not really visible.

This exhibition strives to show that poplar deserves more respect than it has been given. Esherick produced many beautiful poplar pieces. He would mix poplar with other woods, not hiding it, but keeping it where it could be seen. The color variations, rather than being a problem, were used as accents in the wood. The sideboard that he made in 1969 for his neighbors, the Hiestands, is a wonderful example of this effect.

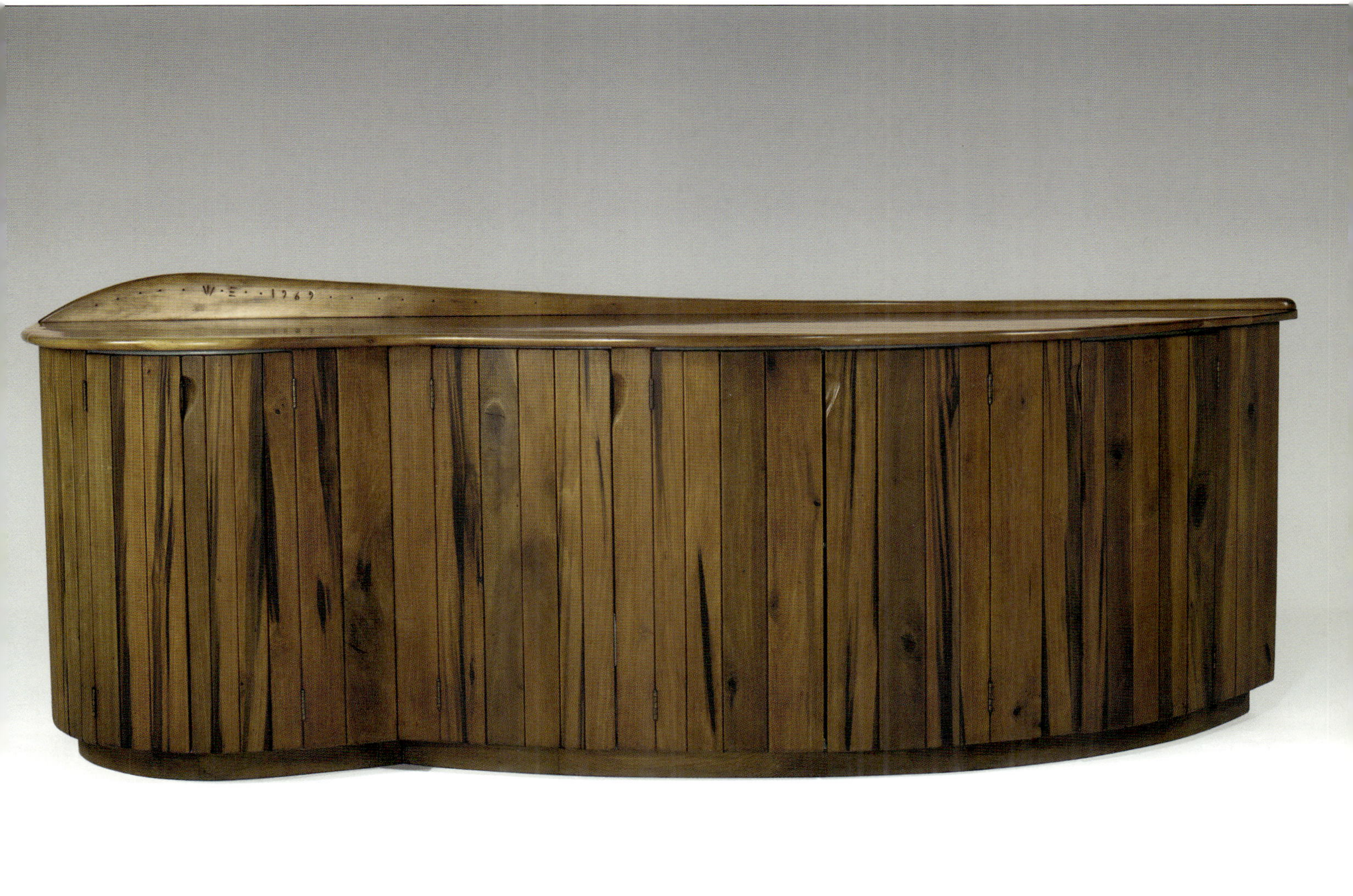

1969 Poplar Sideboard made by Wharton Esherick for his friend and neighbor, Nancy Hiestand. *Photo courtesy of David Rago Arts and Auction.*

Carved poplar end of the sofa in Esherick's bedroom. The sofa was originally made for the Bok House reading room and was included in the Pennsylvania Hill House exhibit at the 1940 World's Fair in New York City. *Photo by Paul Eisenhauer.*

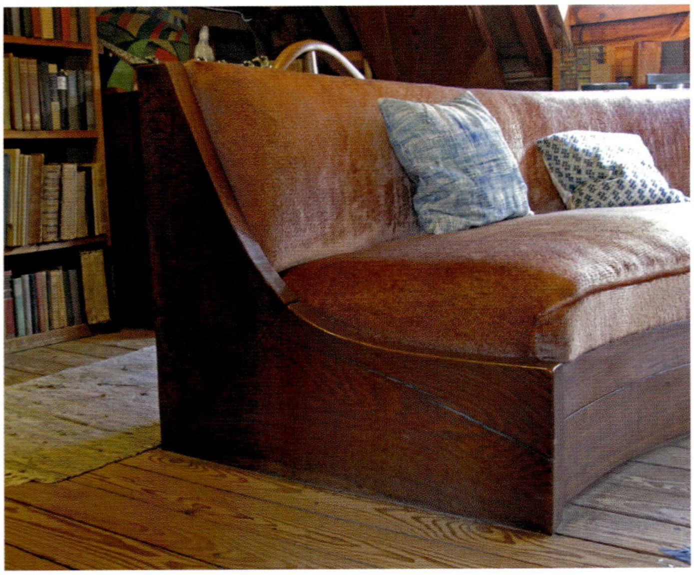

Esherick also took advantage of the long and wide boards that were plentiful in this fast-growing, straight tree. He used poplar for the large end blocks of the sofa included in the 1940 World's Fair in New York, which is now in the Studio bedroom. Wide poplar boards were also a favorite for paneling, as seen in the wall paneling and window screen that Wharton made for Larry and Alice Seiver's home in Villanova, Pennsylvania.

The artists in this show have risen to our challenge. The body of work is clearly diverse and beautiful. Some have designed pieces that accentuate the color variations in tulip poplar, while others have painted or stained the wood. A few chose not to follow the rules (as artists are wont to do), and used other woods as accents – though all kept the poplar as the central element of their work. Woodturners have produced wonderful pieces that range in style and complexity. Furniture in the exhibit ranges from traditional to modern, from rustic to refined. Natural edges and forms mix with imaginative designs. The direct influence of Esherick is evident in some pieces, while others follow different muses. As one would expect in an Esherick-inspired show, there is plenty of functional sculpture. What is evident in all the work is that the artists have been inspired by this man, this tree and this challenge.

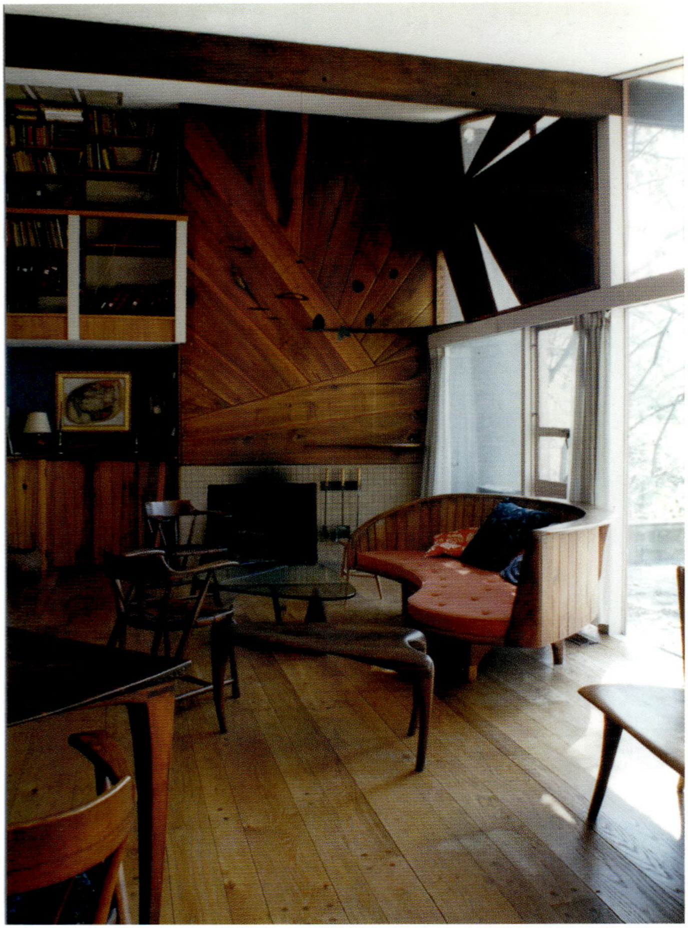

The living room of Lawrence and Alice Seiver with the Esherick's 1960 large poplar panel and window screen. *Photo by Mansfield Bascom.*

End notes

1. Bascom, Mansfield, 2010, *Wharton Esherick: The Journey of a Creative Mind*, New York: Abrams, p.70.
2. There were around 135 rings when the tree was cut down, making it approximately a decade older than Esherick.

THE WORK

Ken Bell

I have a long history of making "things" and have channeled that interest into making baskets. It is important to me that my baskets are attractive and have function. Symmetry, which is the harmony of arrangement, is an integral part of making a basket visually appealing, as well as making it work for its intended use.

I have used different types of wood, but have found white oak to be the best basket wood for my woven baskets. To use poplar for a basket in the style I made for the show, works just fine because this style does not require severe bends. I use white cedar for the bottoms of all my baskets; this helps the basket keep its shape and the cedar does not rot easily.

To take trees out of my woods, and turn the wood into a pretty, functional, and strong basket, is a very satisfying thing to do. Each tree has an unknown potential until it is opened, and folks always have ideas for a new basket, so getting bored is out of the question. I have been making baskets for twenty-two years and will continue as long as I am able.

Poplar Splint Basket (2012)
Tulip poplar, white cedar, leather
10.5" h (without handles) x 10.75" diam.

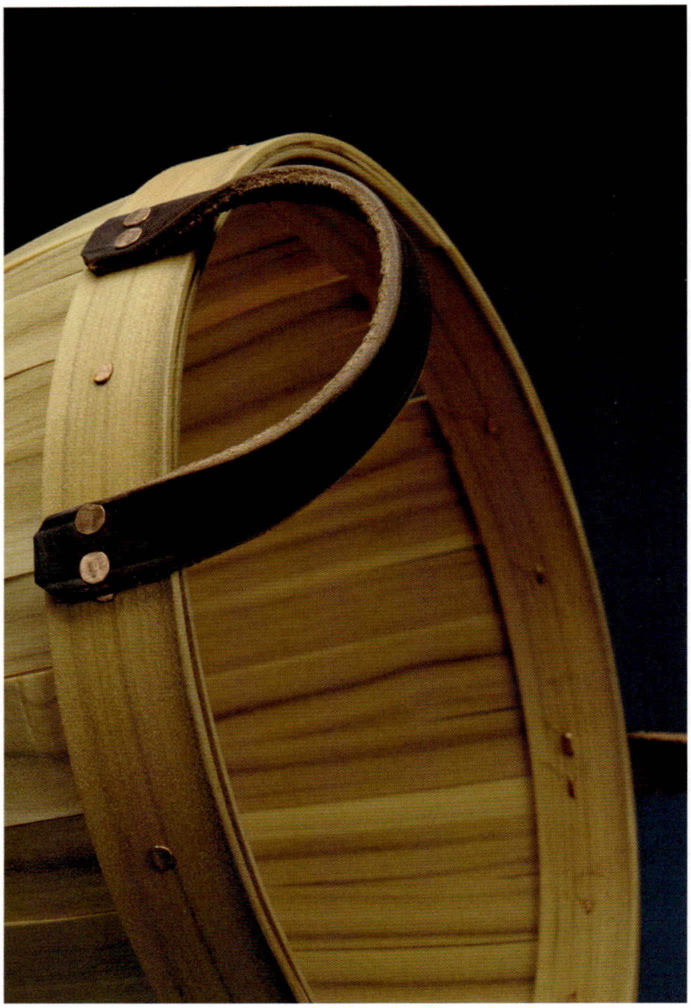

Photo by James Mario.

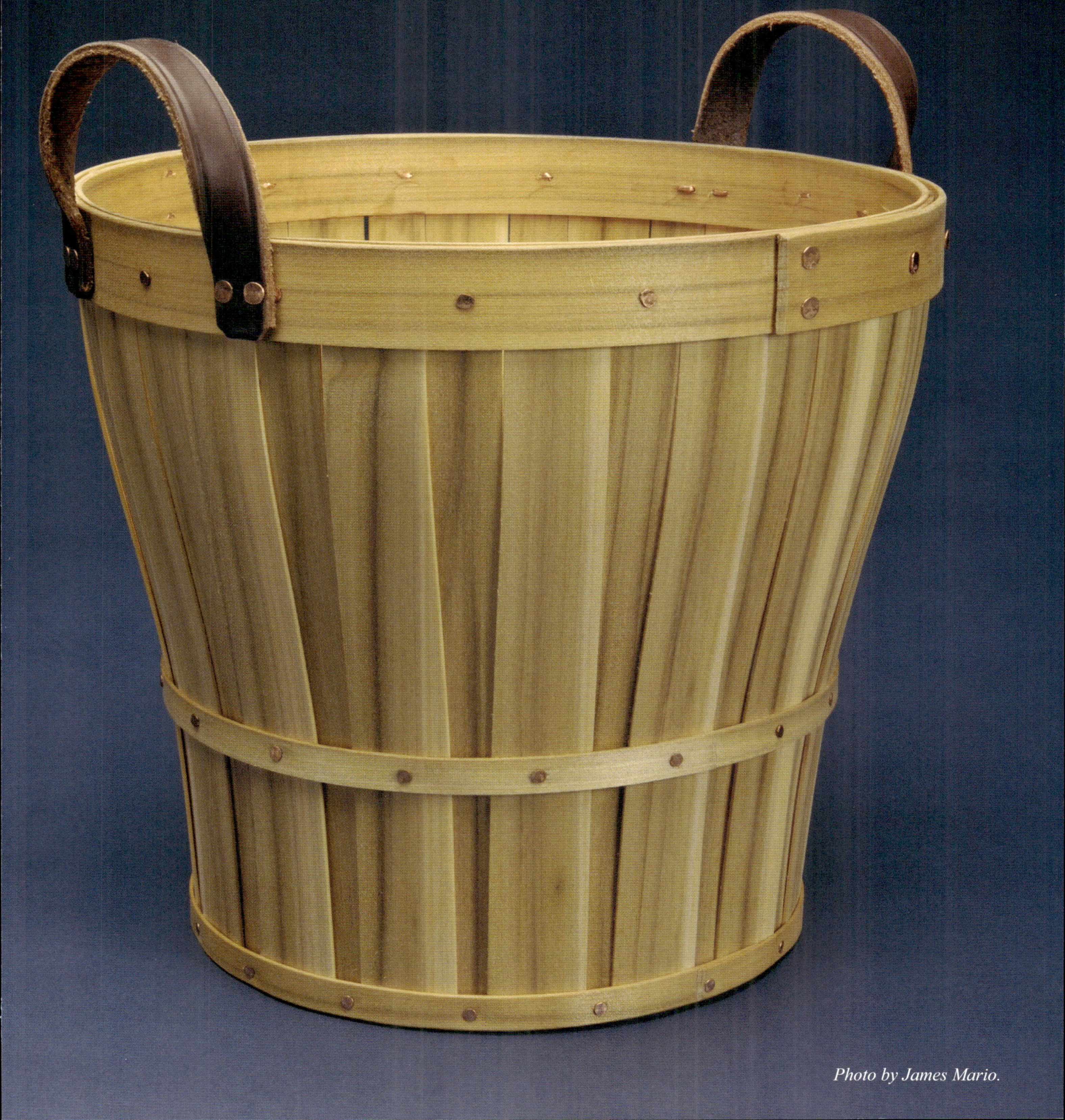

Photo by James Mario.

Michael Biddison

I refer to my artworks as "Shrubbi" which is my own word for transformed rubbish. Rubbish is enchanting. Creating Shrubbi is a process of reincarnation, it is finding, combining, and harmonizing magnetic chunks of stuff, overlapping their stories into new creatures. Rubbish is something that does not exist in nature. Rubbish, garbage, refuse, and trash are modern man-made concepts. Nature uses everything. My art also uses everything. Whether the medium is found wood, ancient architectural fragments, car parts, or discarded Plexiglass, I intend to create experiences through objects and performance that celebrate the creative and soulful possibilities of every day life.

Listening for Boats, an Elemental Throne (2012)
Tulip poplar, copper, epoxy resin, tung oil
26" h x 24" diam.

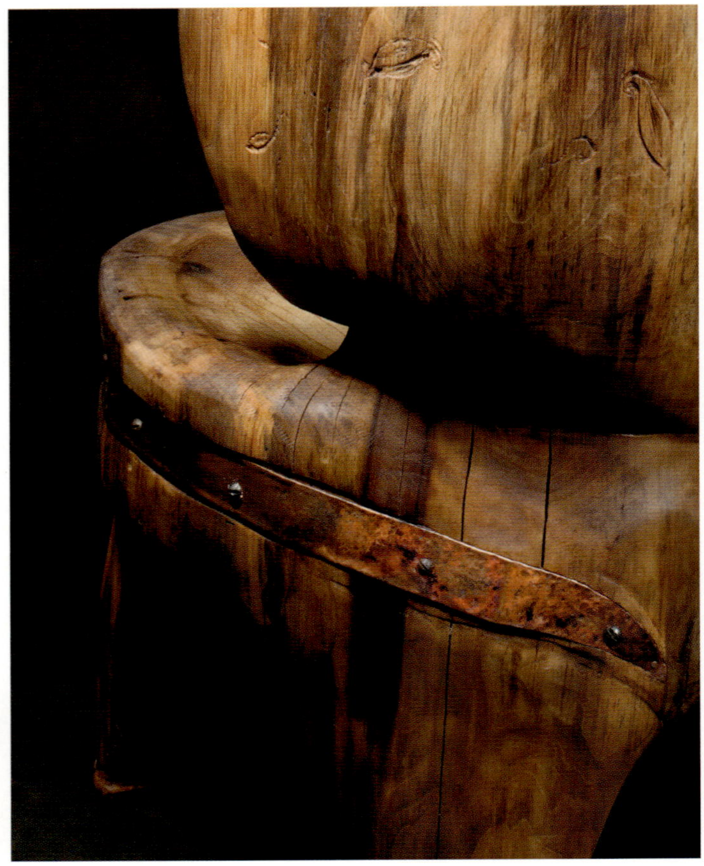

Photo by Jacque Rubin.

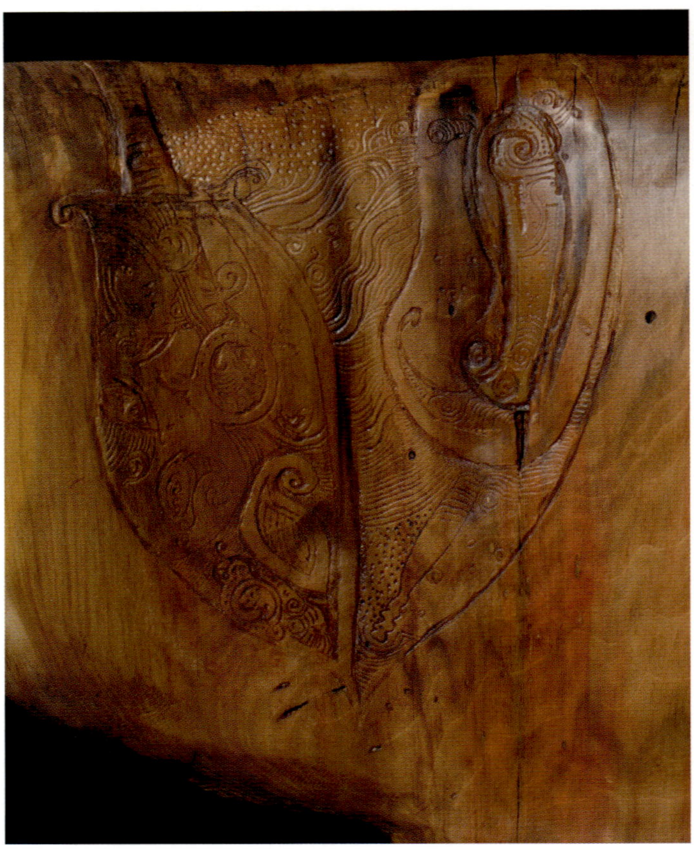

Photo by Jacque Rubin.

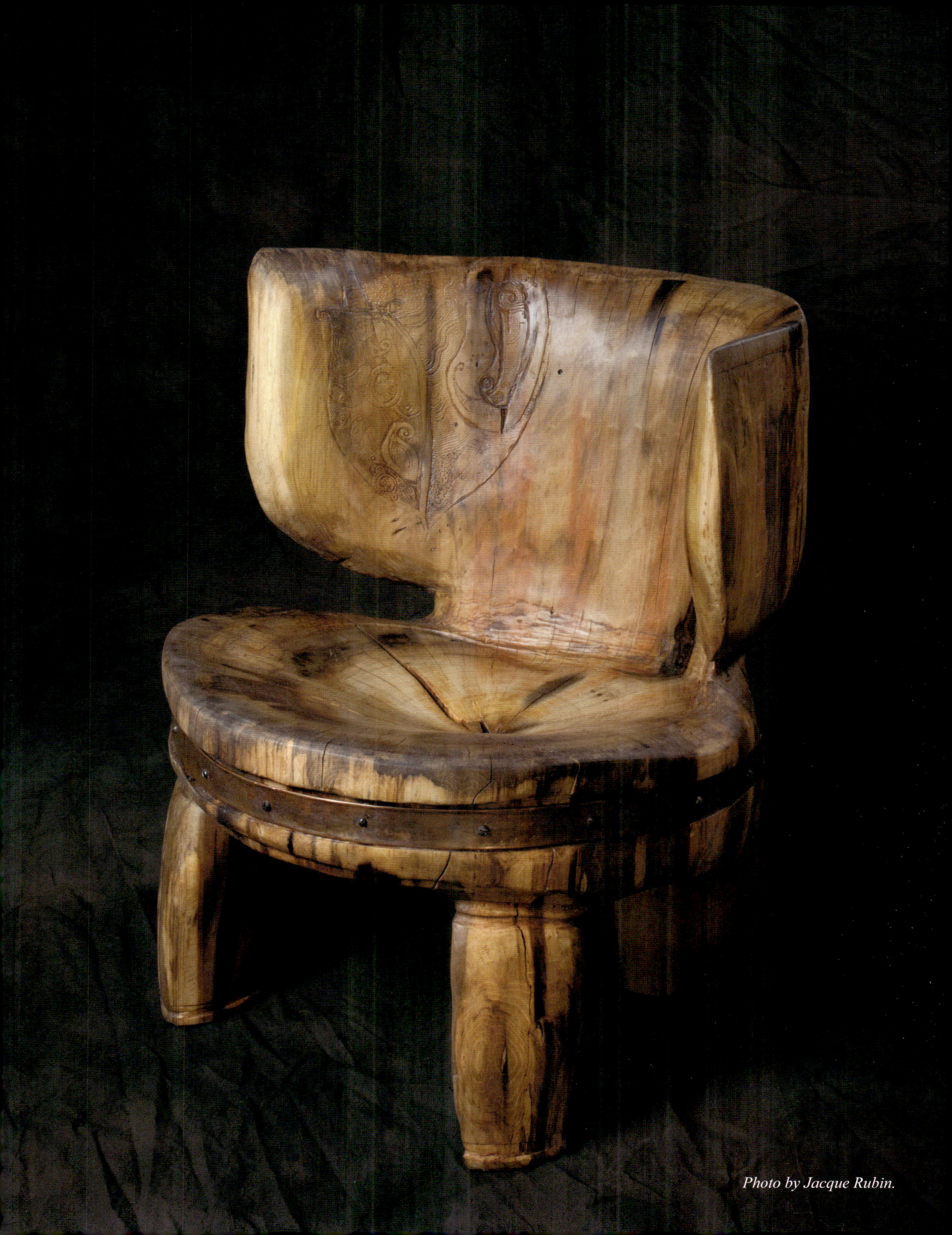

Photo by Jacque Rubin.

Jasper Brinton

We can only imagine the distant past. We can only marvel at the variety of life forms which today share the planet. Speculating about origins has helped me grasp the trope my work seems to formalize. From these beginnings I find openings for the signs I need, ensuring that each intrinsic work contains a viable latent threshold. I love the organic, the sequential aspect of growth and variation. But I'm a child of the modern, an image of the rational, so I reject the edenic illusion that good design is pronounced by anything other than unconsolidated play.

Residua of That Which Was Series (2012)
Ceramic with tulip poplar ash glaze
Average size: 14.17" h x 11" w x 2" d

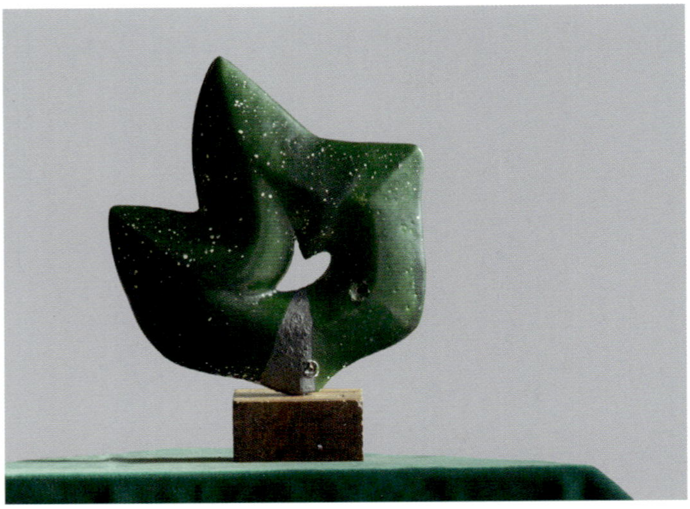

Photo by Jasper Brinton.

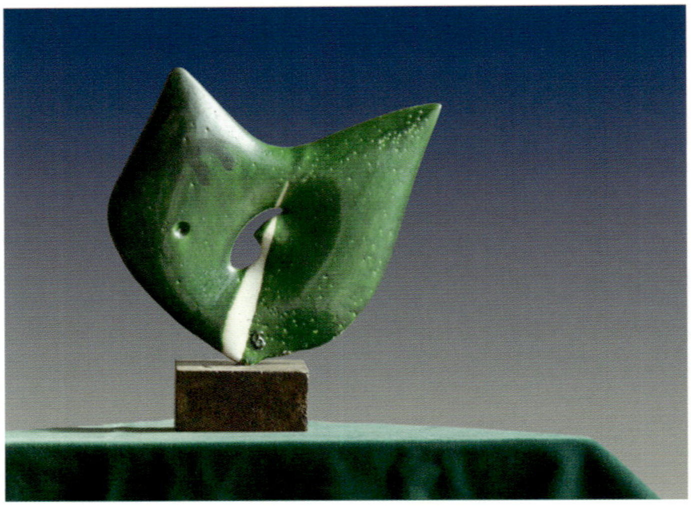

Photo by Jasper Brinton.

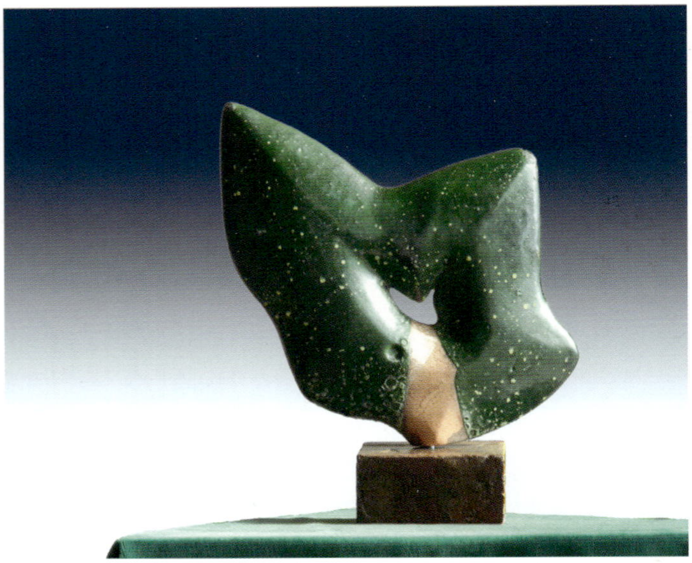

Photo by Jasper Brinton.

Michael Brolly

Art has always offered me a very comforting and grounding place to dwell. When I was young I would spend hours in the basement making things. I should probably say here that the Southwest Philadelphia of my youth was in no way Art Mecca or even an Art Haven; it was a decidedly blue collar type of place. The Art World that I would later discover could have been in another universe and it would have been no more remote than it was to me then.

My work with wood has paralleled this journey. I started in my basement with only the most rudimentary hand tools. I finally got to a wood shop where I could make boards straight and flat at the ripe old age of 26. The teacher was John Stolz and he changed my life. He showed me some of the wonders that could be produced with wood. After he opened my eyes, I was fortunate enough to go to Wharton Esherick's studio and had a tour given by his longtime friend Miriam Philips. Straight and flat went right out the window, for I had found my life path. Since then I have travelled from the familiar into the depths of the wood itself, a new universe as it were. It will be interesting to see just how far I can travel in this universe that Wharton and John gave me my first glimpse of.

Self Portrait of Wharton in Wood (2012)
Tulip poplar and color photograph
24" h x 21" w x 3" d

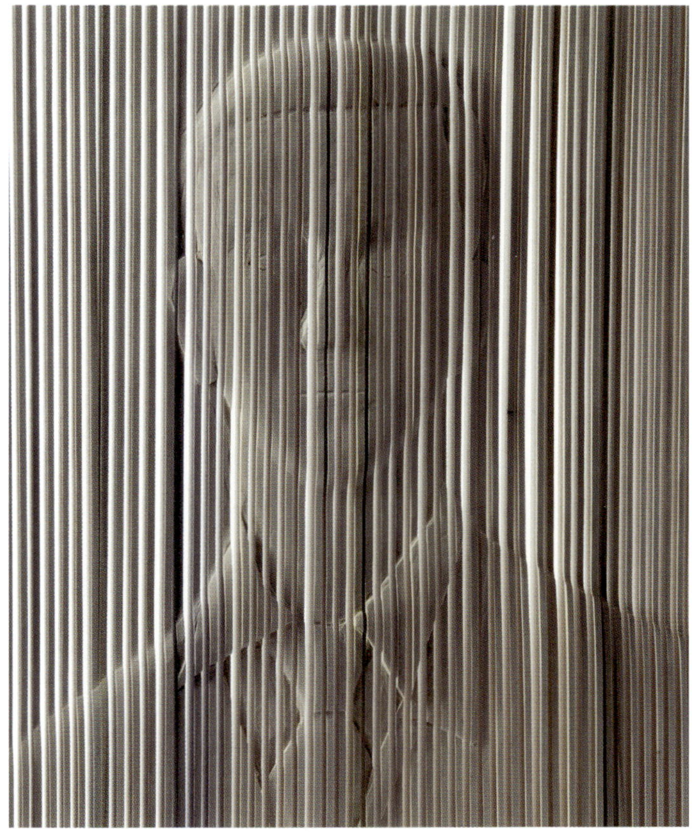

Photo by Donna Chiarelli.

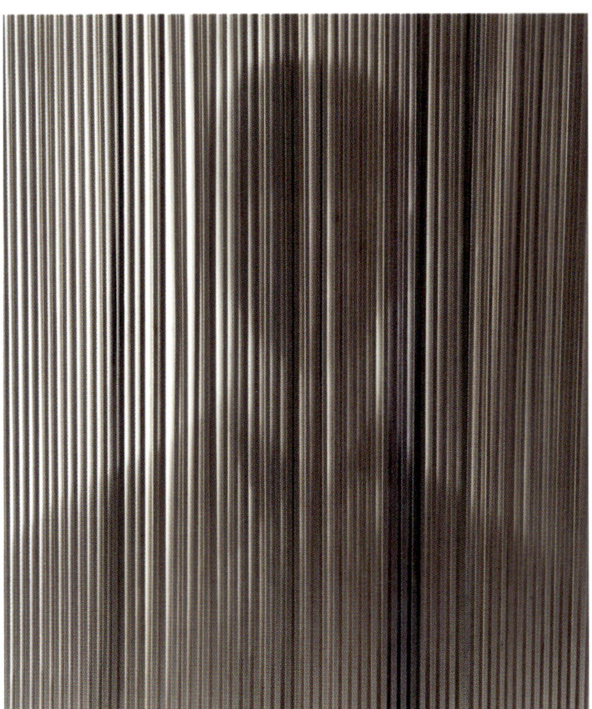

Photo by Donna Chiarelli.

Miriam Carpenter

With enthusiasm, I find contentment in just about any type of creative work. From the time I was very young, I have been attracted to tortured slabs of gnarled wood. My yoga practice also provides me with inspiration, and from time to time one image will play long enough for me to make something of it – like a woodcut for *Poplar Culture*. I was first introduced to woodblock carving and to the exciting world of Wharton Esherick by Mark Sfirri, who continues to be a mentor to me. Through Esherick's work I find freedom, humor, connectivity and bountiful delight.

Karnapidasana (2011)
Woodcut (artist's proof)
Rives BFK paper, Gamblin Relief Ink – Portland Intense Black
Image Size: 10.5" h x 7.75" w
Paper Size: 15.25" h x 11.5" w

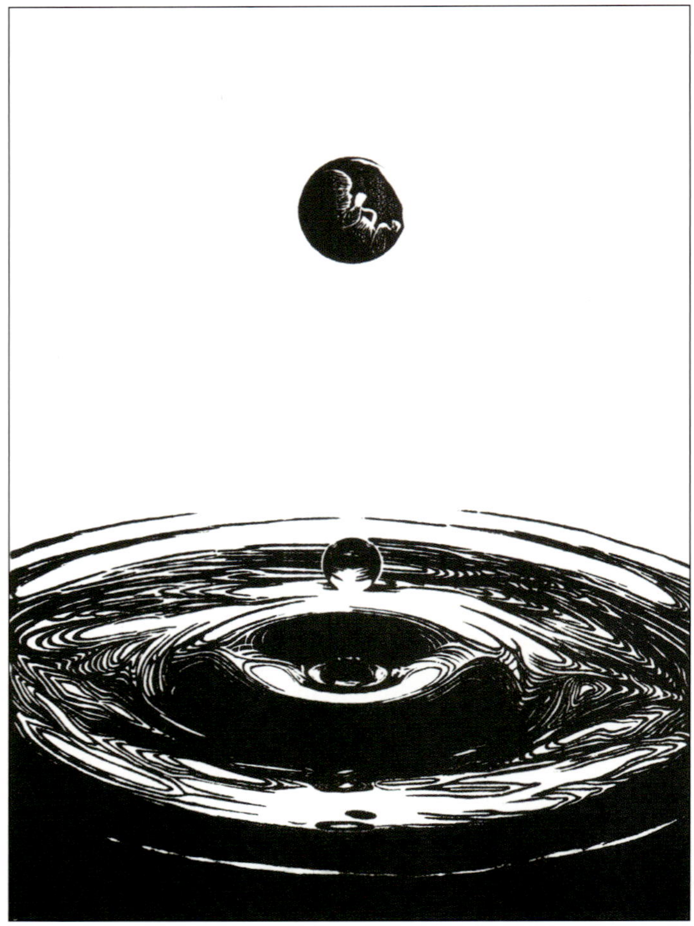

Photo by Mark Sfirri.

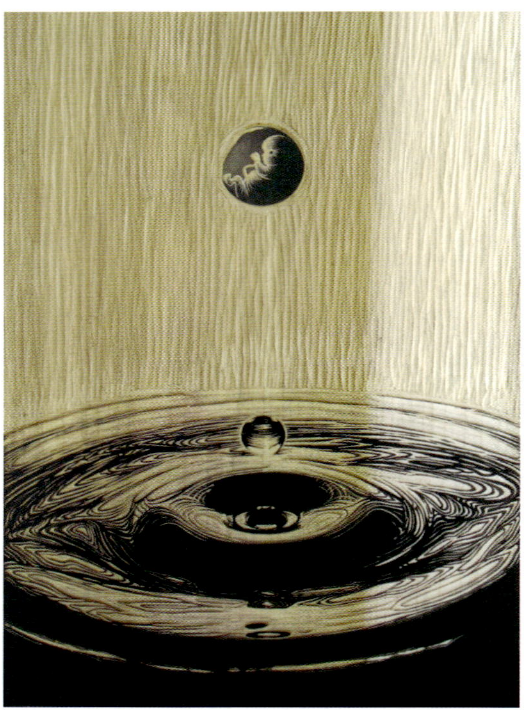

Photo by Mark Sfirri.

Andy DiPietro

As a Design Engineer for the last 28 years I have learned the importance of shape, form and function along with focus on details. My Artist career has allowed me to explore the beauty of shape, form, texture and color without boundaries. My true love is working with wood.

The art of my work is in the shapes I form together with the beauty of the wood I select. My forms and finishes are chosen to showcase the grain flow of the wood. My vessels are textured by sandblasting the surface and enhancing the grain with color dyes and oil finishes.

As a tree ages it becomes more beautiful or refined like a fine wine. I used my sand-texturing technique to open the pores on each annual growth ring to accept a black and red dye treatment. Then I finished off the surface with a soft gloss oil to give the appearance of a fine red wine.

Wine Vessel (2011)
Tulip poplar, dyes
10.5" h x 7.5" diam.

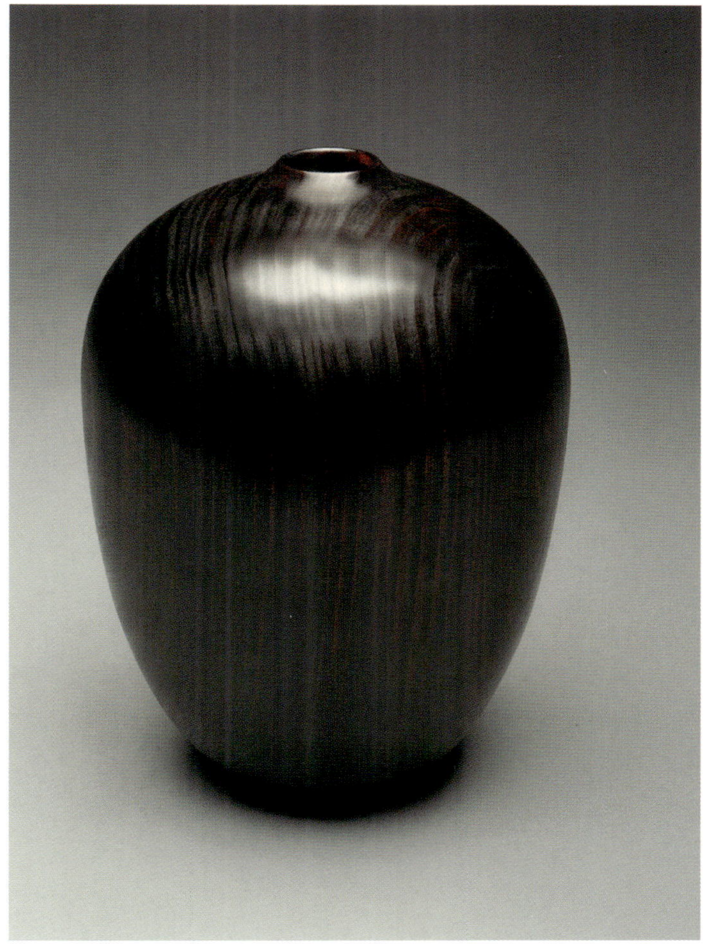

Photo by James Mario.

Ron Durr

Through the email system, I became aware of the request to use some of the poplar wood from a tree being removed from the Museum site as a safety move and make something with it to be sold for the benefit of the Museum. I visited the site the day the tree was felled by professionals and was given two branch logs with which I could create some pieces. The two pieces pictured in this publication are the result of my efforts.

One piece in the hourglass shape is constructed in an open segmented style and the various colors are a selection of heart wood (dark) and sap wood (toward the bark). No foreign wood has been incorporated here.

The hollow form or vase is done in the pierced fashion showing a few geometrical designs.

Hourglass Form (2011)
Tulip poplar
11.5" h x 7" diam.

Pierced Hollow Form (2011)
Tulip poplar
8.5" h x 5.5" diam

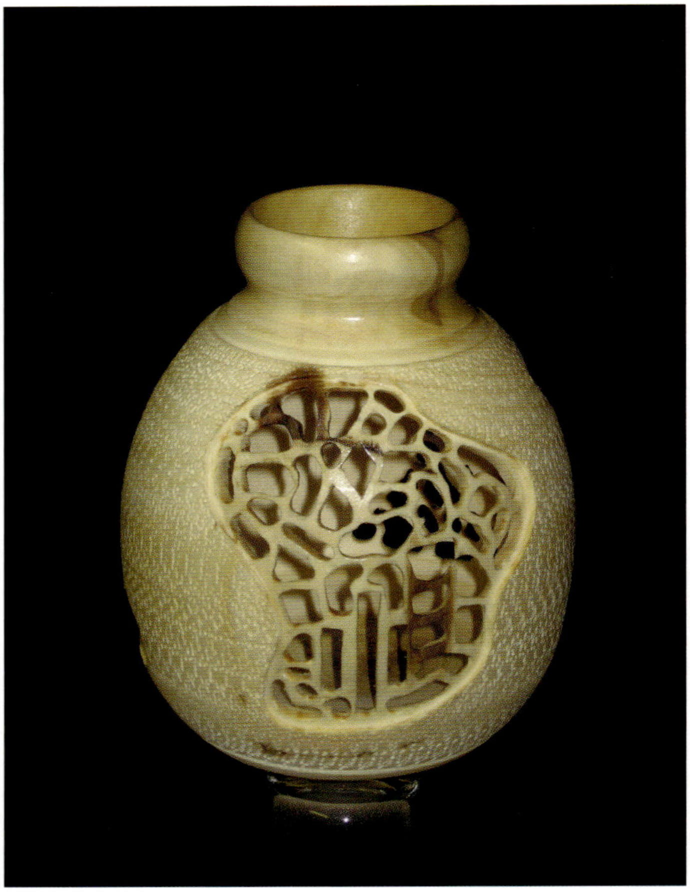

Photo by Ron Durr.

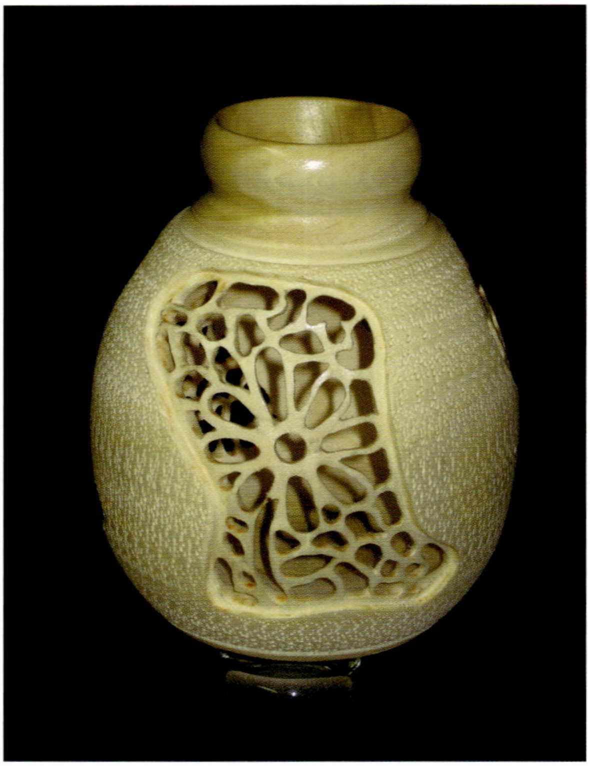

Photo by Ron Durr.

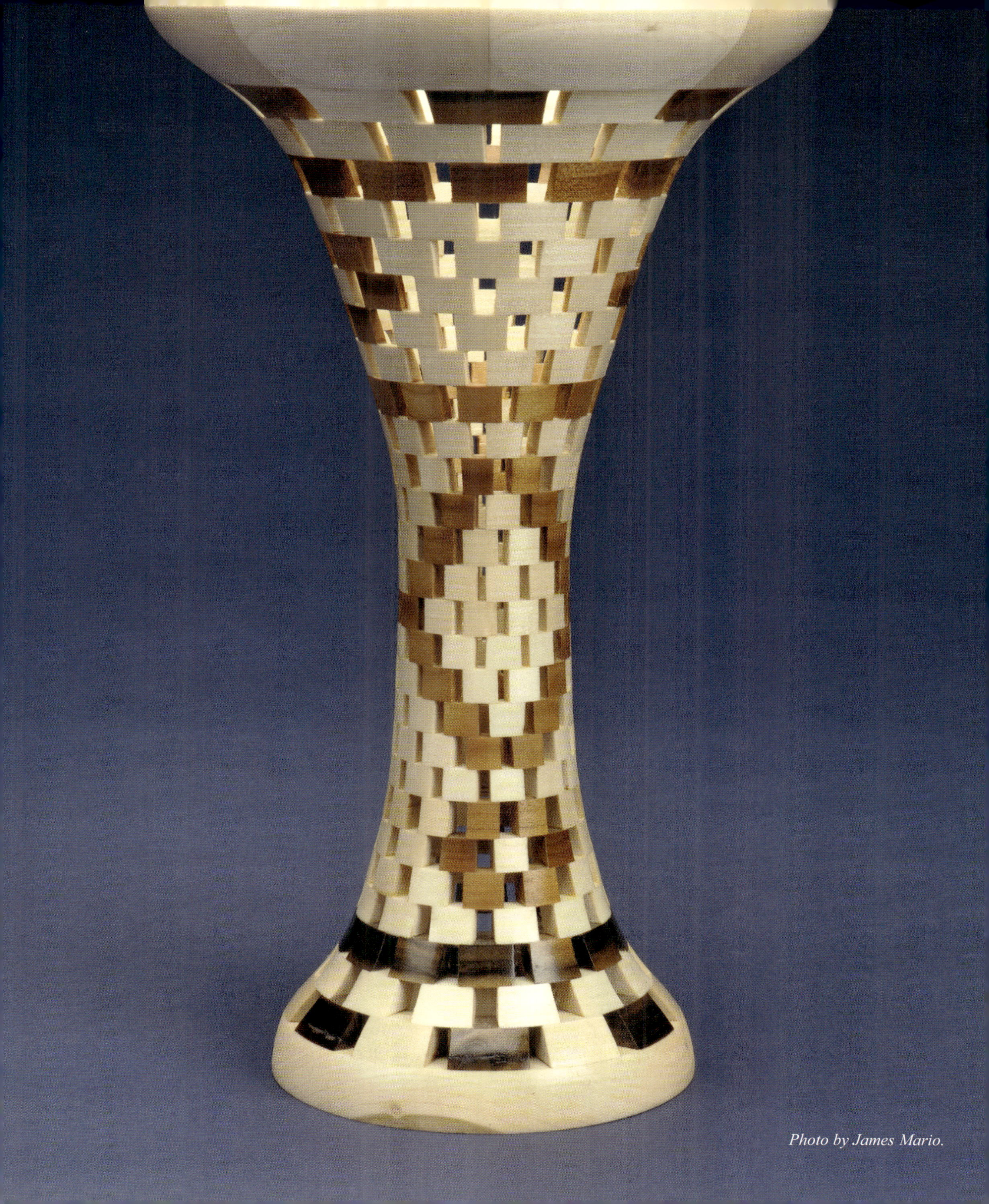

Photo by James Mario.

Chuck Dyke

Recently, much of my work has been in the tradition of the Appalachian chain carvers, including the present piece, *The Ravages of Time*. It's a variation on the traditional "ball in cage" motif. But inevitably, in these days of conceptual art, there are some interwoven narratives in the piece: time, measurement, evolution (the double helix), thus life and death, growth and decay (of the Tulip Poplar).

The Ravages of Time (2011)
Tulip poplar, glass, polycarbonate, sand
10.5" h x 4.38" diam.

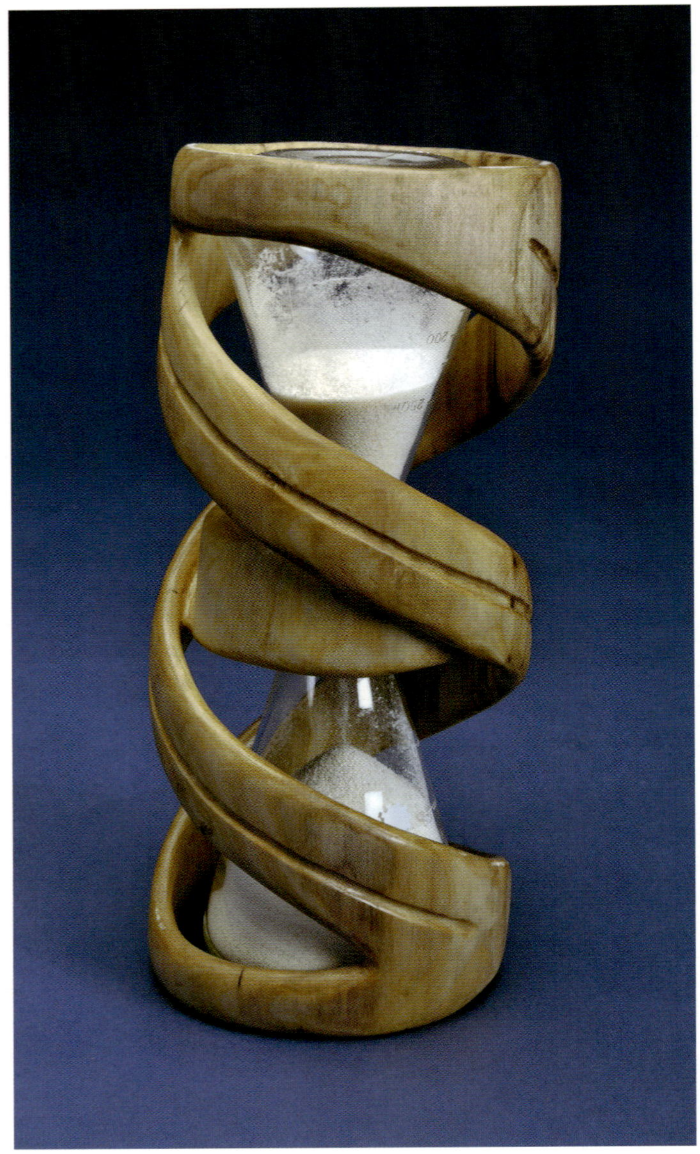

Photo by James Mario.

David Ebner

I approach my art intuitively as well as intellectually, drawing inspiration wherever I find it. I've explored a variety of directions and themes over the years, but each piece is treated as an art object with concern for my material and honesty to its inherent qualities. For me, one's creative ability is demonstrated in the diversity of the pieces and what one learns from change. For this show, I chose to make one of my MFA Benches. The inspiration for this piece came from one of my early studio pieces, the Renwick Stool, first made in 1974. Wharton's painted horse *Cheeter*, made in 1935, is the inspiration for my use of blue milk paint as a finish.

MFA Bench (2012)
Tulip poplar, blue milk paint
16.5" h x 36" l x 15" d

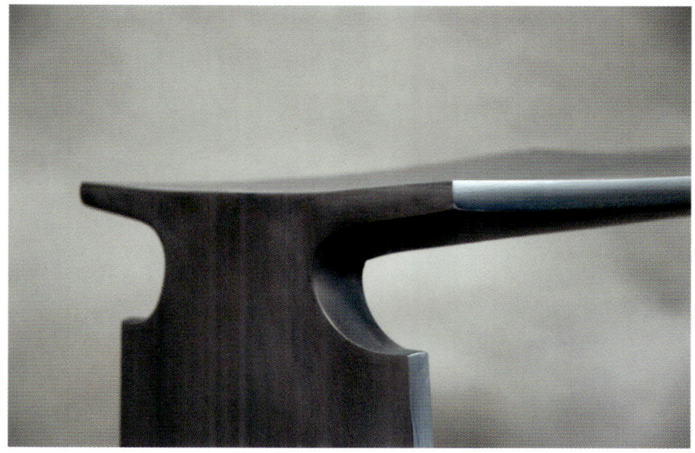

Photo by LuAnn Thompson.

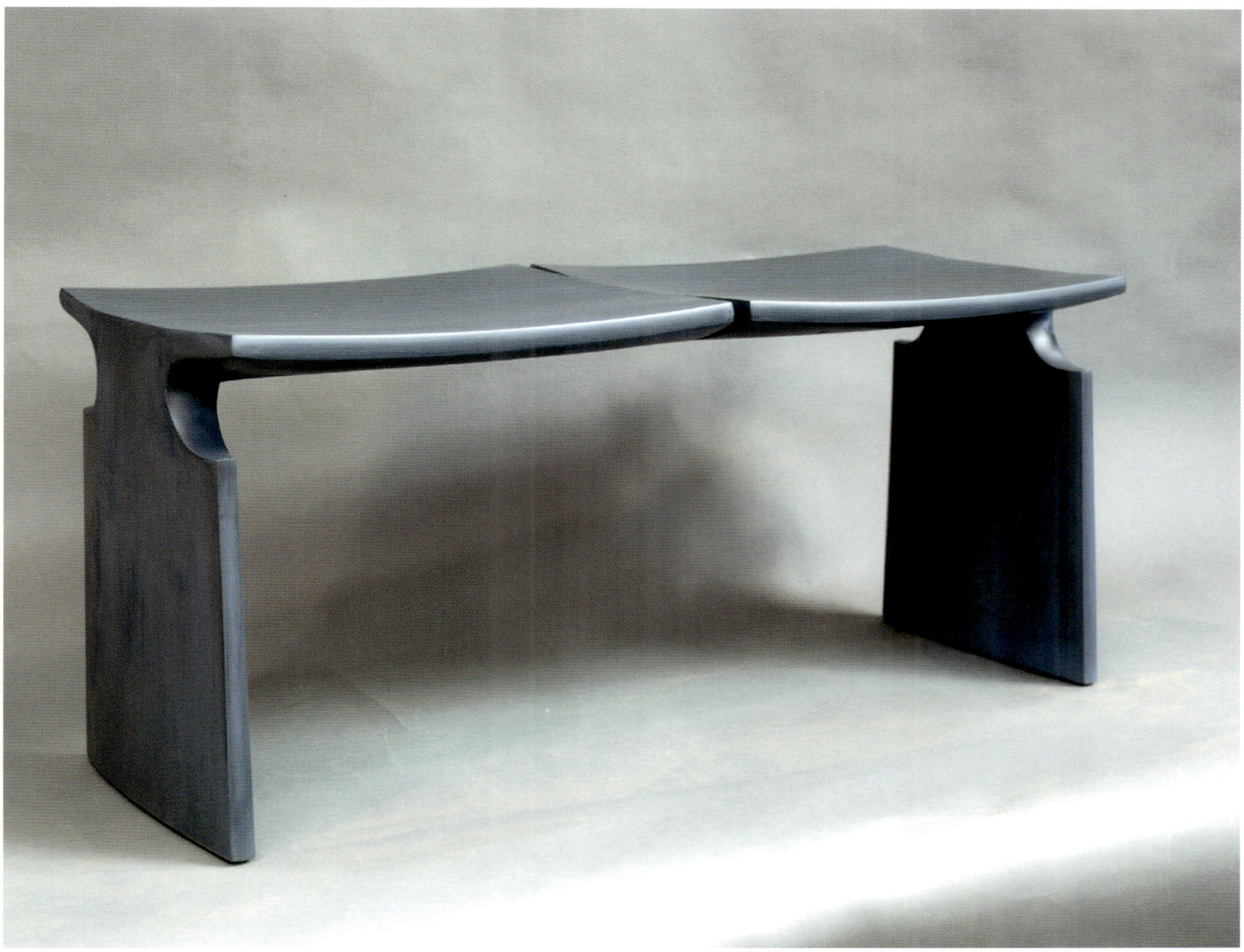

Photo by LuAnn Thompson.

Craig Edelbrock

As an amateur woodworker and a novice, I am swayed by Esherick's highly stylized approach to wood sculpture, particularly in pieces like *Cat in the Grass*. I set out to carve a bird with sinuous curves, and to shun ornamentation and detail in favor of pure stylized form. The bird and base are all poplar, stained with lightfast dyes. The base is finished flat and is weathered, while the bird is buffed with carnauba wax to a glossy shine.

A small poplar spoon inspired by Esherick's own wooden kitchenware: simple, graceful curves, and above all useful.

Bird on a Base (2012)
Tulip poplar
8" h x 9" l

Small Spoon (2012)
Tulip poplar
7" l x 2" w

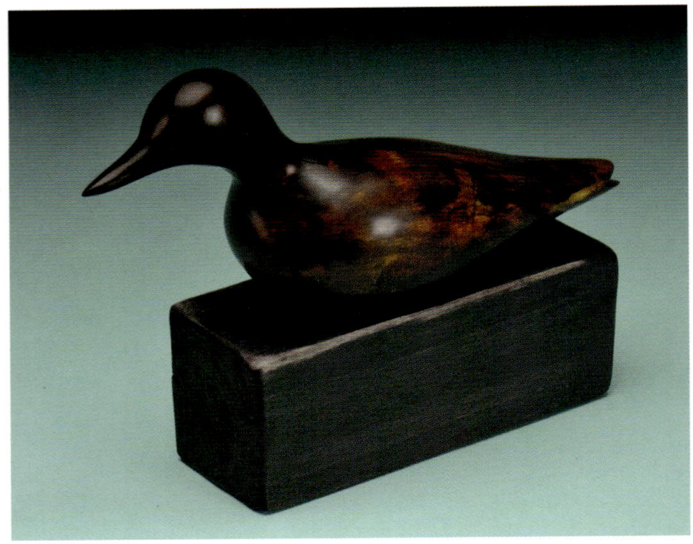

Photo by James Mario.

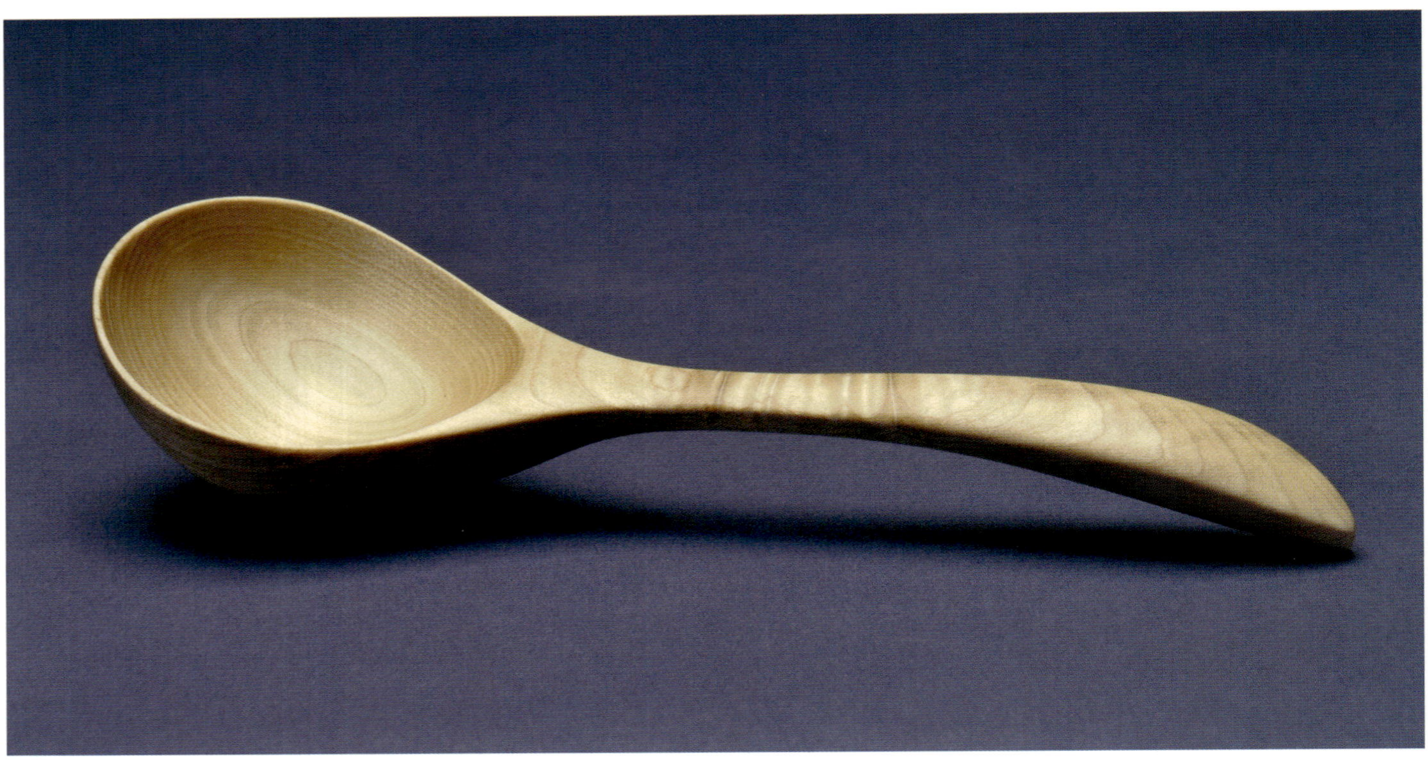

Photo by James Mario.

Paul & Jesse Eisenhauer

This display shelf came from our desire to honor the tree by using its natural form. The inverted "h" shape of these forked branches reminded us of Esherick's *S-K Chair* and his straight *Library Ladder*. We combined the forms, keeping the natural shape of the forks for the supports and the natural edge of the shelves. The warp created when the split branches dried created challenges, but provides an asymmetry that seems in harmony with Esherick's organic ethos.

Struttin' (2012)
Tulip poplar
63" h x 38" w x 21" d

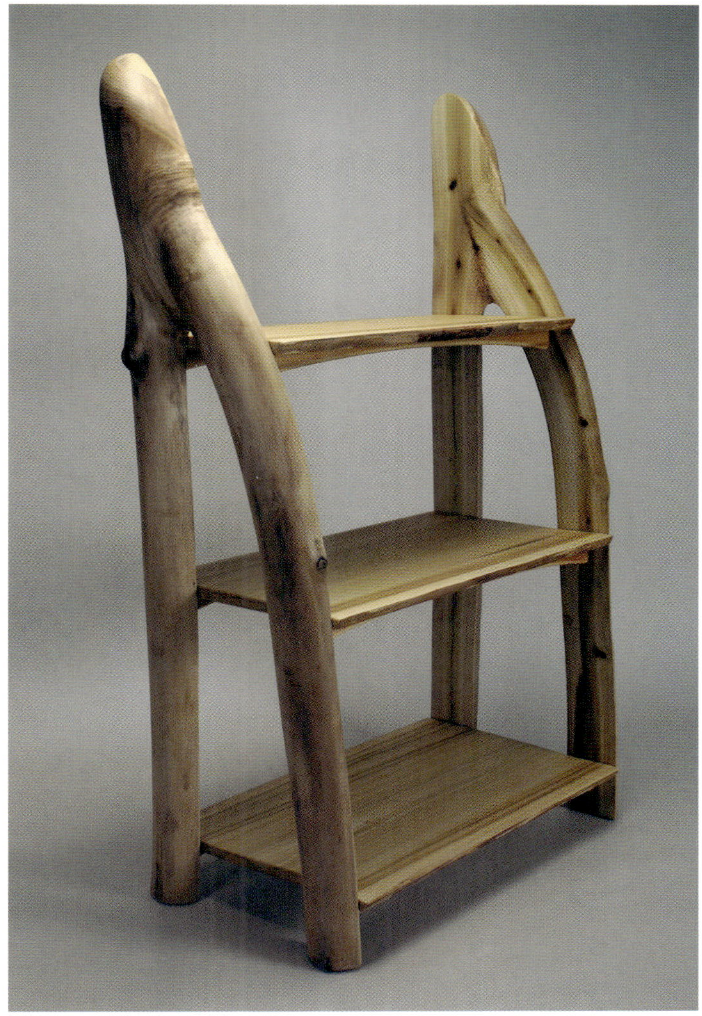

Photo by James Mario.

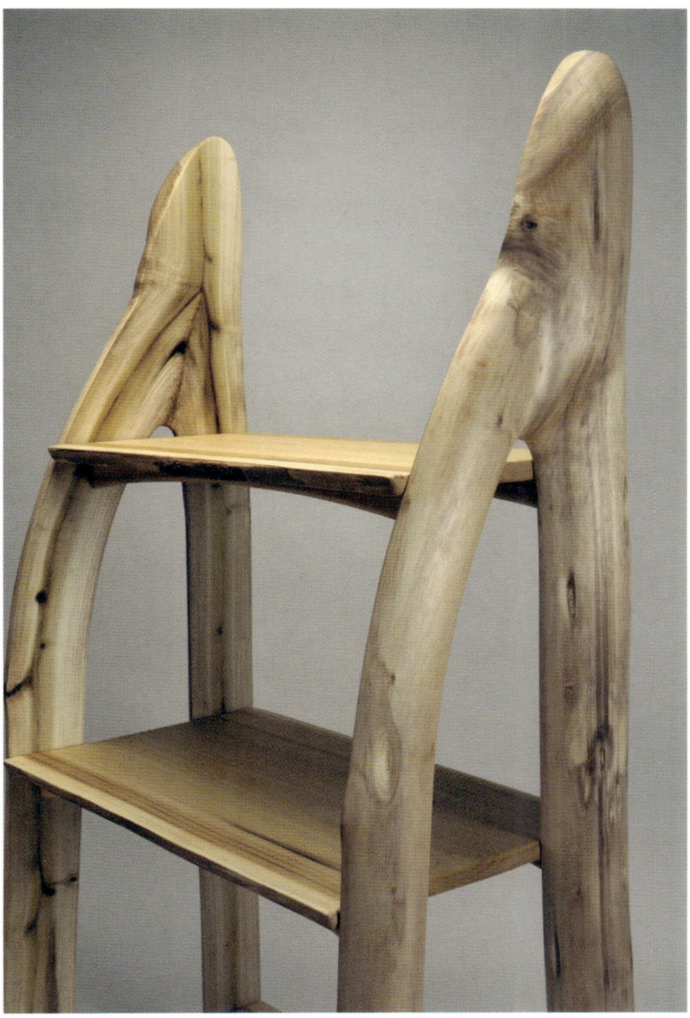

Photo by James Mario.

David Ellsworth

The most significant element that has inspired my work over the past three decades would be the *sphere*. While the sphere is universally recognized as a symbol of life and wholeness, I find that it is also an extremely difficult form to design from, simply because it is too perfect, too complete within itself and, one might even say, too boring an image to bother with.

And yet, consistent with my feelings that wood is the most perfectly imperfect material to work with, it is this inherent perfection of the sphere that is so challenging for me as a designer of wooden forms. And because I focus on "line as volume" rather than "line as shape," manipulating the sphere in any number of ways including stretching, squashing, squeezing, and pulling can yield an unlimited number of subtle, yet powerful design opportunities. The resulting forms provide a foundation for a whole new vocabulary in understanding the vessel form. Combined with the dynamics and complexity of wood grain and color, elements of this language would include movement, poise, sadness and joy, unity and indifference, energy, passivity, and what is most important to my work...pulse.

Esherick Sphere (2012)
Tulip poplar, acrylic base
12" h x 12" w x 11.5" d

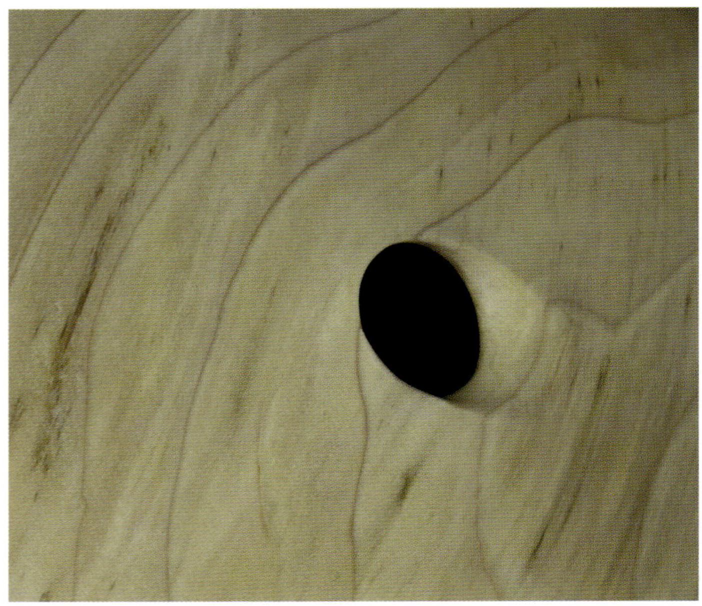

Photo by David Ellsworth.

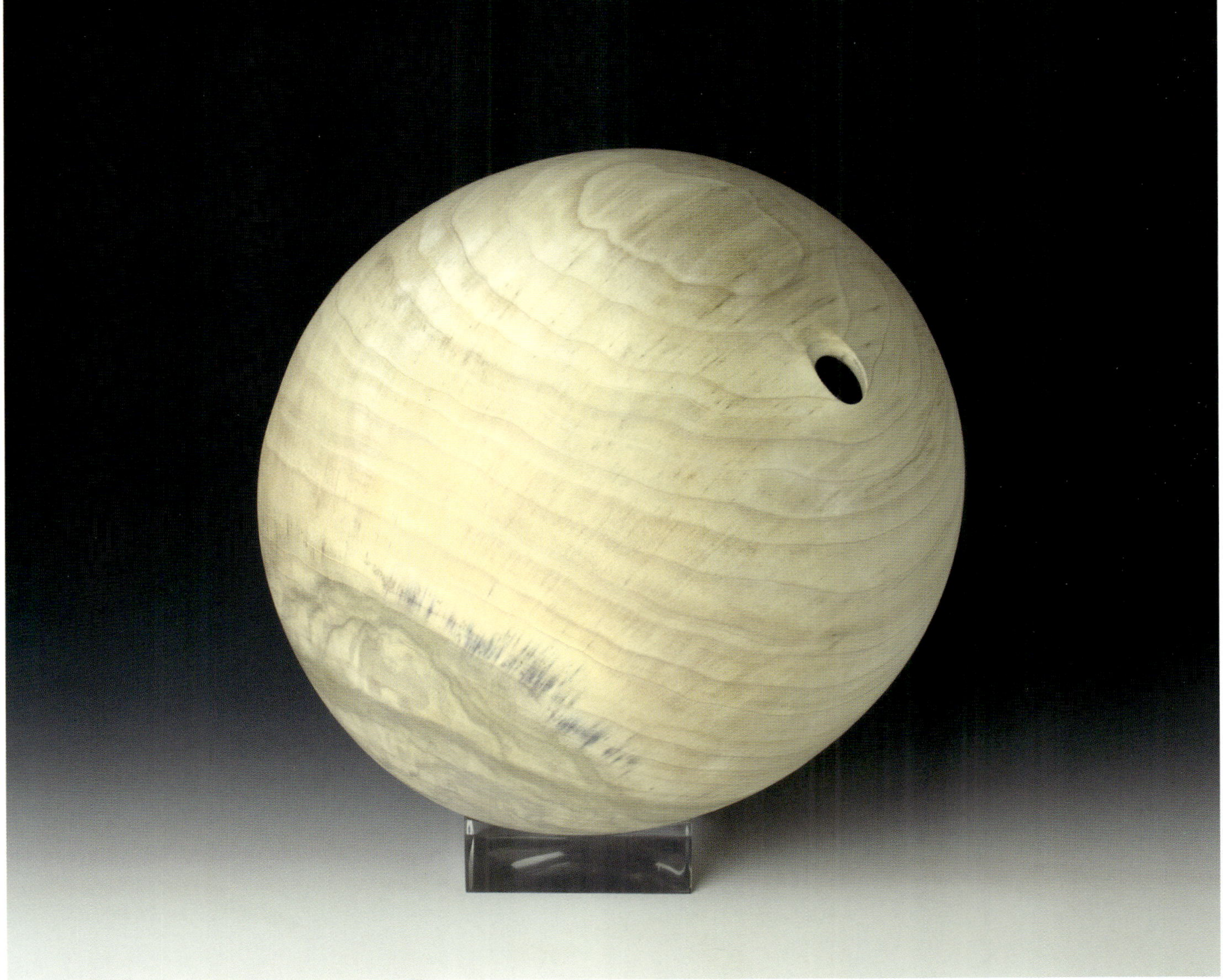

Photo by David Ellsworth.

Philip Hauser

I emphasize the natural beauty and the imperfections of whole pieces of wood. Mother Nature produces an infinite variety of interesting shapes and contortions, and my goal is to work with the natural flow to create pleasing pieces of turned wood. I am committed to creating traditionally shaped pieces for everyday use as well as for decoration. (below and following page)

Natural Edge Bowl (2012)
Tulip poplar
3.5" h x 8" diam.

Natural Edge Bowl (2012)
Tulip poplar
5.5" h x 6.5" diam.

Natural Edge Bowl (2012)
Tulip poplar
7" h x 3" diam.

Pencil Box (2012)
Tulip poplar
5.5" h x 3" diam.

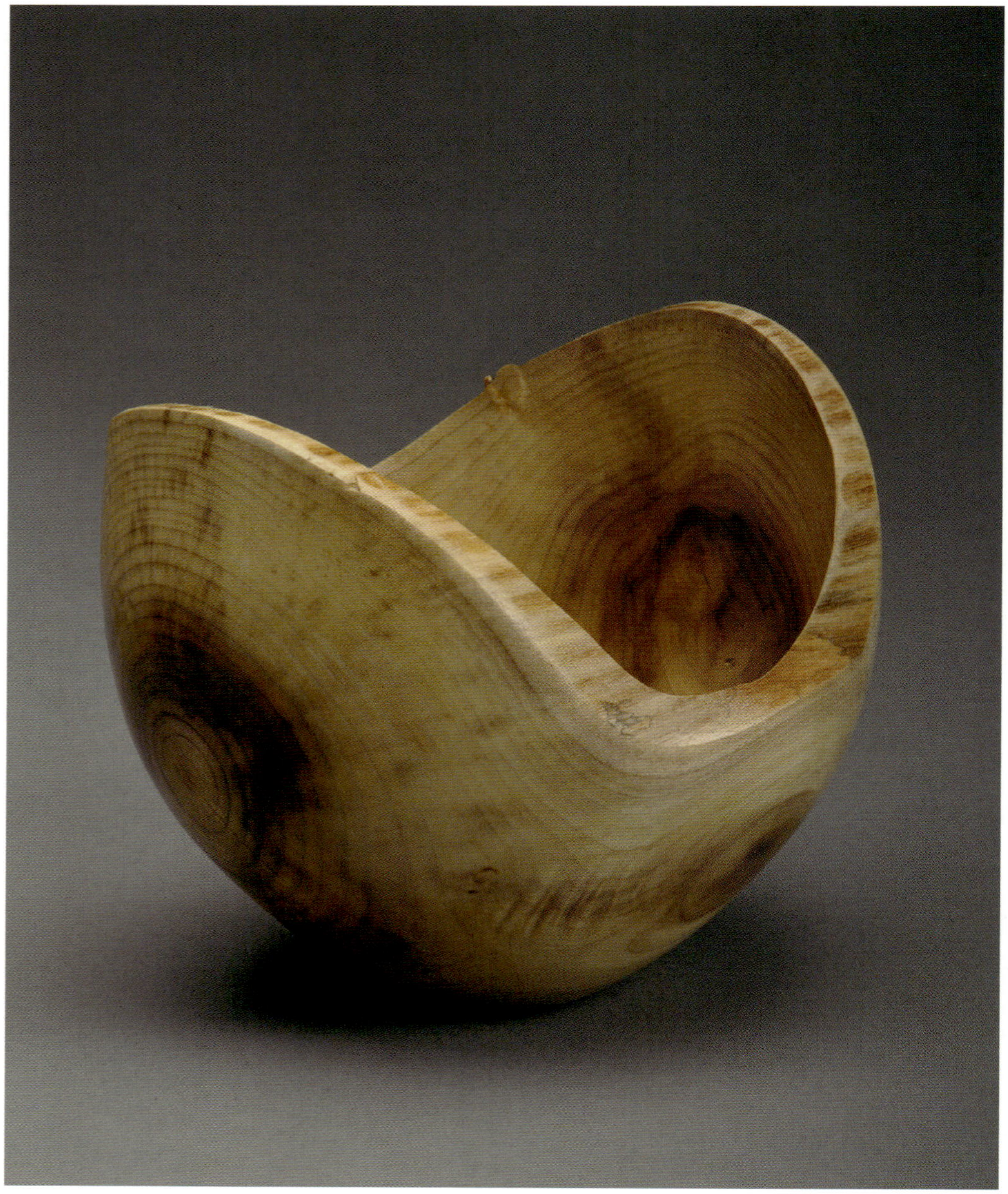

Photo by James Mario.

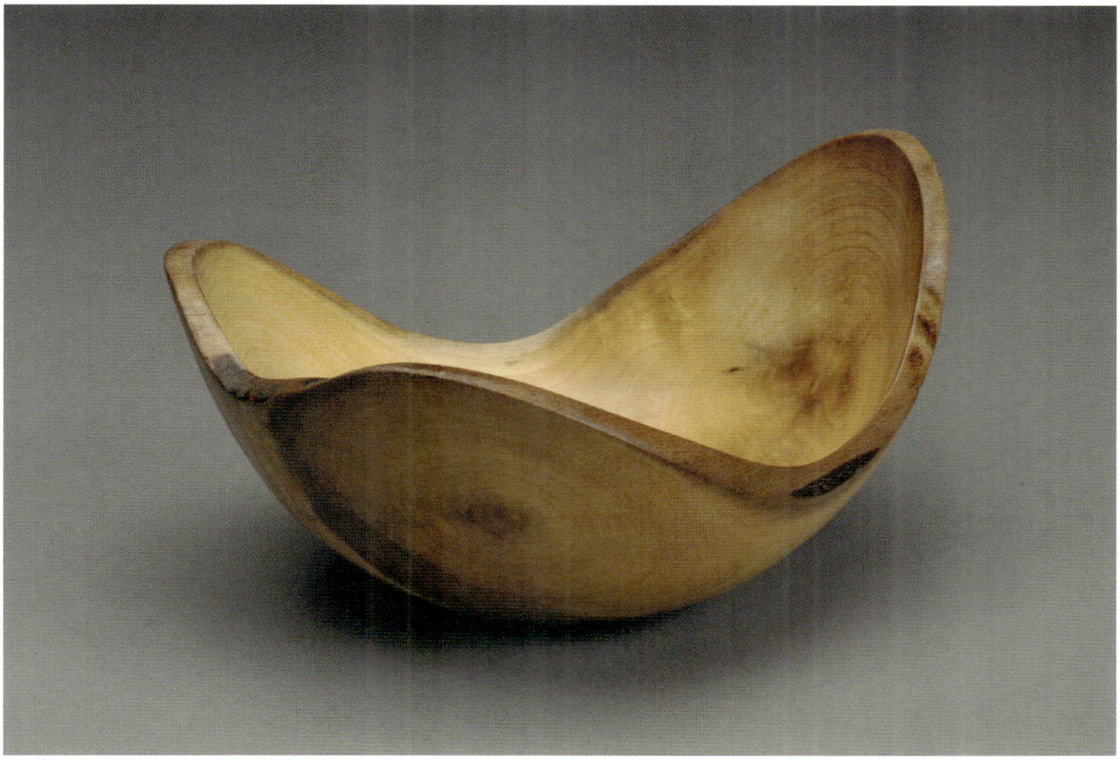

Photo by James Mario.

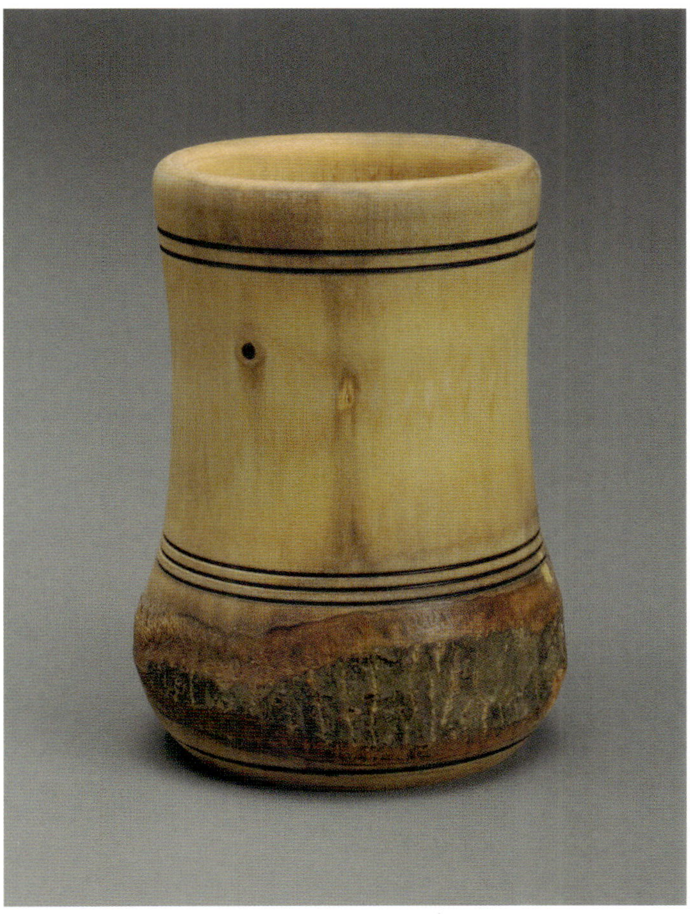

Photo by James Mario.

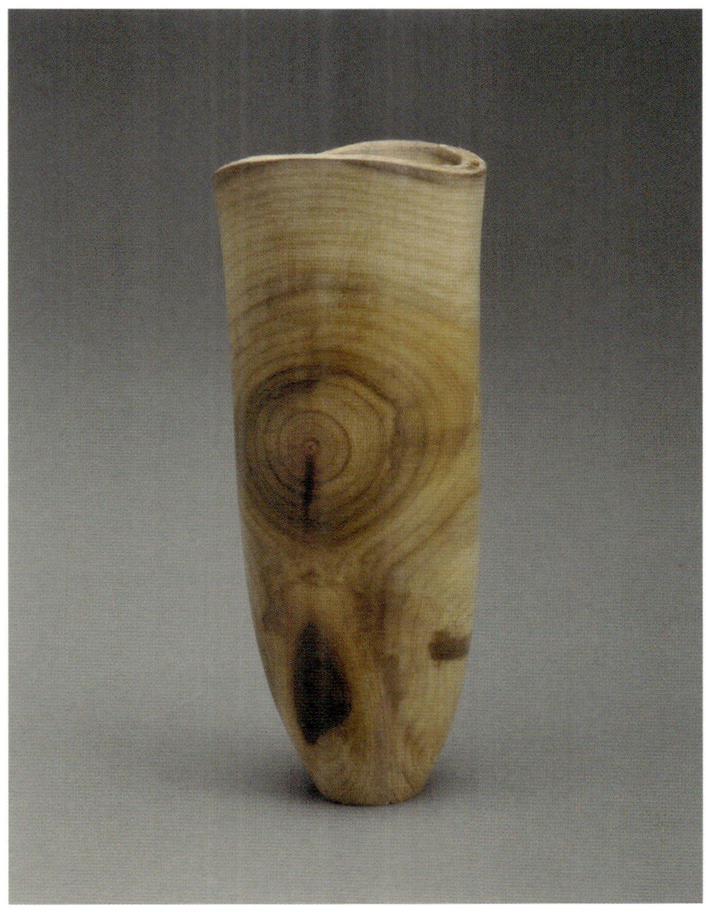

Photo by James Mario.

Carolyn Hesse

As an artist who has worked as a wooden boat builder, and who has built boats that currently sail on Barnegat Bay in New Jersey, I feel a special affinity for Wharton Esherick's life and work. I feel that the *Poplar Culture* project dovetails beautifully into my own life and work. This piece continues my exploration of the straight line, and retains the essence of the tree as a natural shape. Making this piece was an opportunity to approach the formal issues in my work from an opposite creative process than what I normally use; namely, a reductive approach instead of an additive approach.

Breach II (2012)
Tulip poplar
21" h x 93" w x 3" d

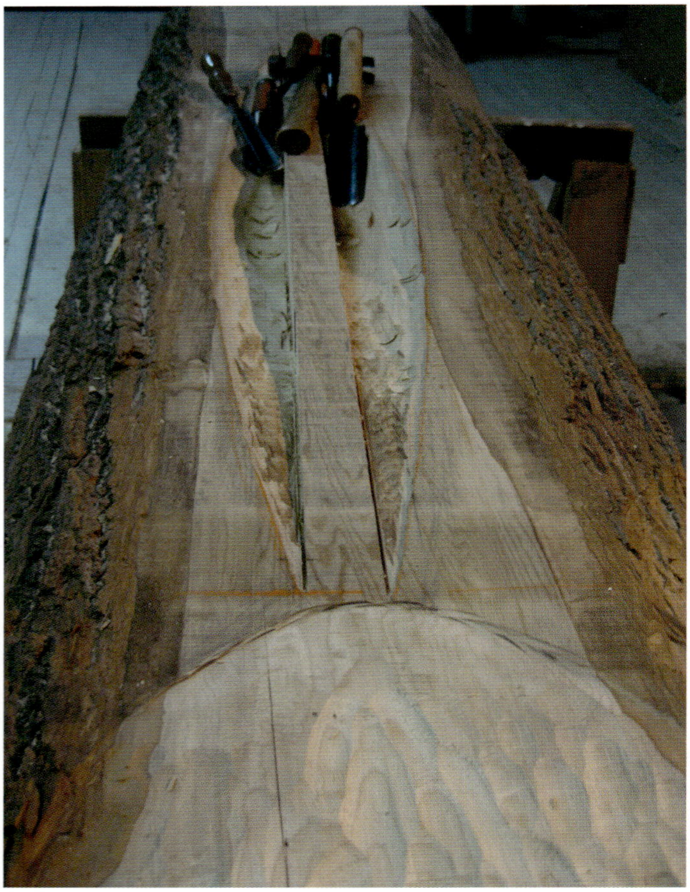

Carolyn Hesse has been traveling, and her piece was not far along when the catalog went to press. We include these photos of the work in process to give a sense of the direction of her piece. *Photo courtesy of Carolyn Hesse.*

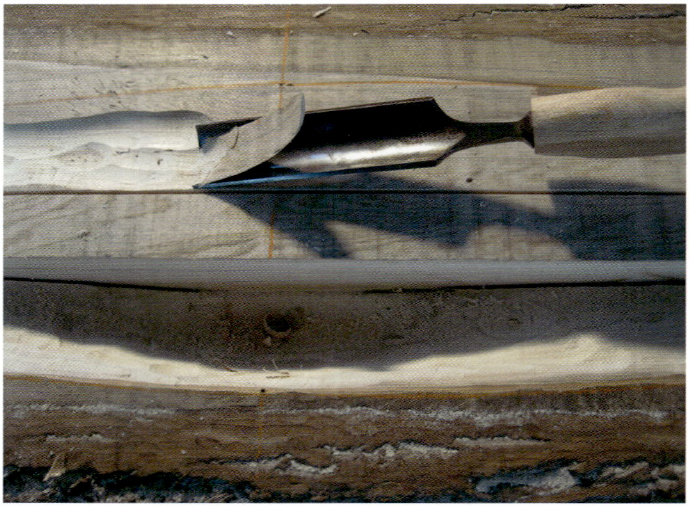

Photo courtesy of Carolyn Hesse.

Roger Justice

In that Wharton Esherick fostered studio craft through his application of the principles of sculpture to common utilitarian objects, this bowl attempts to pay tribute to his uncanny ability to meld the beauty of nature with the utilitarian functionality he found in many of the pieces he produced.

The boldness of this piece recognizes his decisiveness while the earthy, natural look of this piece embraces his ability to bring the beauty of the outdoors to the pleasure of everyday living.

Nature's Gift (2011)
Tulip poplar
2.5" h x 6.75" diam.

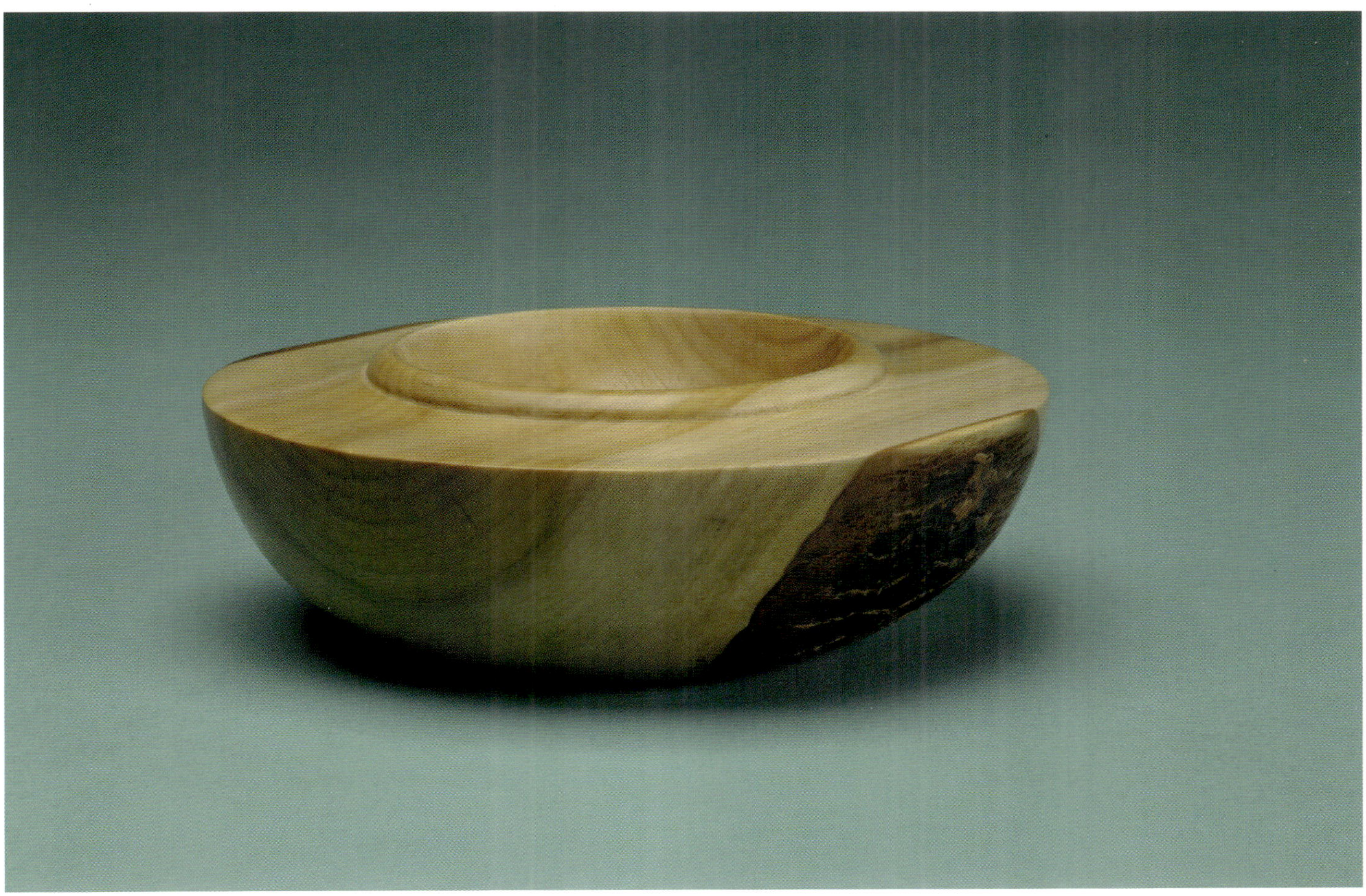

Photo by James Mario.

Ray Kelso

A wise friend once explained to me that the experience of art was far more important to being an artist than knowing the language of art. And although I may not be as familiar with terminology as other artists, I have experienced much in a thirty five-year career as a self-taught woodworker: I observed widely, paid attention to details, and learned from everyone.

I do not feel bound by the confines of the straight line or by any of the other conventions of classical furniture design. In fact, many walks in the woods have taught me that a straight line and a flat plane are not natural occurrences but are man-made devices created to provide a sense of simplicity and order for our lives. I believe that furniture, perhaps even more than the structures in which we place it, is such an intimate part of our lives that it needs to manifest the natural and playful world of which we are a part. I attempt to do just that in each piece that I create. Like a walk in the woods, I stray from the straight line and the sharp corner. And like trees that provide raw material and much of the inspiration for my work, my furniture begs to be touched. I attempt to instill a sense of playfulness in each piece, all the while being conscious of the fact that it must function as intended. If my work raises the spirit and brings a smile to the face, then I have been successful.

Esherick once said that he should be able to create something beautiful from what grows in his own back yard. I don't know that I have been as successful as he might have been, but hopefully he would have approved.

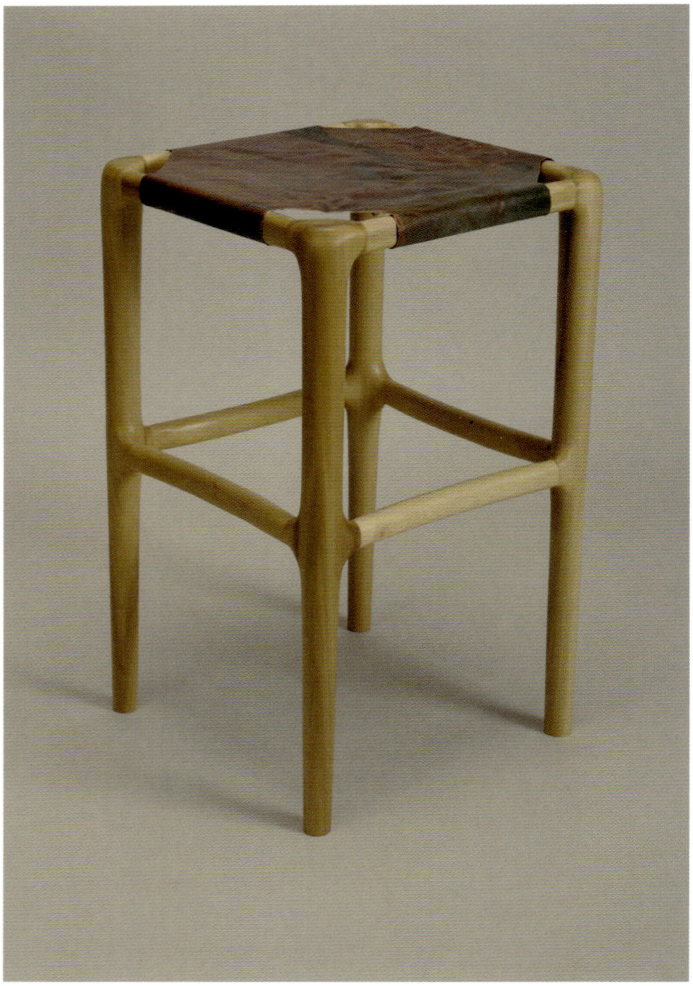

Stool (2012)
Tulip poplar, copper cap from Esherick poplar tree
24" h x 14" w x 14" d

Photo by James Mario.

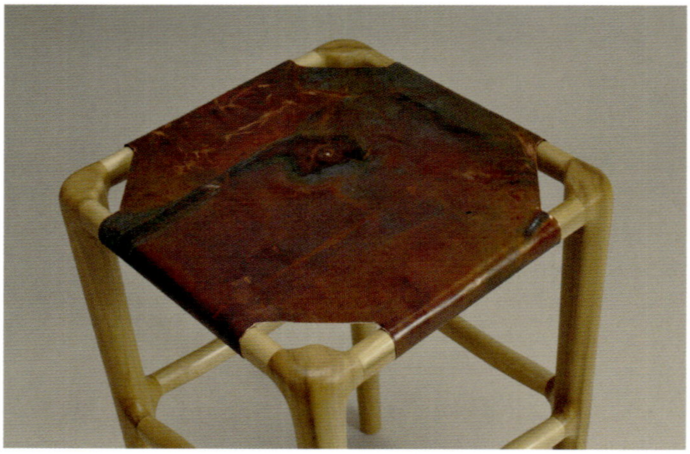

The colors on seat, which is made from the copper that covered the top of the poplar tree, come from the contact with the wood and with the oxidation of the copper. *Photo by James Mario.*

Brian Kolakowski

I have spent the last year focused on exploring carving technique with only hand tools as well as conceptual approach formulated in what I call Abstract Anatomy; blending my loves of anatomy, jazz/improvised music, science, nature, love, silliness, dreams, abstract, fractals/ math, spiritualism, poetry, graffiti and bright colors from my childhood in the '80s and much more.

to love is to save (2012)
wall relief
Tulip poplar, paint
21" h x 68" l x 1.5" d

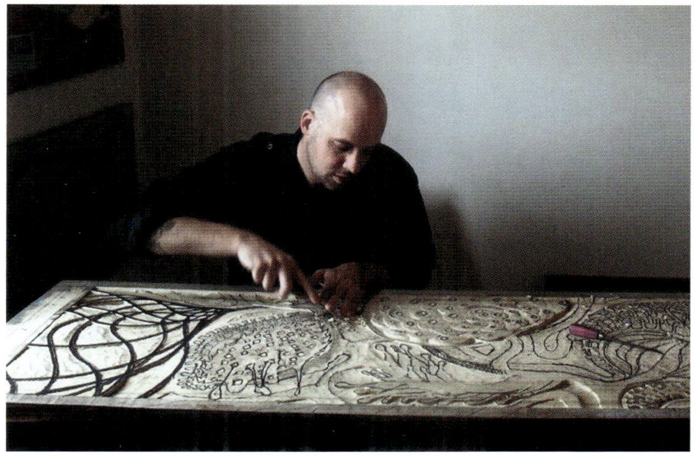

Photo by Karen Riley.

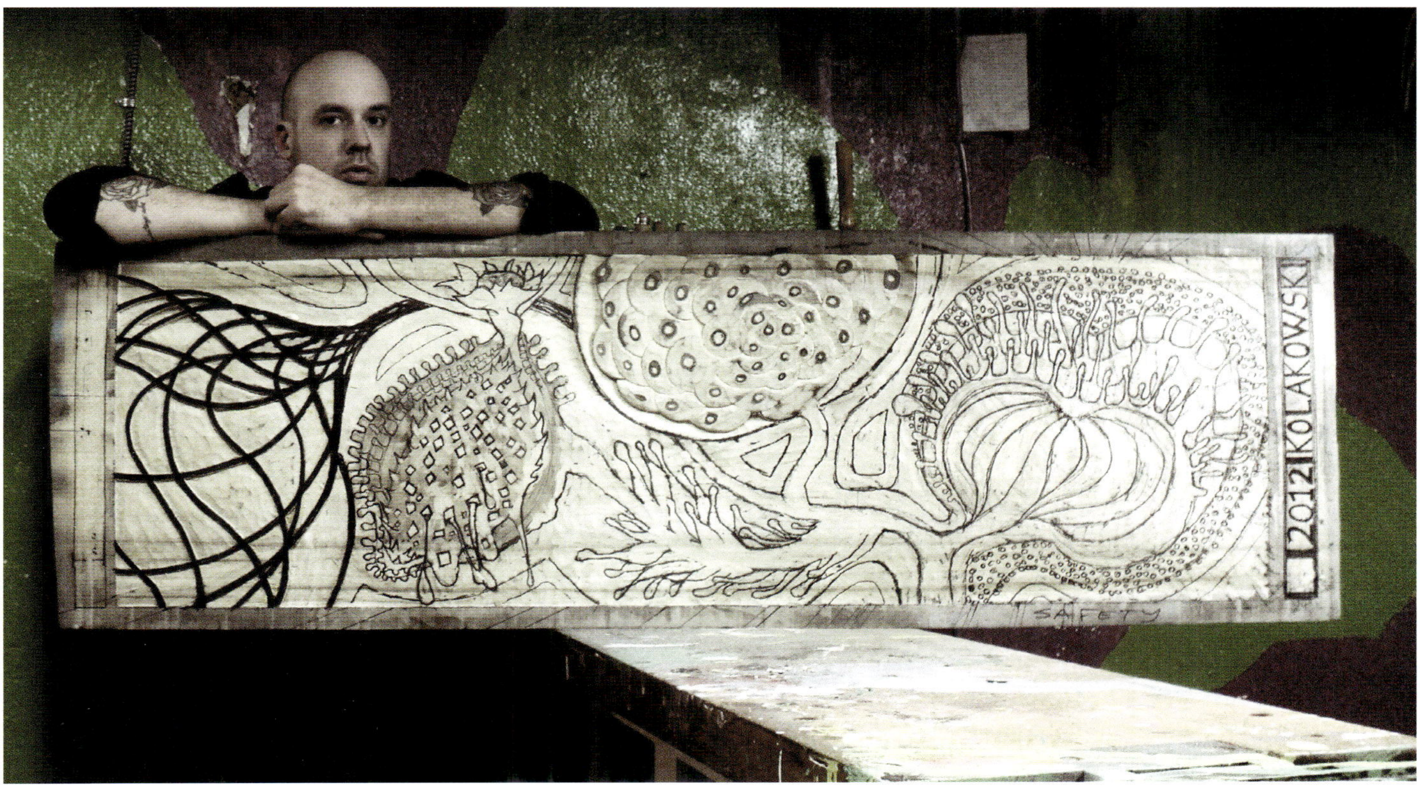

The size and scope of Brian's piece did not allow for it to be finished before the catalog publication deadline. Here you can see the concept drawing he is working from. *Photo by Karen Riley.*

Jack Larimore

Liriodendron Tulipifera, *Whartonia*
remembered Poplar
in ruin, still beautiful
her sensuous spirit speaks
I am blessed…
on that day
I was listening

Lessons from the Poplar (2012)
26" h x 26" w x 61" d
Tulip poplar, steel, brass

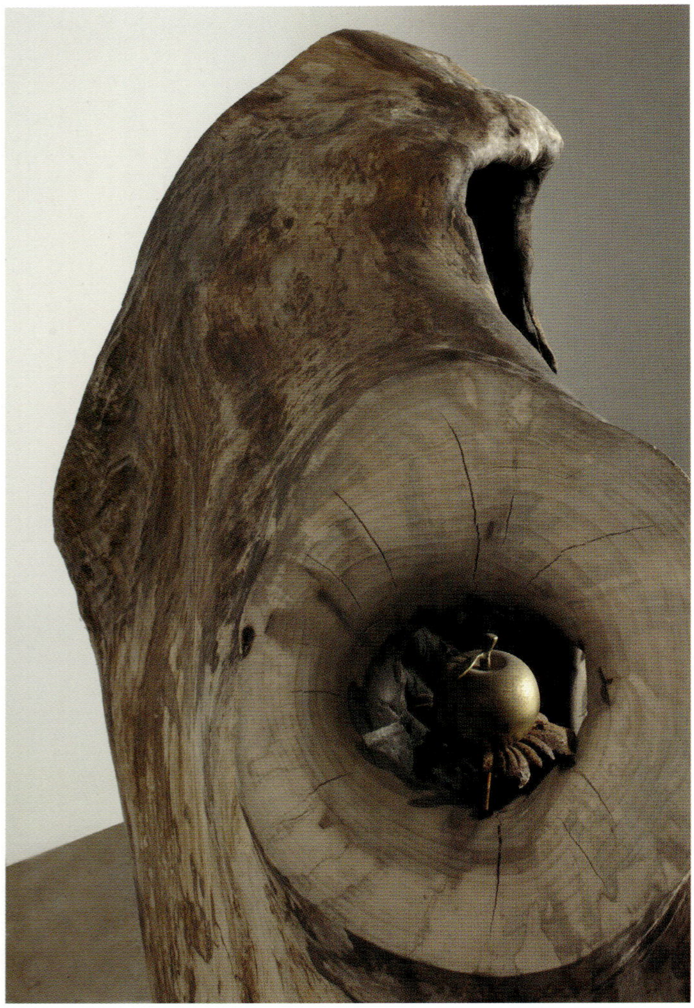

Photo by John Carlano.

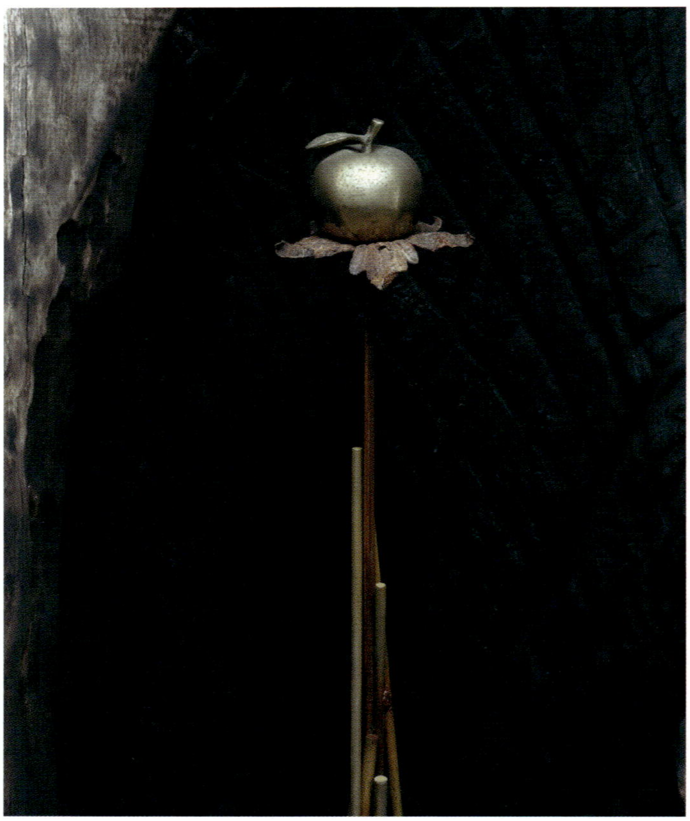

Photo by John Carlano.

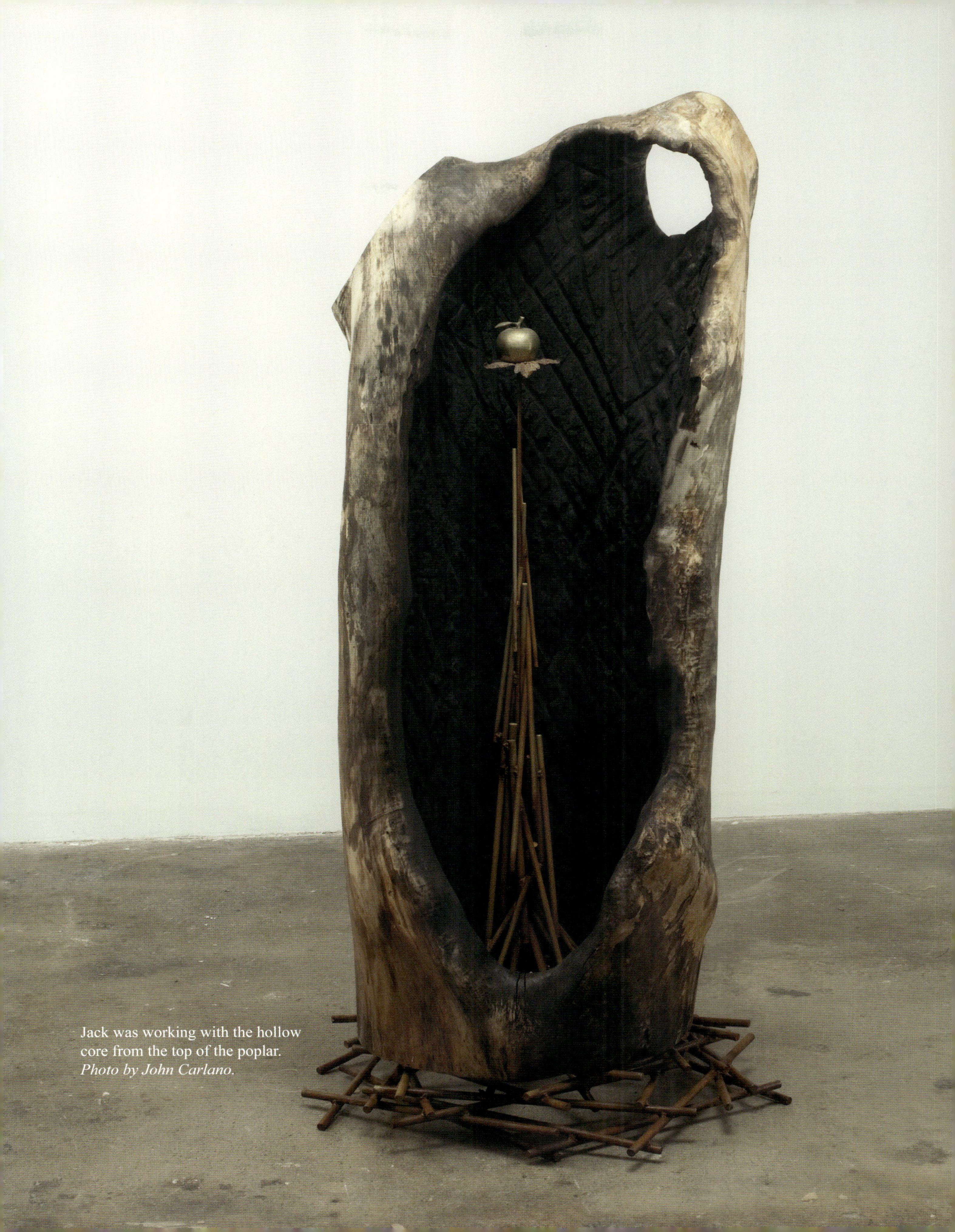

Jack was working with the hollow core from the top of the poplar. *Photo by John Carlano.*

Stephen Leichner

Bringing out the highest potential in a given piece of wood is what keeps my lathe humming and me happily engaged. The sculpted, wavelike edge of *The Hills of Chester County* is reminiscent of the panoramic view of the rolling landscape that Wharton enjoyed from his deck. The bowl was cut from a half log on the trunk about 30 feet above the ground. Further, it reflects his design philosophy of avoiding straight lines and symmetry. Also echoing this paradigm are the two smaller bowls. The rim of one curves outward while the other curves inward; Hence *Vessel: Extrovert* and *Vessel: Introvert.*

The Hills of Chester County (2011)
Tulip poplar
6" h x 19" diam.

Vessel: Extrovert (2011)
Tulip poplar
2.5" h x 11" diam.

Vessel: Introvert (2011)
Tulip poplar
3" h x 11" diam.

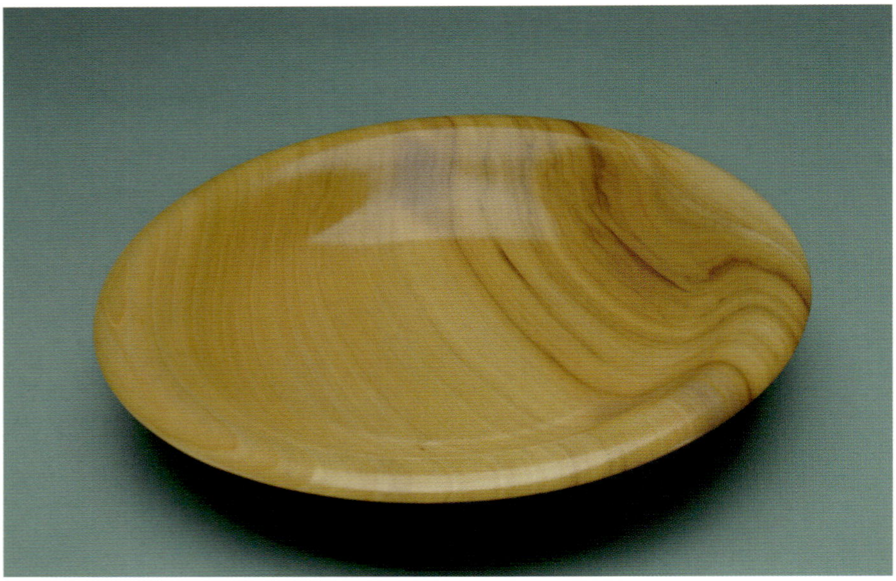

Photo by James Mario.

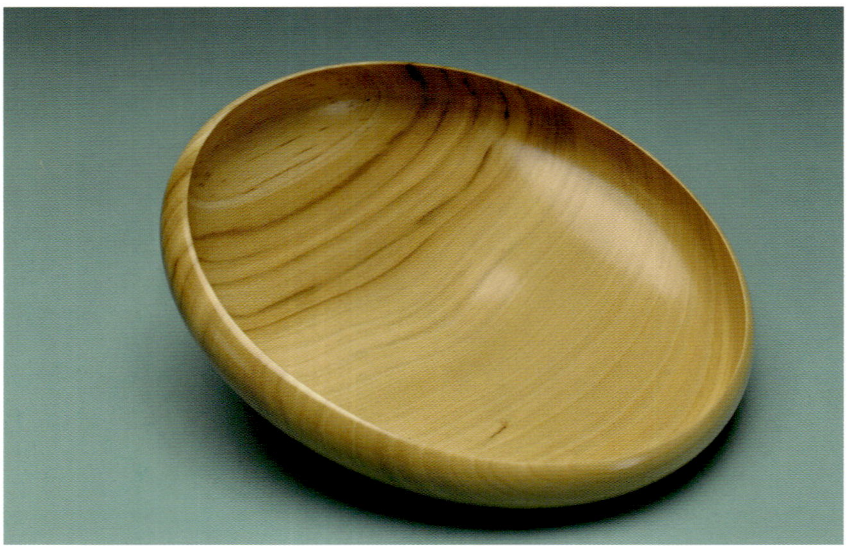

Photo by James Mario.

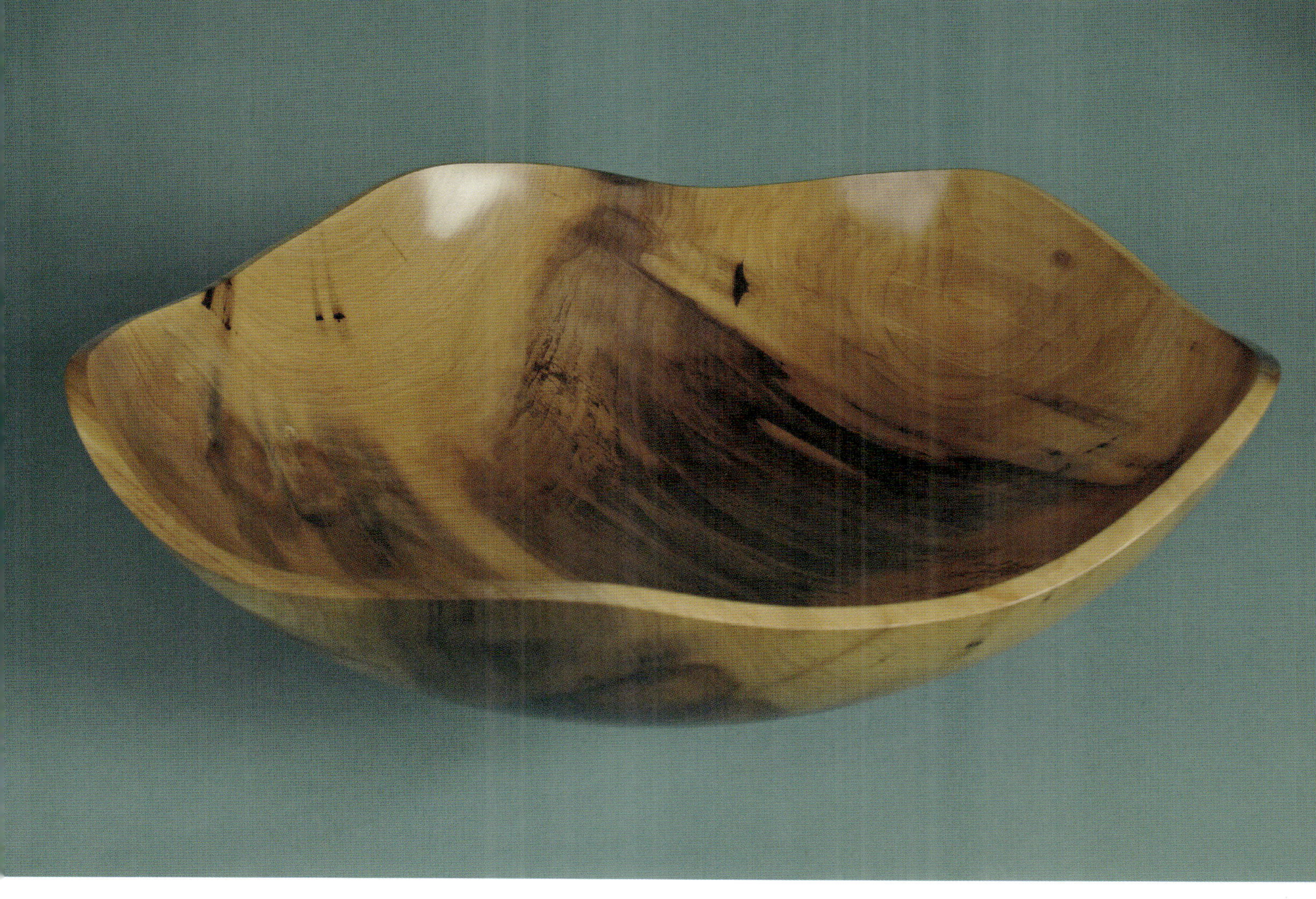

Photo by James Mario.

Steve Loar

My work has been important to the field of contemporary woodturning in its extended explorations of color, texture, complex composition, exploration of narrative, and attempts to concretize music. *Bird Encased* is a somewhat playful diversion from my current Lingham Series that are exercises in extreme restraint. A bend in the limb allowed for an unexpected bit of gesture. In addition to Esherick, I was looking at the sensibilities of the sculptor Constantine Brancusi and turner Rude Osolnik.

Bird Encased (2012)
Tulip poplar, partially bleached, paint/dye
17" h x 7" diam.

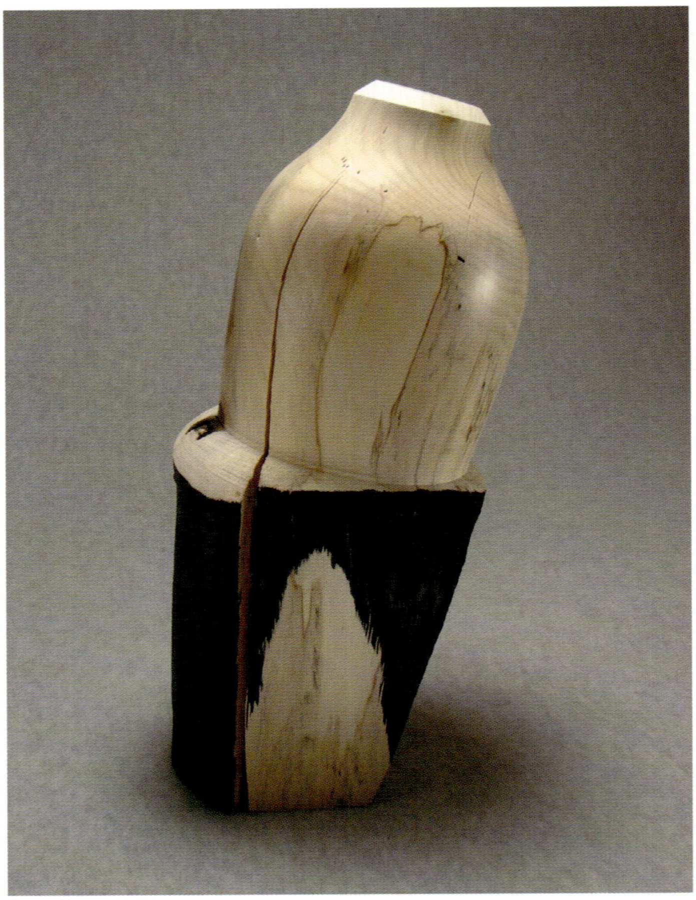

Photo by Steve Loar.

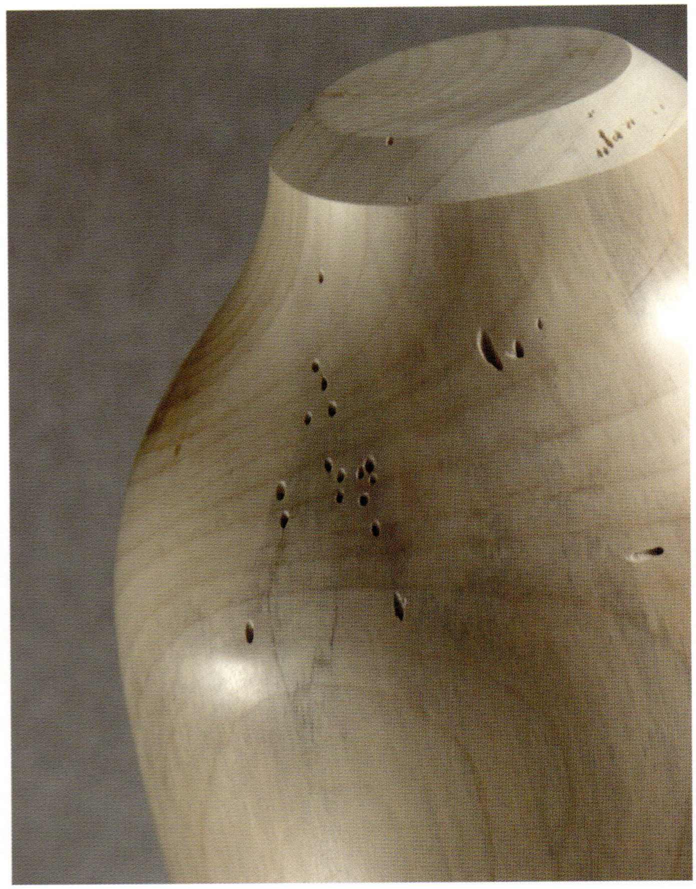

Photo by Steve Loar.

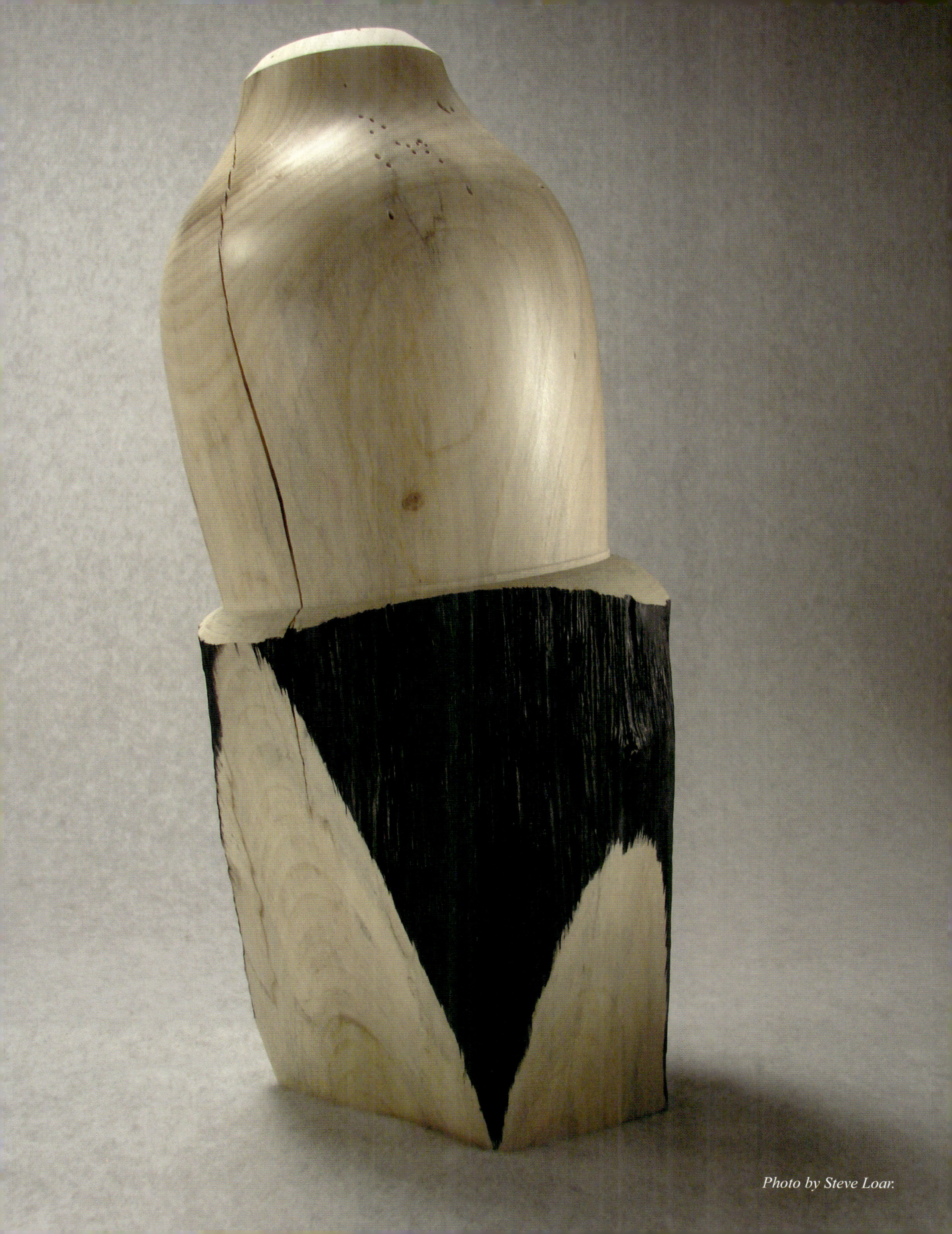

Photo by Steve Loar.

George Manns

Quite often a tree is more than just the source of raw material for the projects I undertake. In this case, my goal was to preserve the tree, literally, in a form Esherick himself might recognize. An interesting shape far up the trunk drew my eye, though it didn't initially suggest the shelving unit it became. The piece serves as a snapshot of a particular tree, incorporating holes left by sapsuckers and tree climbers, the knobby end of a broken limb, and growth rings. Truss rods strengthen the shelves, and a hidden compartment adds extra storage, though its main purpose is to surprise and delight. It also gave me the opportunity to include magnets in the design!

Gone But Not Forgotten (2012)
39" h x 50" w x 20" d
Tulip poplar, oil finish

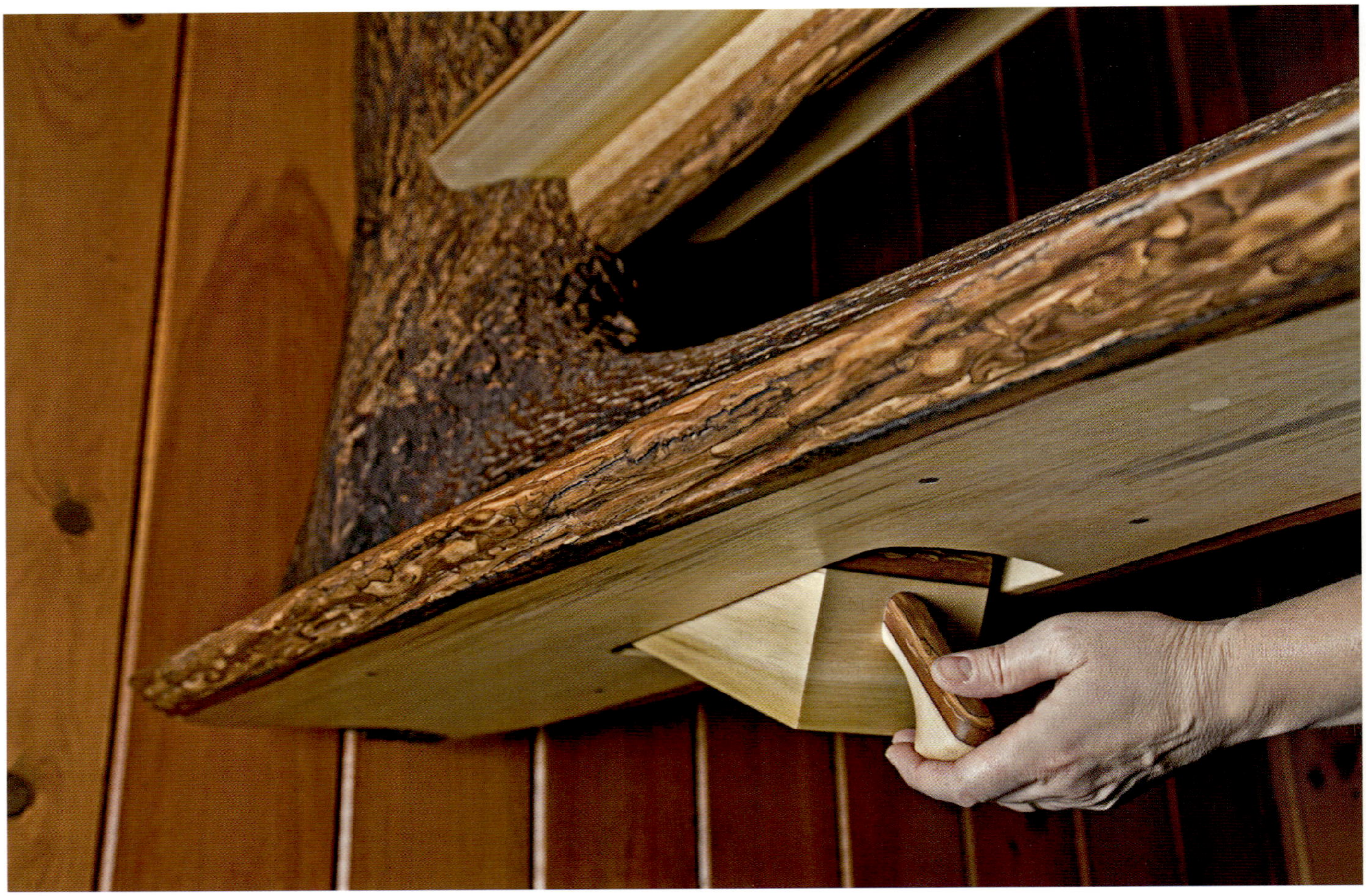

Photo by Jess Badgley.

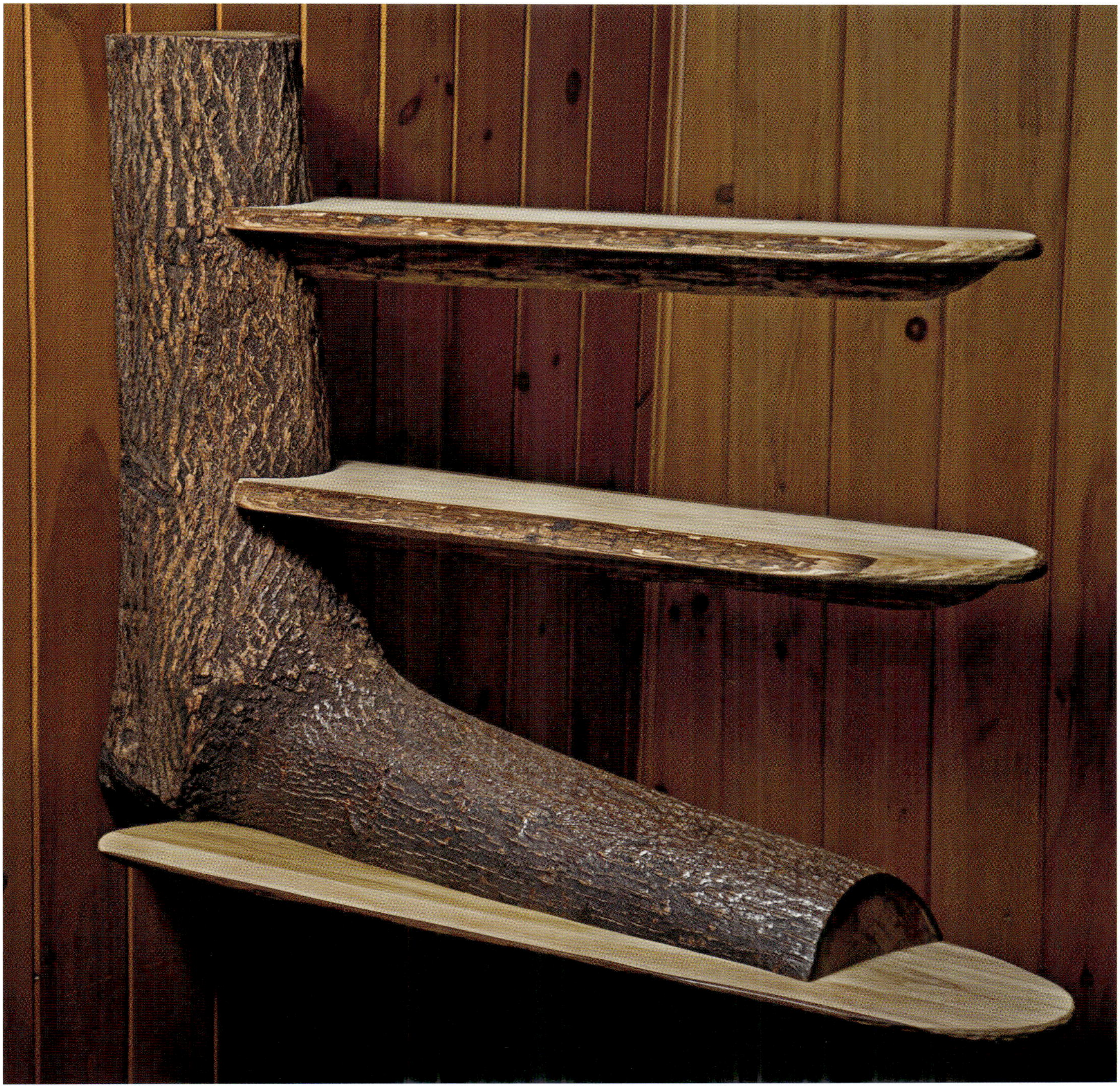

Photo by Jess Badgley.

James Mario

After receiving my piece of poplar wood to do my project for the *Poplar Culture* Exhibit I asked myself, "What Would Wharton Do?" Wharton Esherick avoided using right angles or straight lines, and went to extremes to create very unorthodox designs.

My sculpture is free in design, demanding the viewer to look under, through, up, and around to see the movement, textures and little surprises dictated by the raw original shape, color, and natural decay and beauty of the wood.

The two bowls were initially drawn on the same piece of wood, but then cut apart and designed separately. Wharton's philosophy of not using right angles and straight lines guided my design.

Reaching (2011)
Tulip poplar
29" h x 17" w x 14" d

Curvy Linear (2011)
Tulip poplar
2.75" h x 16.75" l x 10.75" w

Quadrupedia (2011)
Tulip poplar
2.75" h x 17" l x 8" w

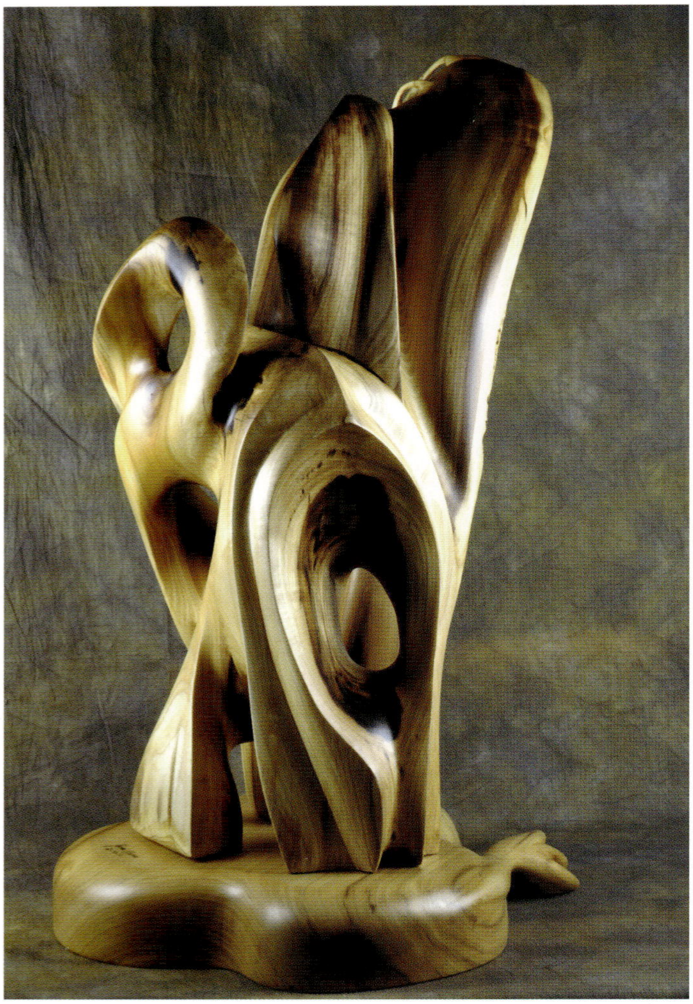

Photo by James Mario.

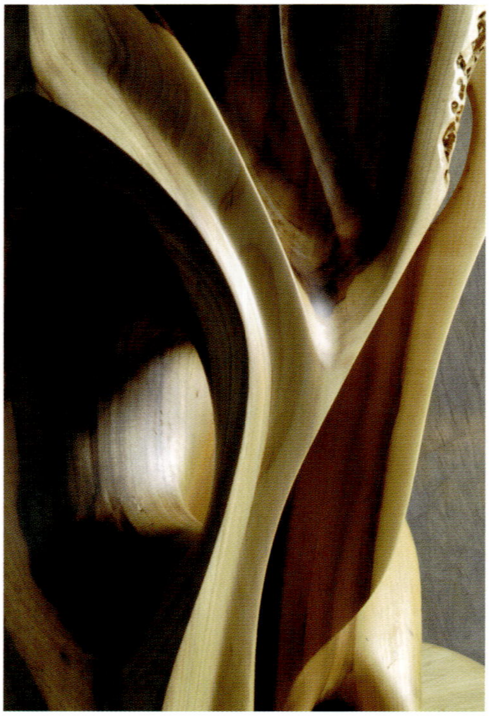

Photo by James Mario.

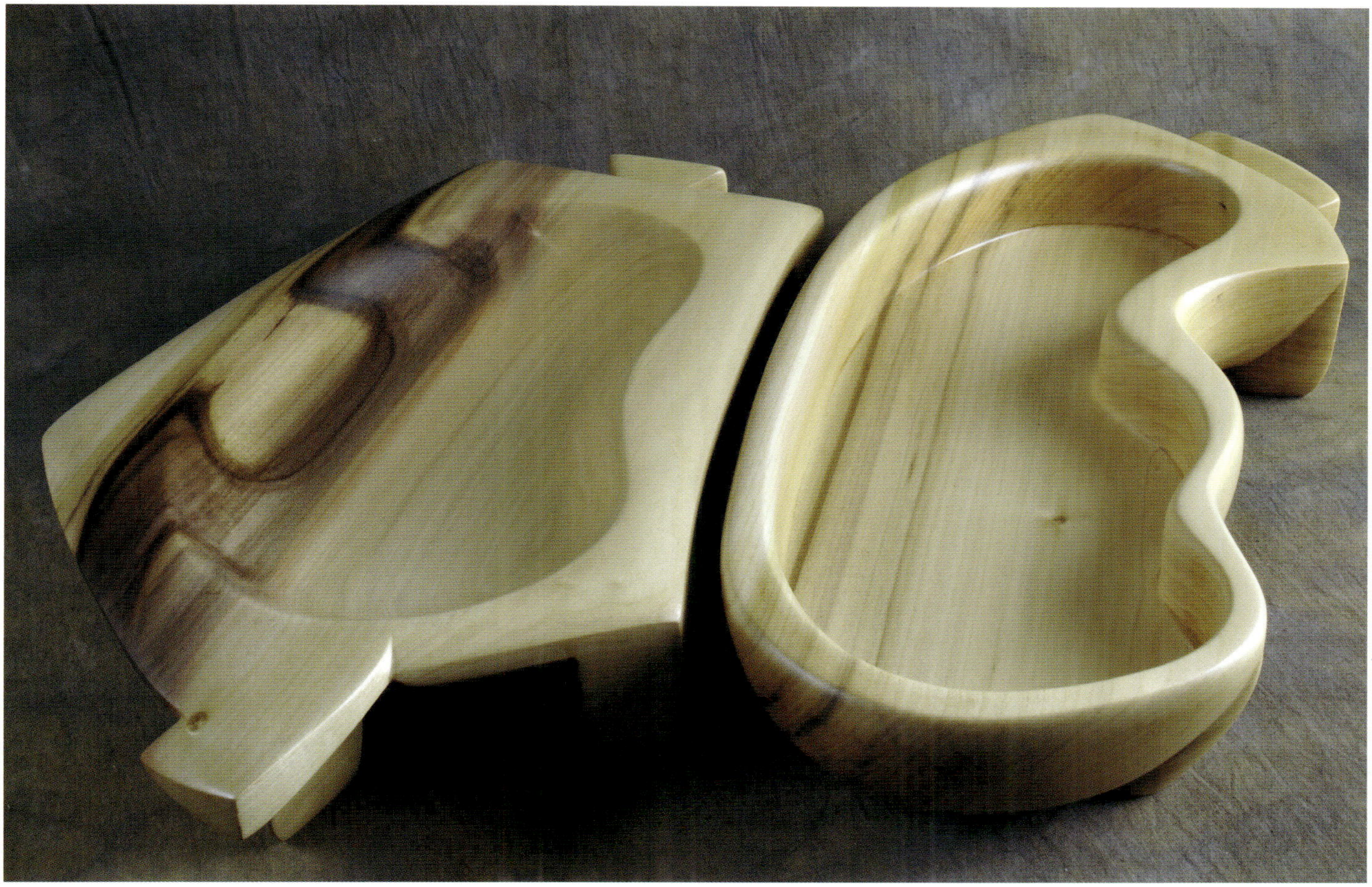

Photo by James Mario.

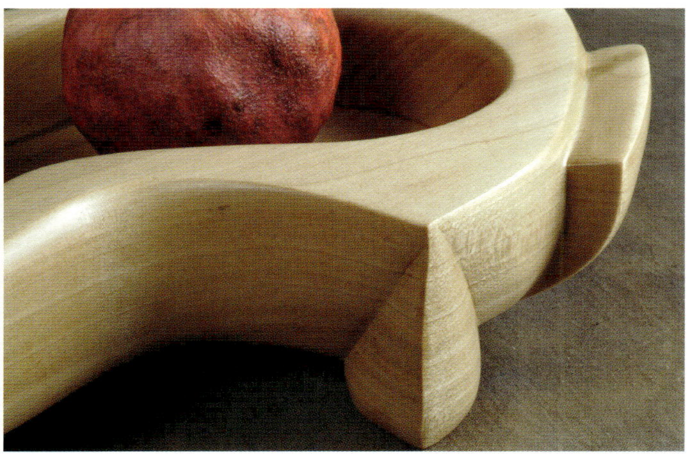

Detail of *Curvy Linear*. *Photo by James Mario.*

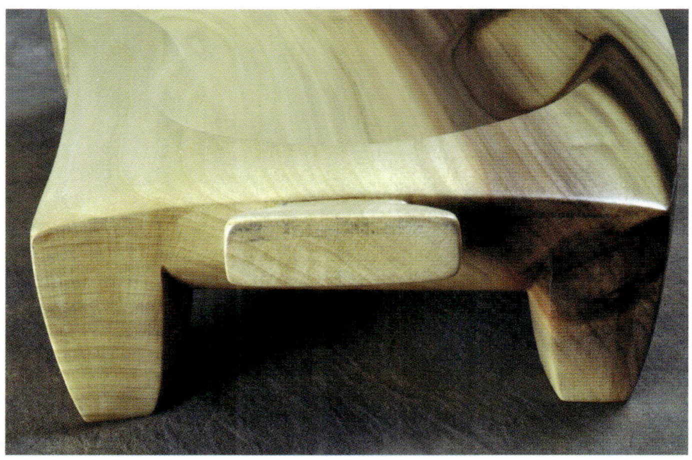

Detail of *Quadrupedia*. *Photo by James Mario.*

John Matthews

Just out of high school in Lancaster County, with a desire to pursue the trade of furniture making, a friend drove me to visit the Wharton Esherick Museum. The transformative experience led me to earn a degree in fine arts so that I could take control of designing my own work, and from there to a career as an art educator working in clay and other sculpture media.

Since that time, I've introduced the Esherick studio to several hundred high school and university students through field trips. I find it continually rewarding to witness the silent awe and delight on the faces of these soon-to-be Esherick admirers as they enter the uncharted realm of his studios, living spaces, furniture, and collections.

The realization when Wharton Esherick decided to transition from his fine arts training to that of woodworker, is the period I've considered through my ceramic work for this exhibit. Using terra cotta clay, local clay slips and glazes utilizing the remaining ash from the burnt poplar wood chips, these thrown platter forms are both functional and sculptural. I borrowed technical and decorative techniques in clay from Esherick's friend, Henry Varnum Poor, and fused these with Wharton's expressive carving and block printing marks. I believe Esherick utilized a chisel on his buzzard desk, as he had earlier wielded brush with pigment on canvas.

Tulip Poplar (2012)
Terra cotta clay, clay slips, poplar ash glazes
1.75" d x 10.37" diam.

Tulip Poplars (2012)
Terra cotta clay, clay slips, poplar ash glazes
1.75" d x 10.37" diam.

Poplar Woods (2012)
Terra cotta clay, clay slips, poplar ash glazes
1.5" d x 10.75" diam.

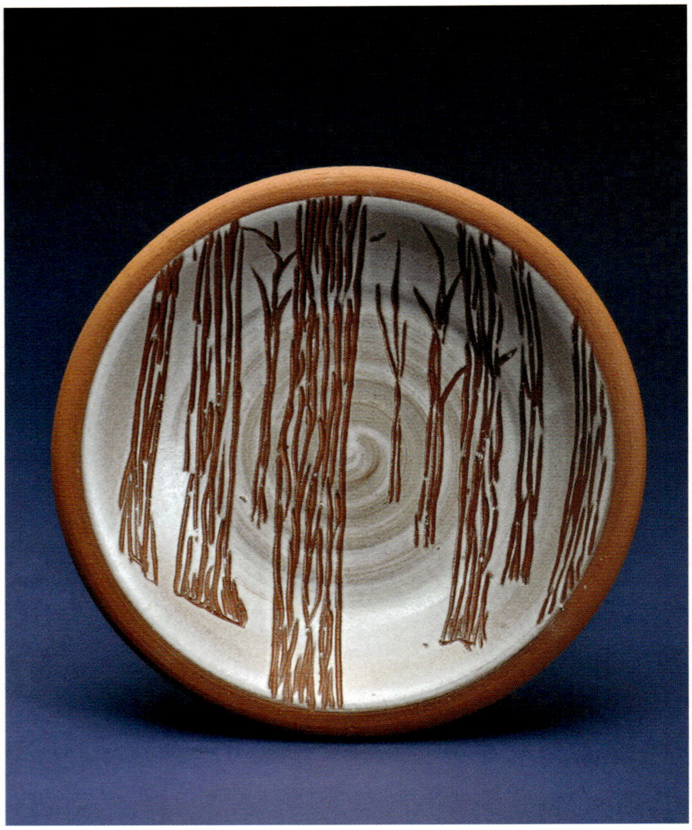

Photo by James Mario.

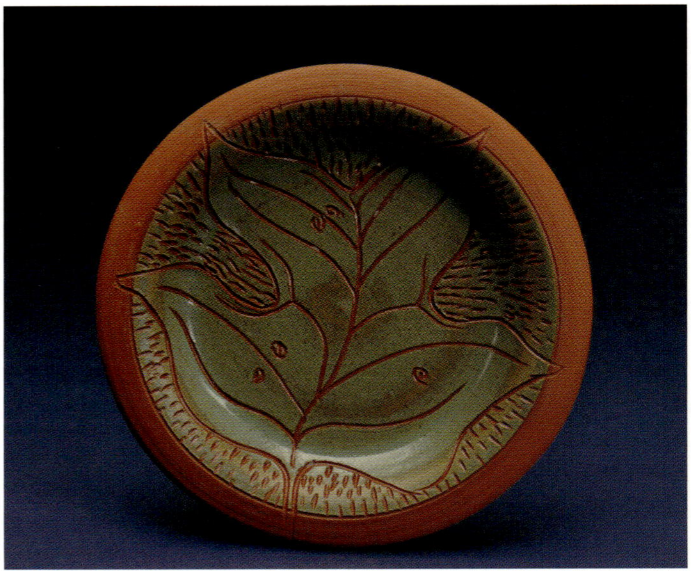

Photo by James Mario.

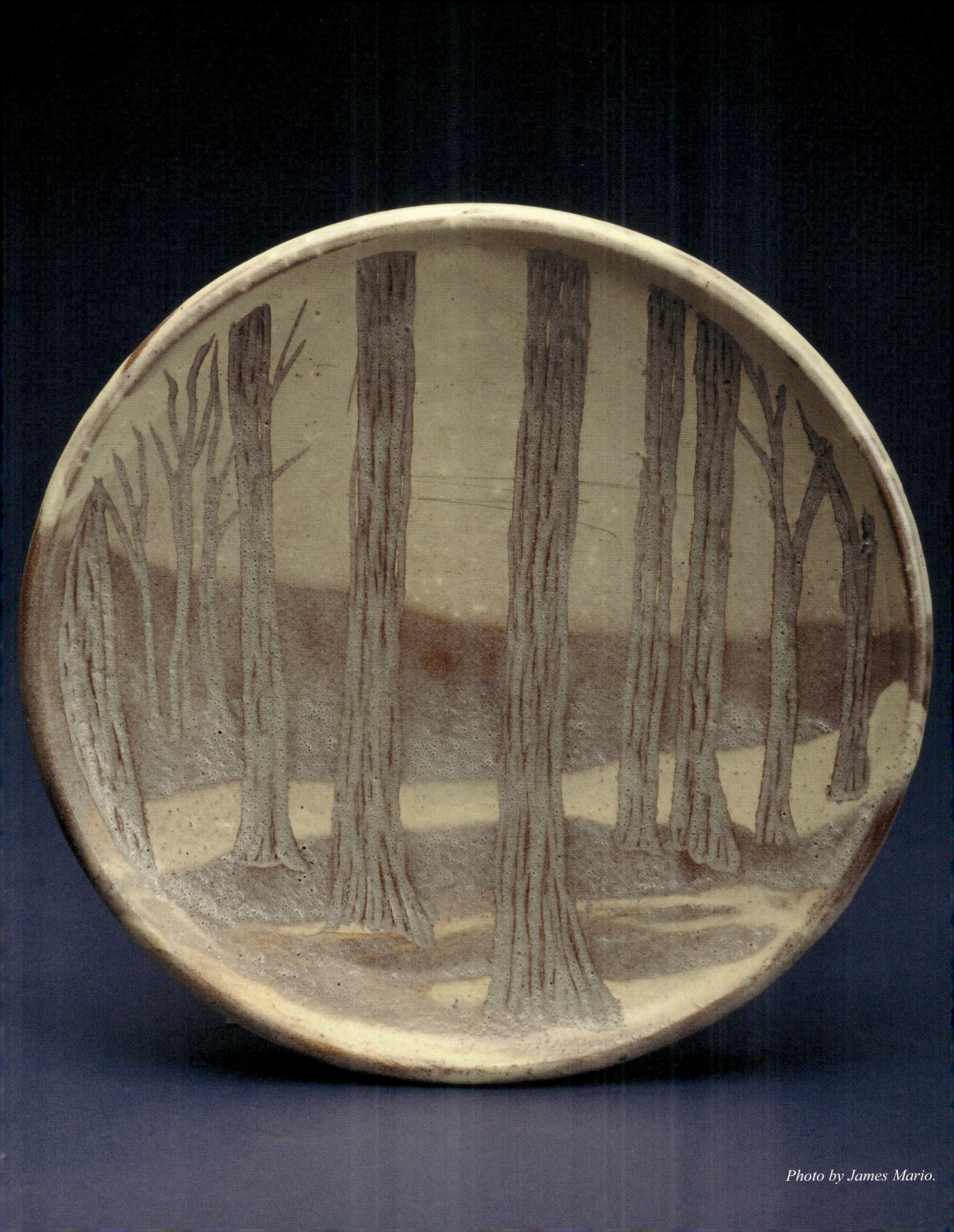

Photo by James Mario.

Alphonse Mattia

I owe so much to Wharton Esherick as an influence and for being the patron saint of all things splintery and inky. His work was the first I saw by a professional artist/woodworker in the late sixties when I was an art student in Philadelphia. Over the years Esherick's sculpture, furniture, and woodcuts continued to excite and inspire me in different ways as I matured in my career.

I chose to do a woodcut because I have always wanted to explore this process, again because of Esherick's work, but I kept putting it off. The invitation to *Poplar Culture* gave me a real incentive to do that. The bonding friendships W.E. had with those close to him and his life-long connection to the Hedgerow Theater seemed an intriguing theme for me to explore. *Steppin' Out* depicts Wharton, Louis Kahn, and Mima on the steps of Hedgerow. Somehow I don't think it requires any stretch to imagine them on a warm spring evening in that very setting. The imagery may seem familiar because Esherick used the Hedgerow entrance and steps as a source in many of his drawings, prints, and wooden objects. I used a combination of laser and hand cutting to produce my image.

Steppin' Out (2012)
Woodcut
Ink on Paper
Image size: 11" h x 7" w
Paper size: 15.12" h x 11.12" w

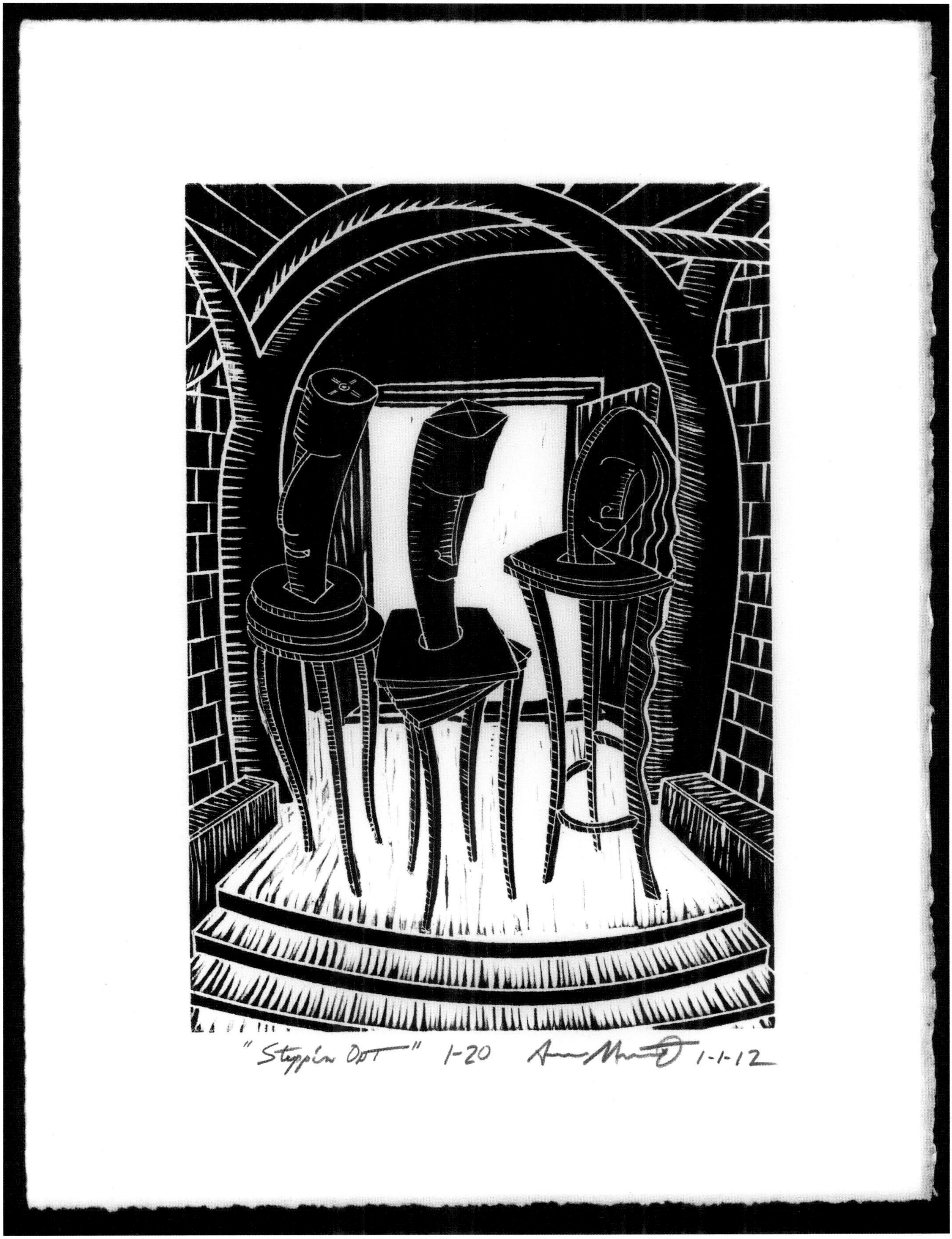

Photo by Alphonse Mattia.

Aurora McFee

This reductive woodcut harks on explorations of trades. The concept of craft and self sufficiency is something I value highly within myself and others. These assets are bound to tradition, ritual, mythology, and history – in the past, often defining whole societies. Textile production, hunting, and farming are no different than woodworking and printmaking in this sense. Many such trades were integral to past societies, but are now rendered obsolete, executed by individuals and machines outside of personable community settings. I attempt to visually and conceptually reunite a sense of intimacy and calm within my work through a pilgrimage to simpler times. (below, opposite, and following page)

Untitled (2012)
Reductive woodcut from tulip poplar block
Image size: 14.5" h x 36" w
Paper size: 24" h x 47.5" w

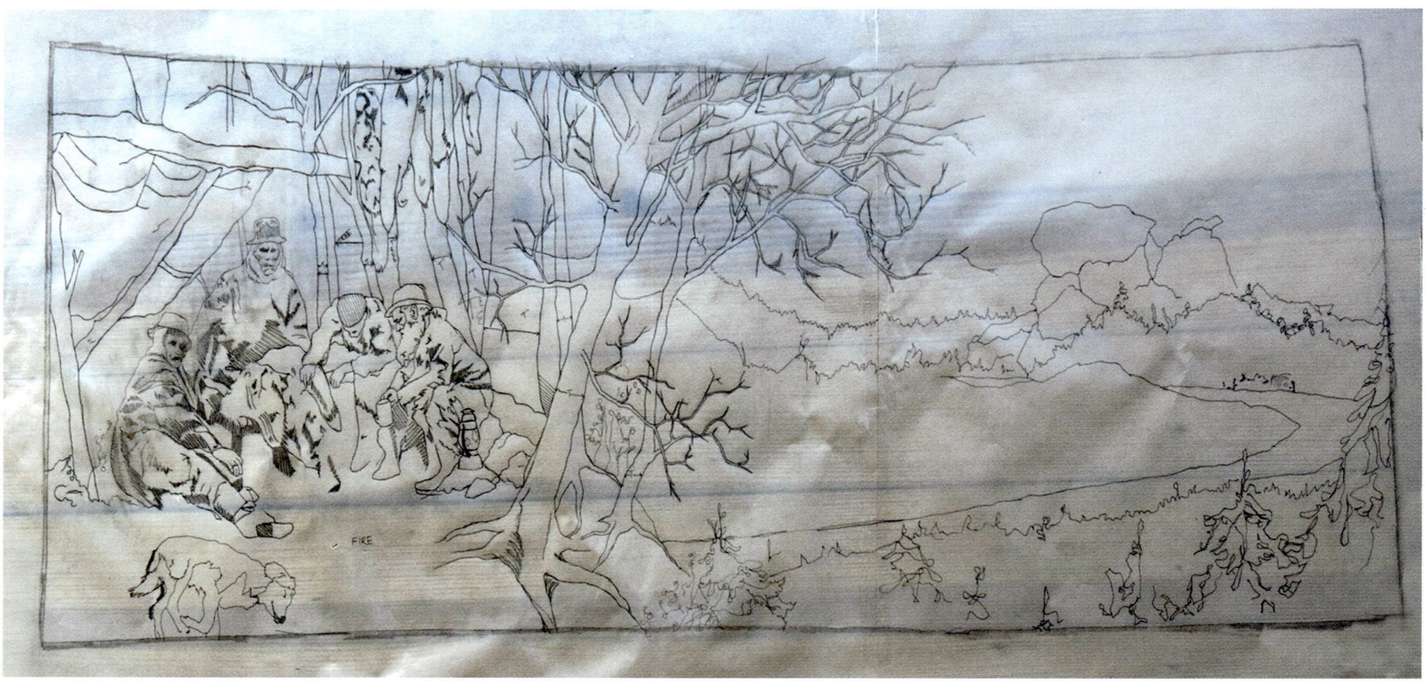

Aurora's reductive woodcut changes the block with each successive printing. There will be four layers, each a different color. The final layer will be printed on Esherick's 1836 Washington Press at the Wharton Esherick Museum. This series of photos shows details of the different parts of the process. This first image is her preliminary sketch. *Photo by Aurora McFee.*

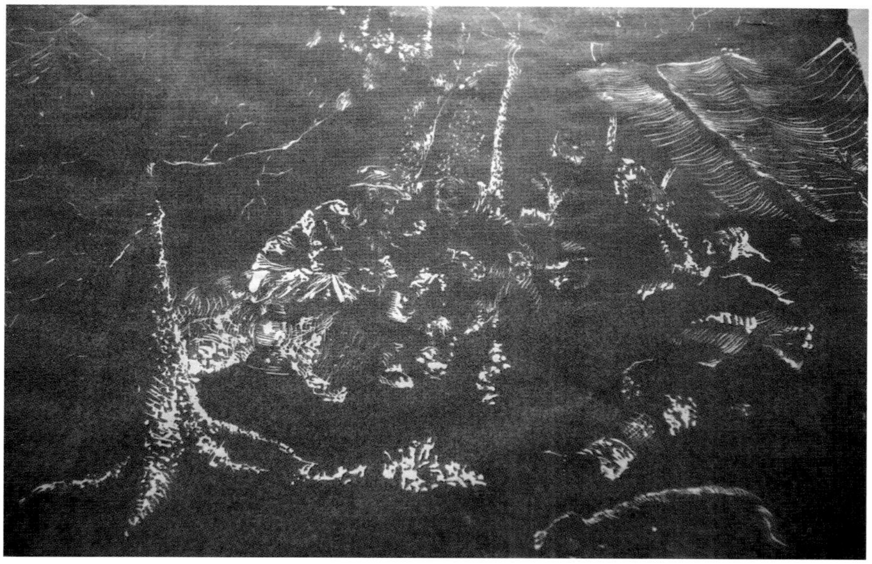

Proof for first color – detail.
Photo by Aurora McFee.

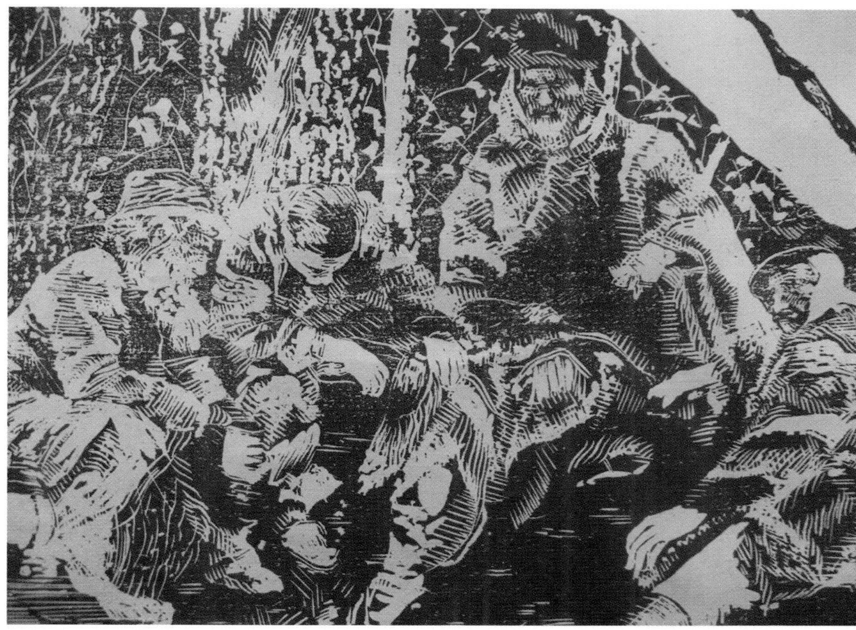

Proof for second color – detail.
Photo by Aurora McFee.

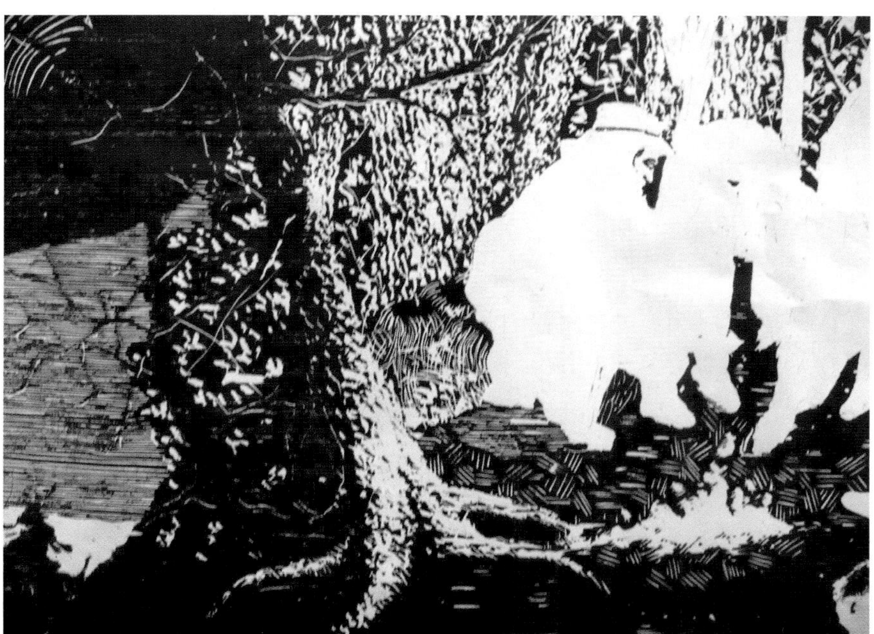

Proof for third color – detail.
Photo by Aurora McFee.

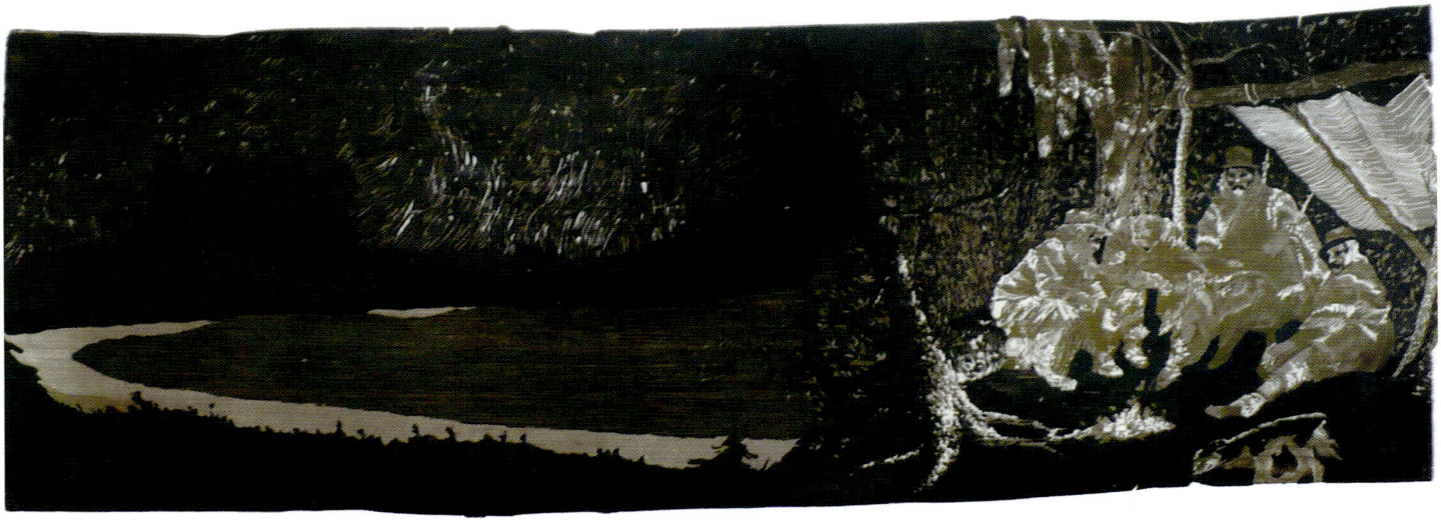

Print after the third layer. *Photo by Aurora McFee.*

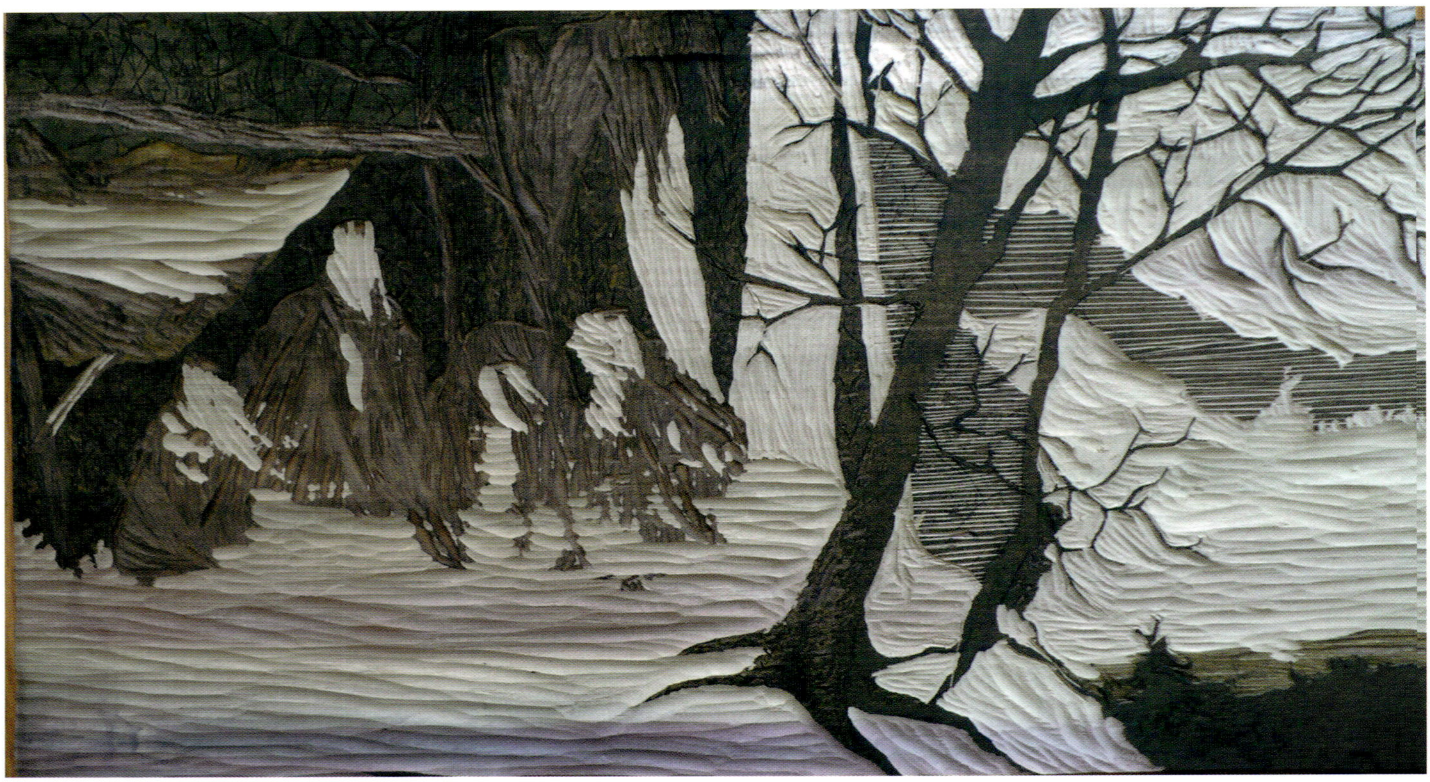

Woodblock for the fourth color – detail. *Photo by Aurora McFee.*

James McNabb

I was honored to be asked to make a piece for the Poplar Culture exhibit, and to work with the Wharton Esherick Museum. Before designing a piece for the show, I felt it was essential to visit the museum and immerse myself inside Wharton's studio. My piece is inspired by Wharton's sculptural approach to woodworking and his dedication to structure and function. The form is stack laminated and shaped with a sculptor's vision. The drawers are hand cut dovetails, and laser engraved with imagery inspired by Wharton's woodcut prints. This piece is my attempt to balance my own design sensibility with the characteristics of Wharton Esherick's approach to making. (below and next page)

JMWE (2012)
Tulip poplar, bacote
43" l x 10" h x 12" d

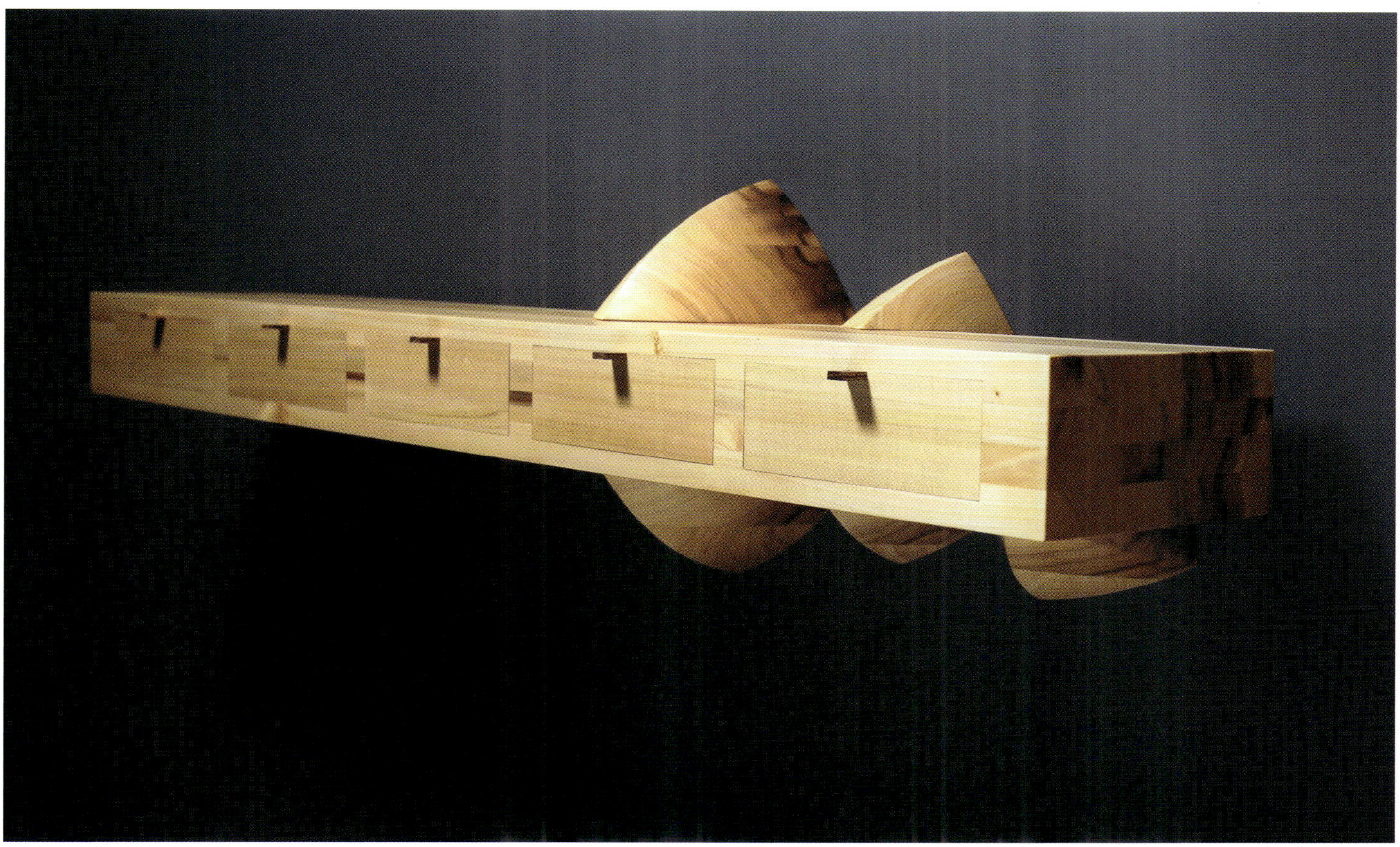

Photo courtesy of James McNabb.

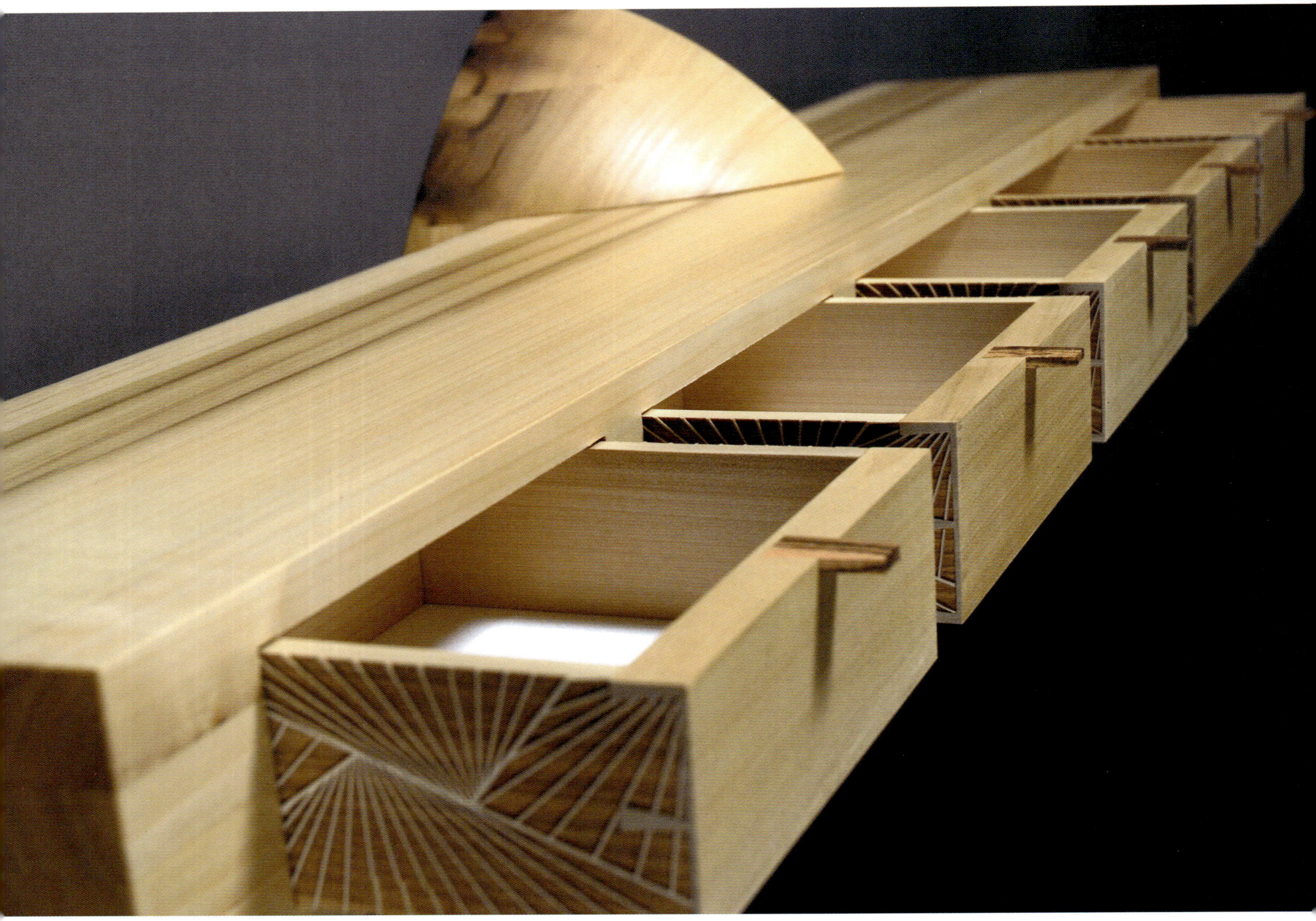

Photo courtesy of James McNabb.

Photo courtesy of James McNabb.

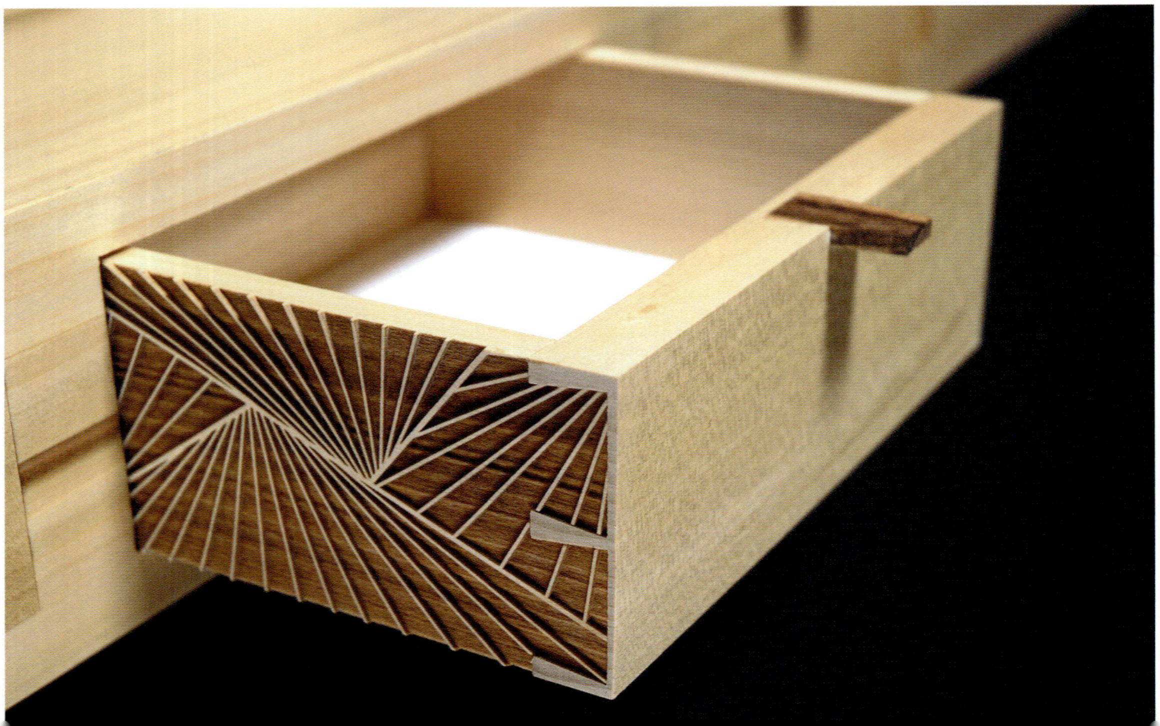

Mira Nakashima

I was honored to be asked to participate in the *Poplar Culture* project celebrating the life of a tree, as well as of Wharton Esherick and George Nakashima. Its sweet smell brought back memories from my childhood. The plank itself looked rather plain, and seemed to be so warped and cracked that I thought, at first, it would be a curved bench bridged by many butterflies. After flipping it over, however, I found that it was flatter, with a knot-hole and several patches of interesting color. I thought that the base should be walnut, and then debated whether to use my design right-side-up or upside-down, as either way looked interesting—so I call it "Reflection."

I feel that I am but walking in my father's awesome footsteps, trying my best to honor him and his traditions of construction and design. Although the majority of our clients prefer interpretations of the "classic" George Nakashima designs, there are always exceptional planks of wood or exceptional usage requests that require the development of something new, which becomes a challenge to "push the envelope"...gently.

At this stage of my life I try to imagine the best way to preserve my father's legacy for the future, as it has been 22 years since his passing. (below and next page)

Reflection Table (2012)
Tulip poplar, walnut
16" h x 100" l x 24" w

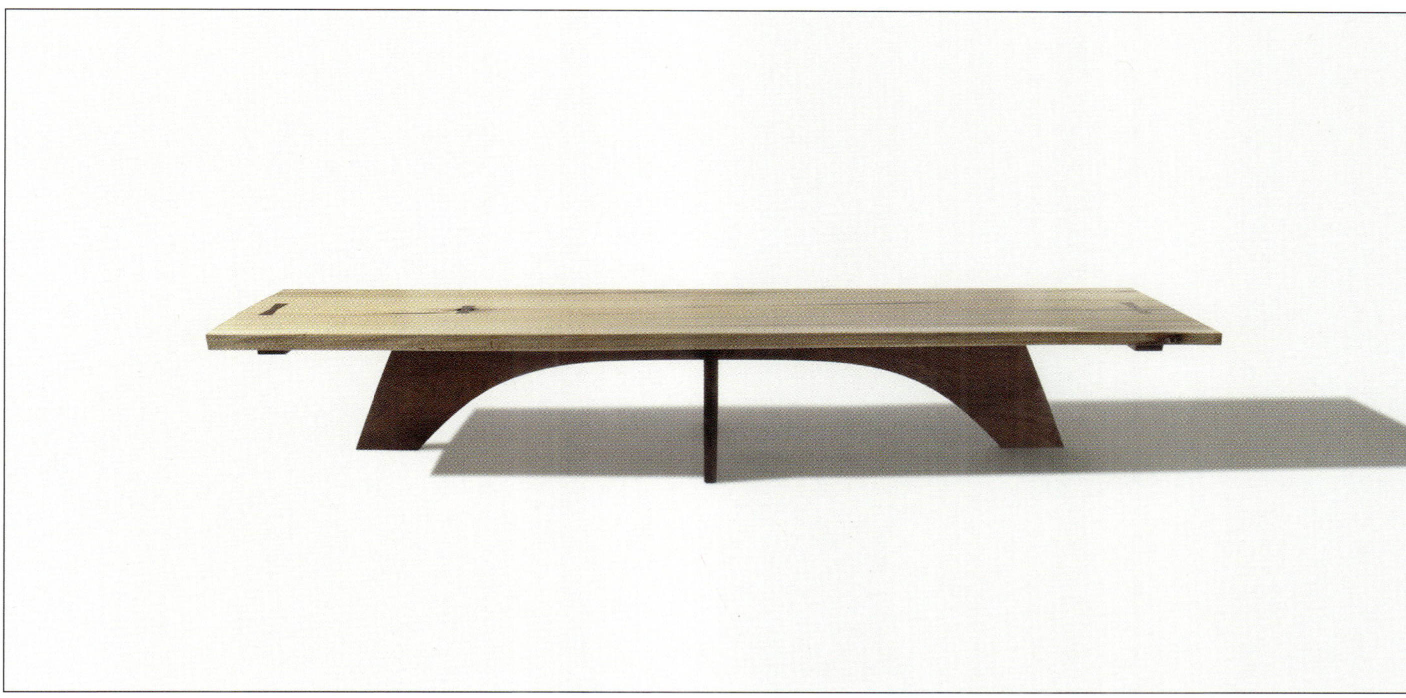

Photo by Christian Giannelli.

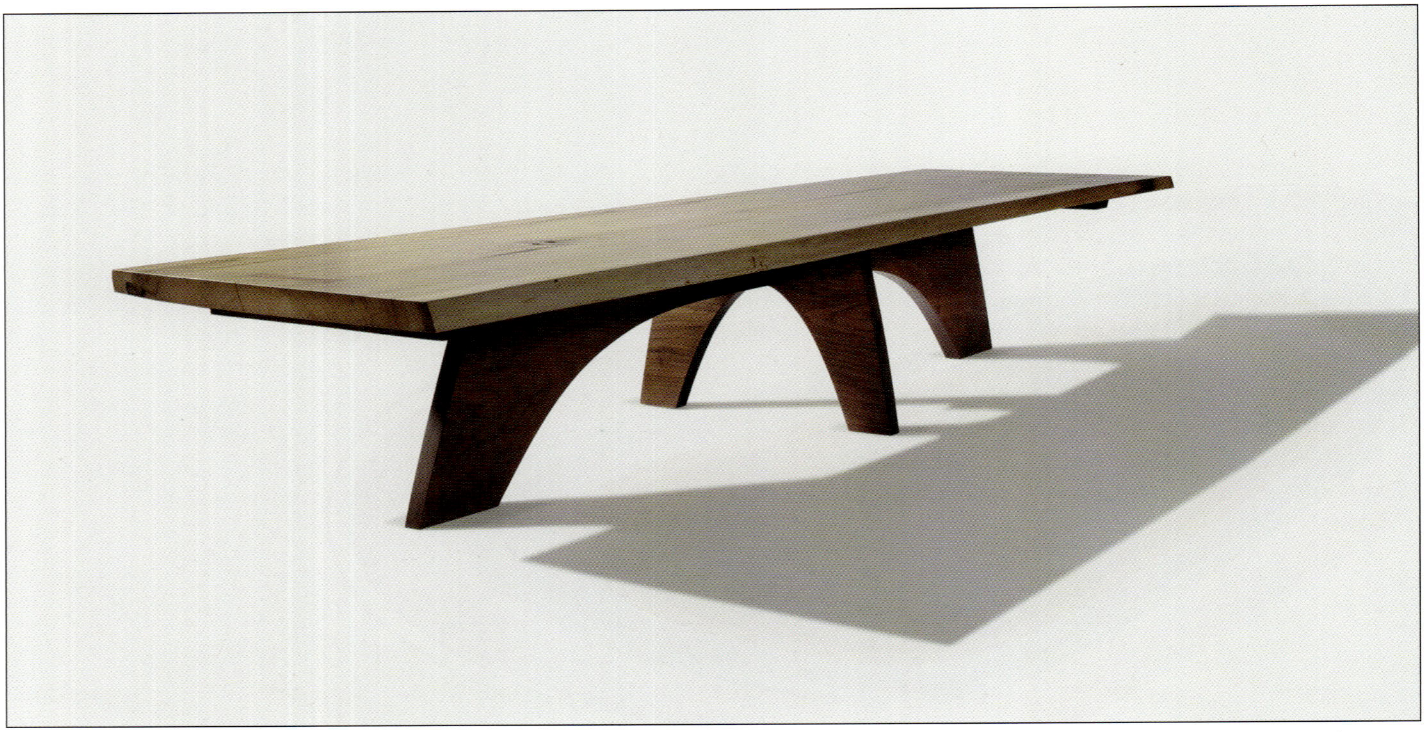

Photo by Christian Giannelli.

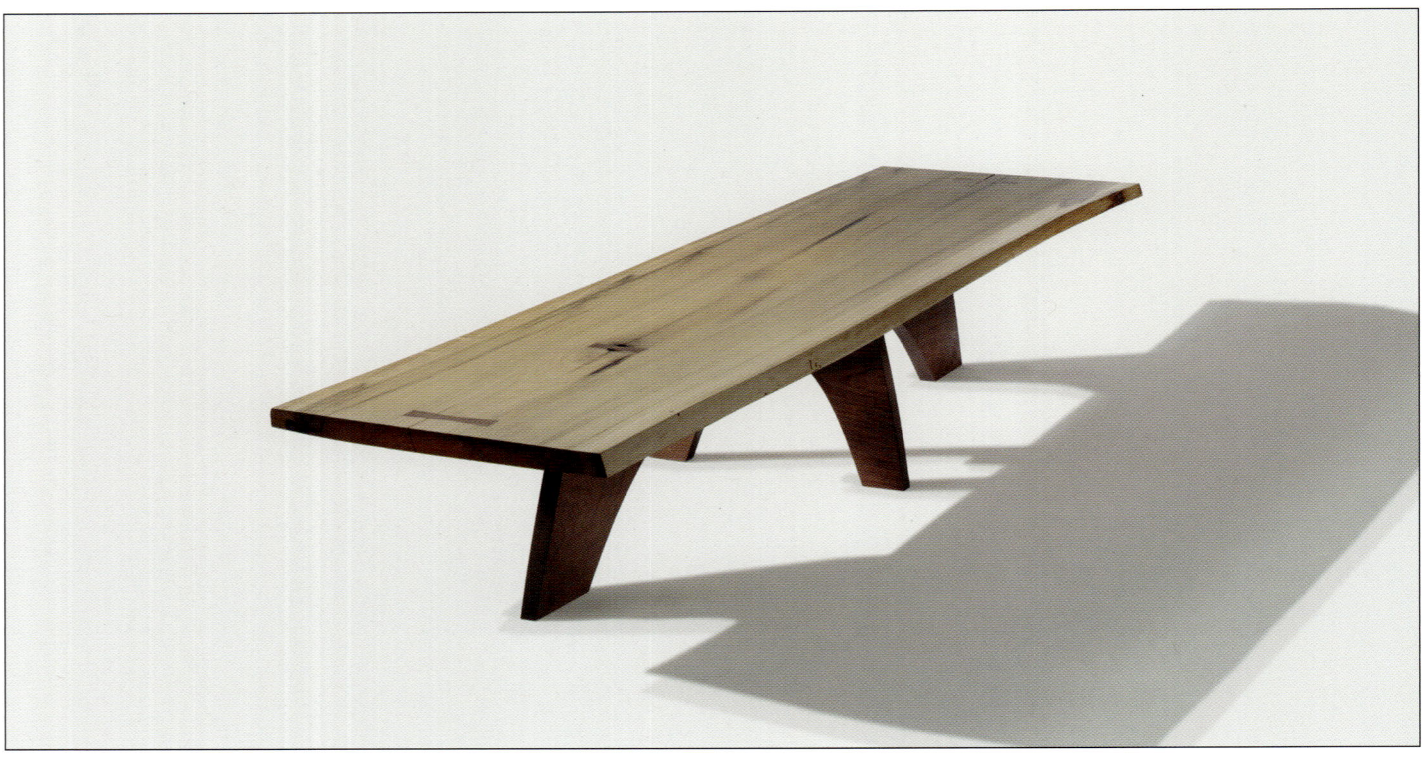

Photo by Christian Giannelli.

Matt Neff

Having had multiple opportunities to interact with the work of Wharton Esherick, both through a project printing a folio of his woodblocks, working on his press, and now through making this piece, I continued to reflect on ideas of memory, different ways of knowing, and the relationship between artists in collaboration. Wharton Esherick's hand as an artist has become a familiar one to me and it is with this familiarity and an interest in collaboration that I approached making this piece.

A Mental Impression Retained (2012)
Ink and pigment on Fabriano paper
38" h x 27" w

Photo by Matt Neff.

Ryan Procsal

I had read about Wharton Esherick in books but I always thought he lived in New England somewhere. After moving to Pennsylvania, I was delighted to find out that Esherick's home was only a few miles away. The Wharton Esherick Museum has been a great inspiration – a kind of religious place for woodworkers.

Candle staff (2012)
Tulip poplar
43.75" h x 18.5" diam.

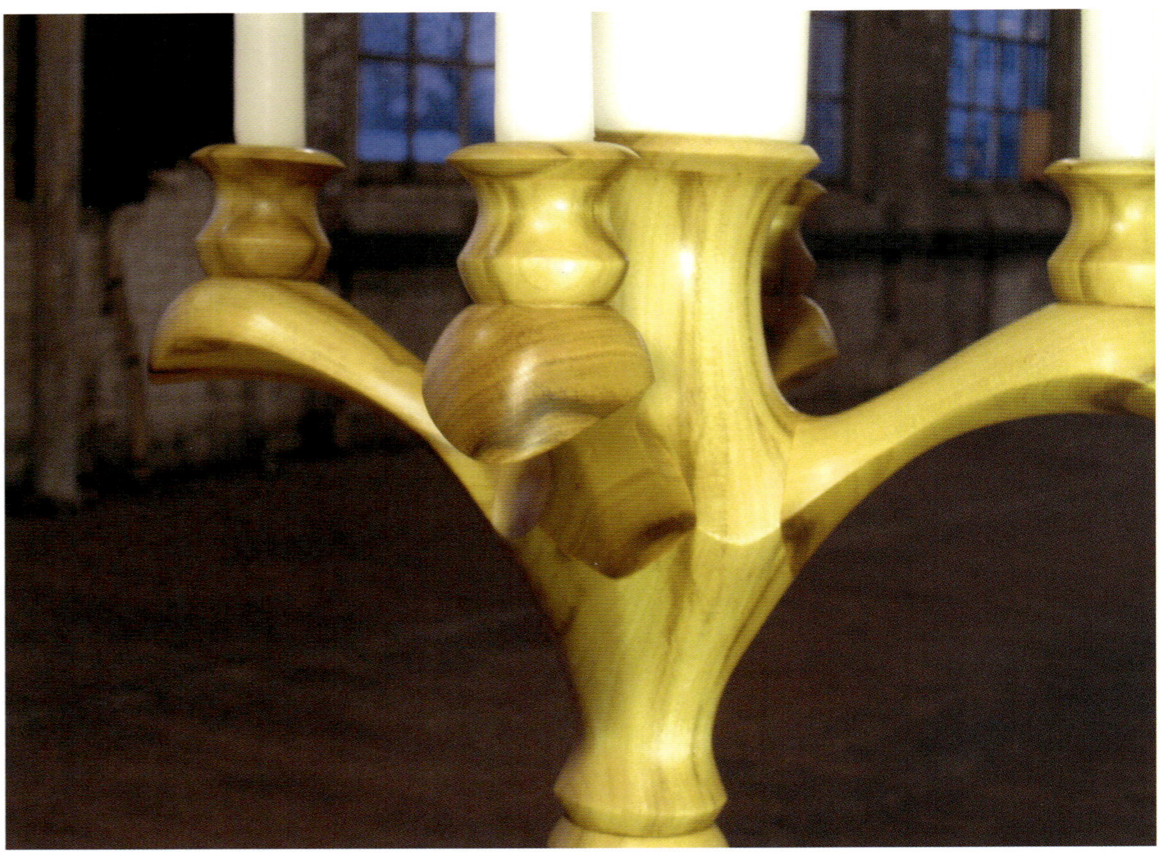

Photo by Ryan Procsal.

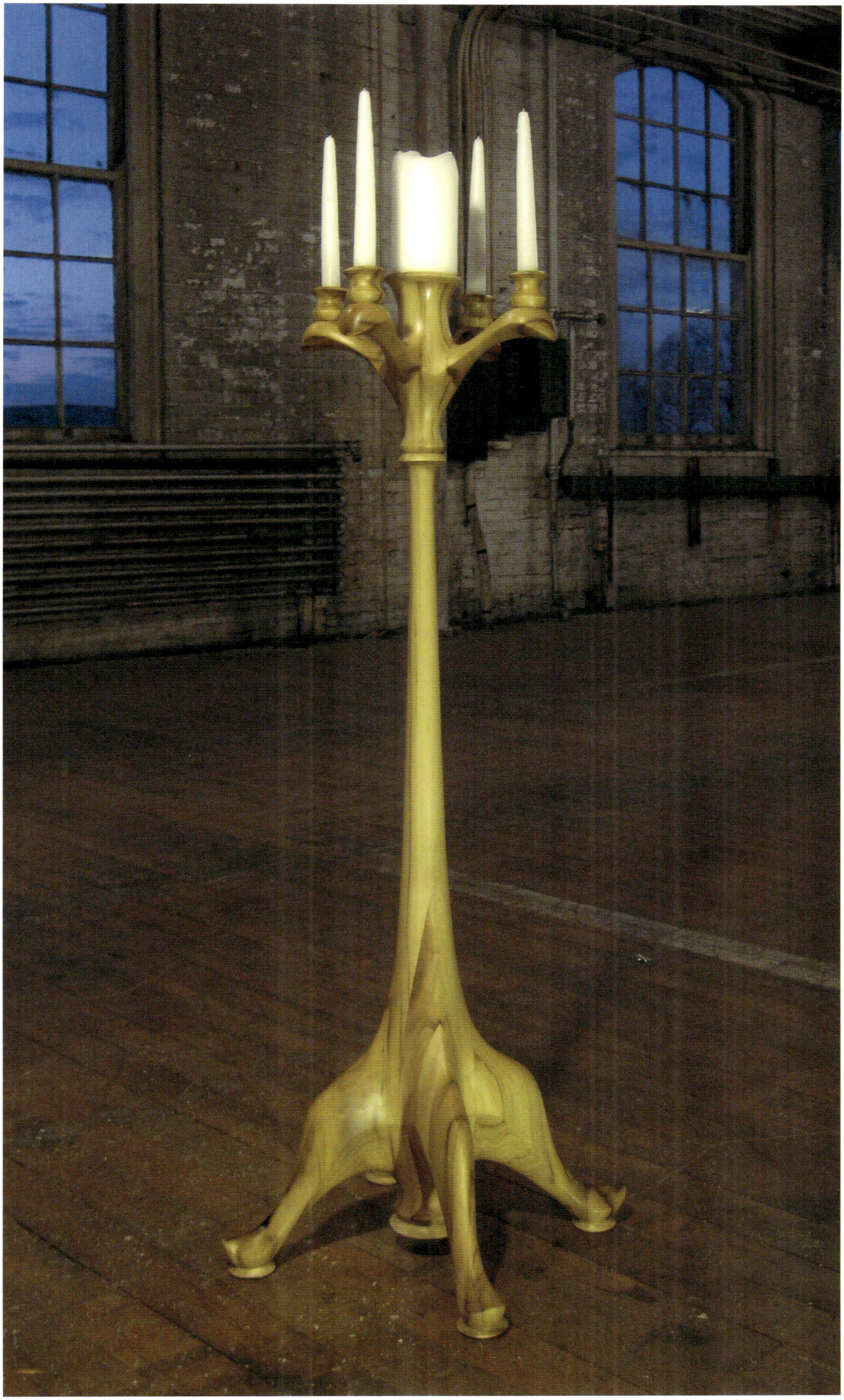

Photo by Ryan Procsal.

Michael Puryear

My choice of wood as a medium of expression is based on its natural warmth and appeal to the hand, along with its technology and traditions. Not having any formal training, my furniture making skills are the result of reading and experimentation.

Design has always had a special resonance for me. The attraction of furniture in particular arose from my early awareness and appreciation of the clarity and directness of Shaker and Scandinavian design. The material culture of Japan, Africa, and other cultures also influences me. Individuals such as Wharton Esherick and James Krenov, particularly in their dedication to their craft, were role models that inspired me.

Yellow Bench (2012)
Poplar, milk paint
16" h x 48" l x 18" w

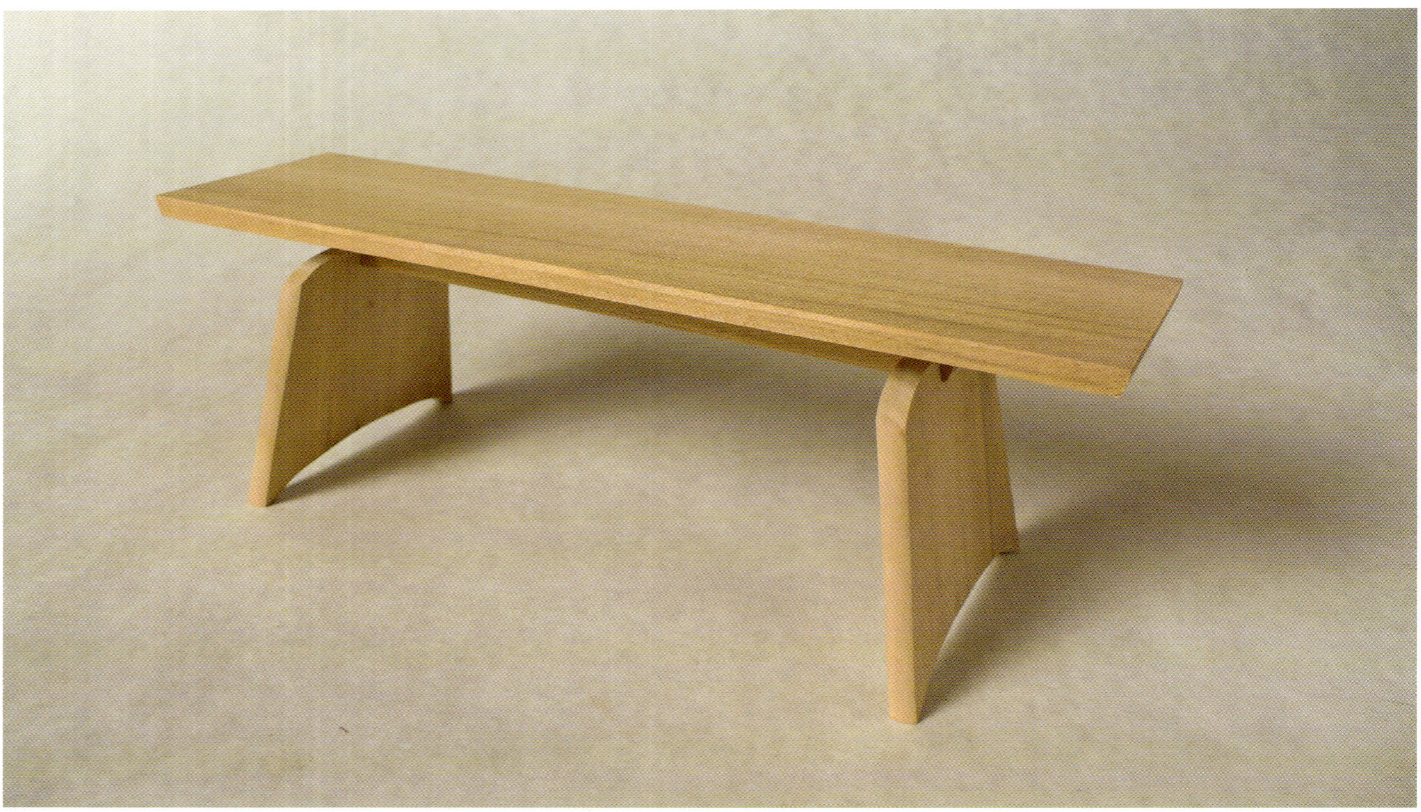

Photo by Michael Puryear.

Norm Sartorius

In the mid-1970s I visited the Wharton Esherick Museum at the suggestion of a friend. My hope for a career as a wood artist grew as a result of seeing Wharton's home, studio, and work that day.

For *Poplar Culture*, I took my inspiration from two of Wharton Esherick's sculptures and one piece of his furniture.

The beautiful curves of *Spring Beauty* and the stocky character of *Head of Dreiser* yielded my first two contributions. Spoons are usually rounded but in the last case the repeated triangles of the *Fischer Sewing Cabinet* demanded a greater departure from my typical work. (below and following two pages)

Spring Beauty Spoon (2012)
Tulip poplar
10" l x 2" w x 2" d

Head of Dreiser Spoon (2012)
Tulip poplar
9.5" l x 2" w x 2" d

Fischer Sewing Cabinet Spoon (2012)
Tulip Poplar
9" l x 3" w x 1.5" d

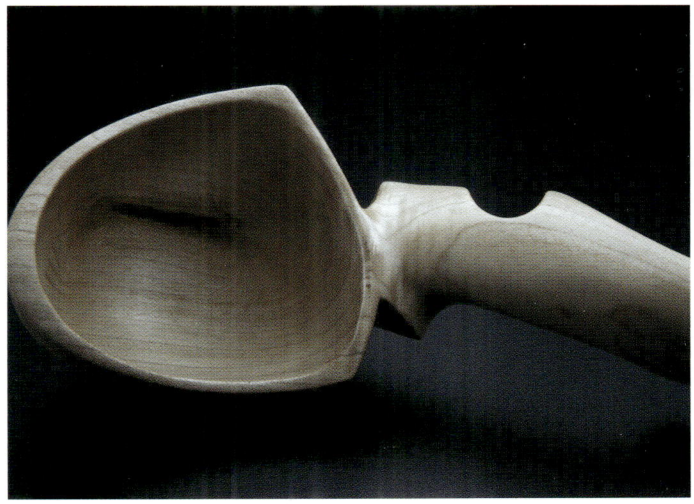

Head of Dreiser Spoon. Photo by Jim Osborn.

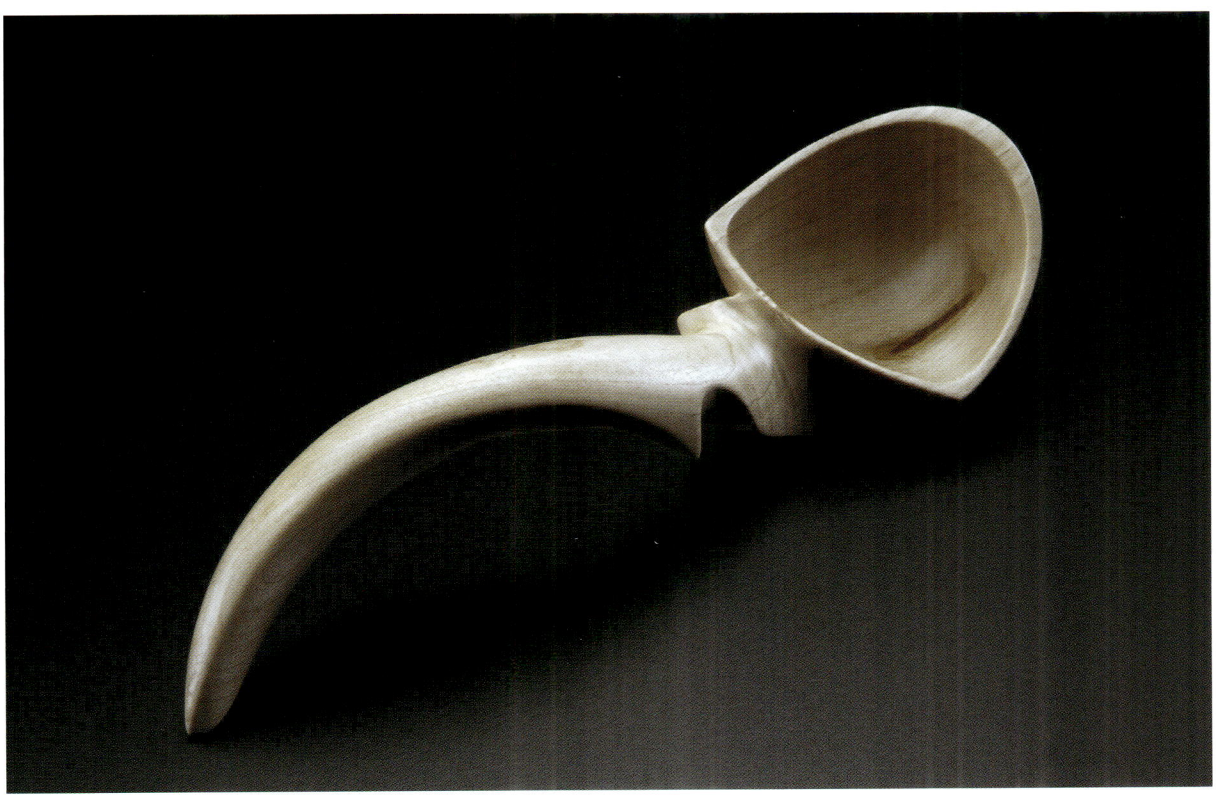

Photo by Jim Osborn.

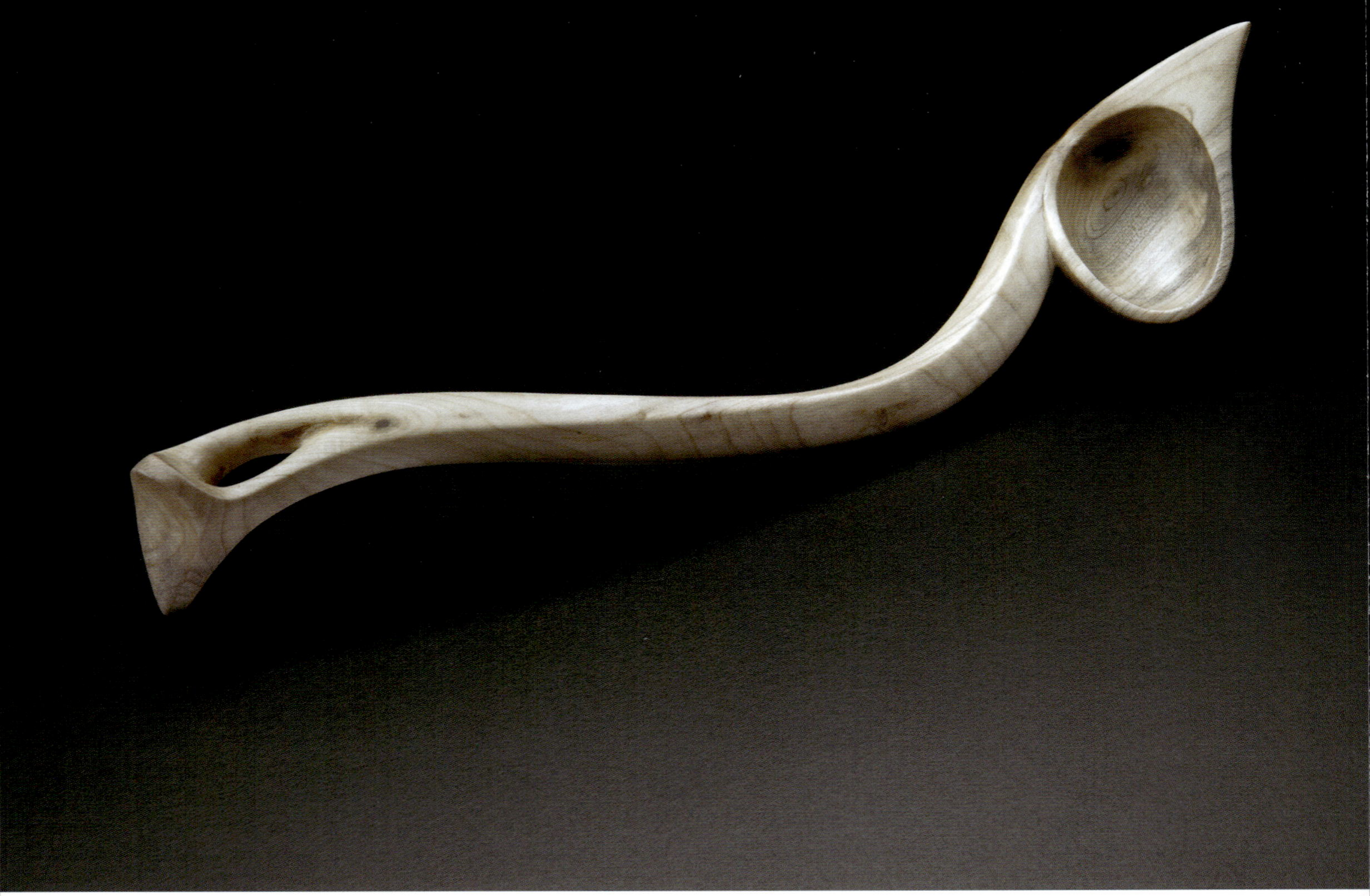

Spring Beauty Spoon. Photo by Jim Osborn.

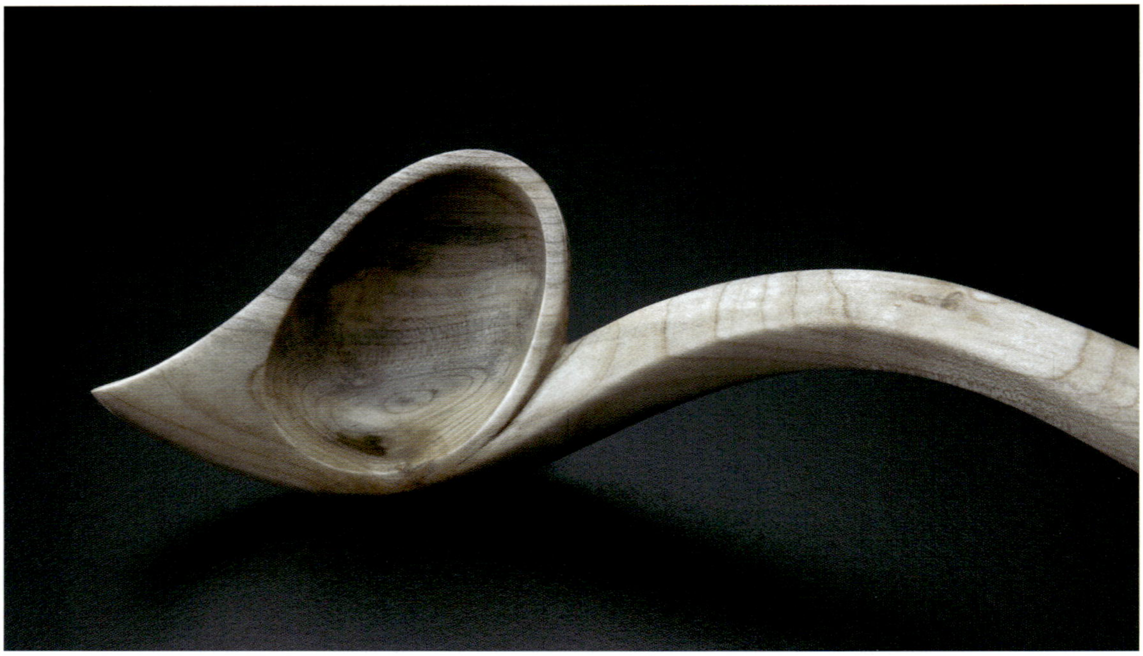

Photo by Jim Osborn.

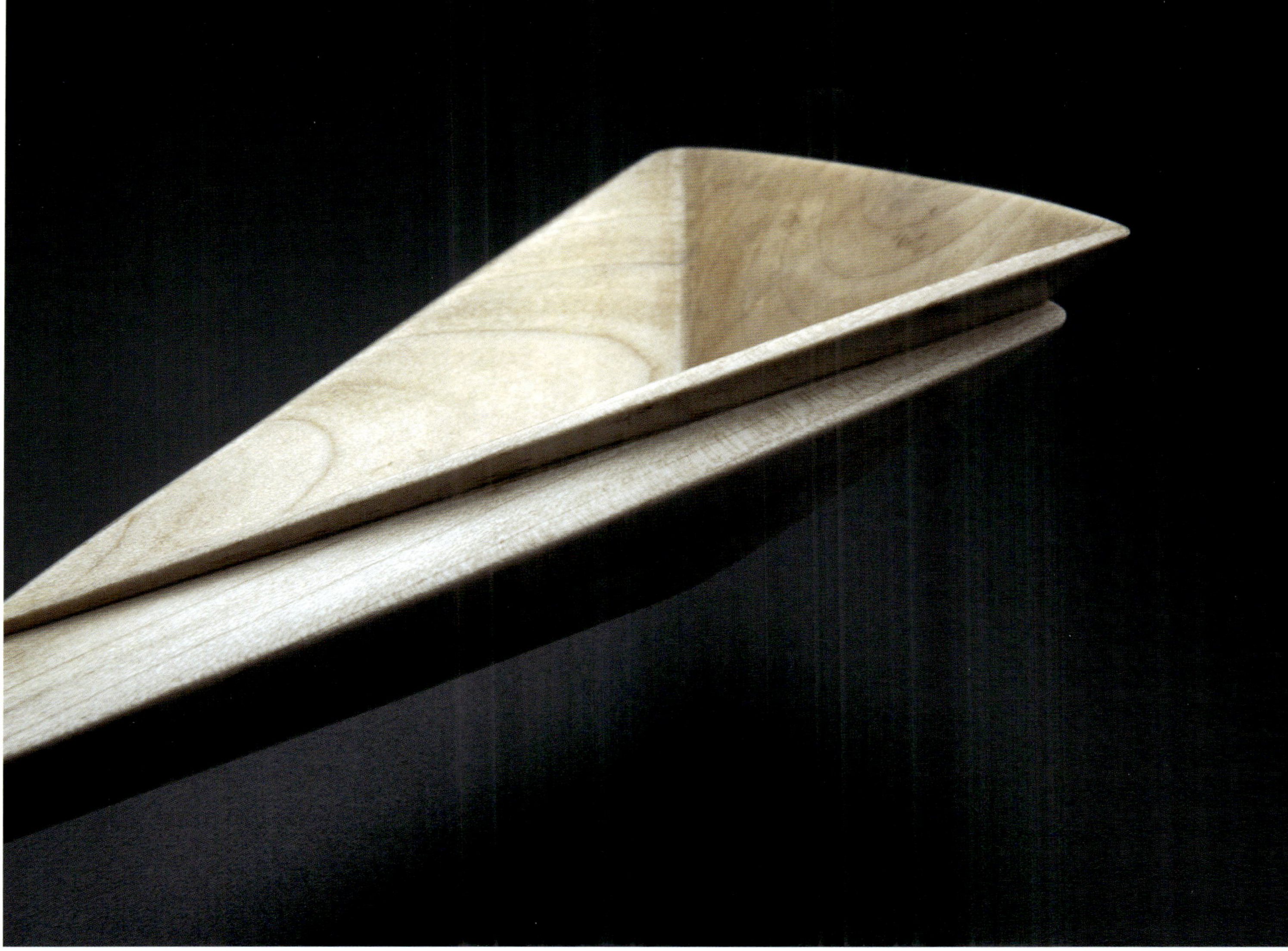

Fischer Sewing Cabinet Spoon. Photo by Jim Osborn.

Sandra Scicchitani

The sources that inspire my work range from the experience of place, to the insight of mythic traditions, to my love of nature and natural forms. I use the elements of shape and color as the foremost means of translating my perception of the stillness, the mystery, and the beauty of these sensations into a visual expression. I work abstractly without establishing specifics of place, time, or object, creating work that transcends a local identity allowing it to express the innate spirit of the human condition.

Water Dance (2012)
Woodcut
Image size:10.5" h x 7.75" w
Paper size: 15.25" h x 11.25" w

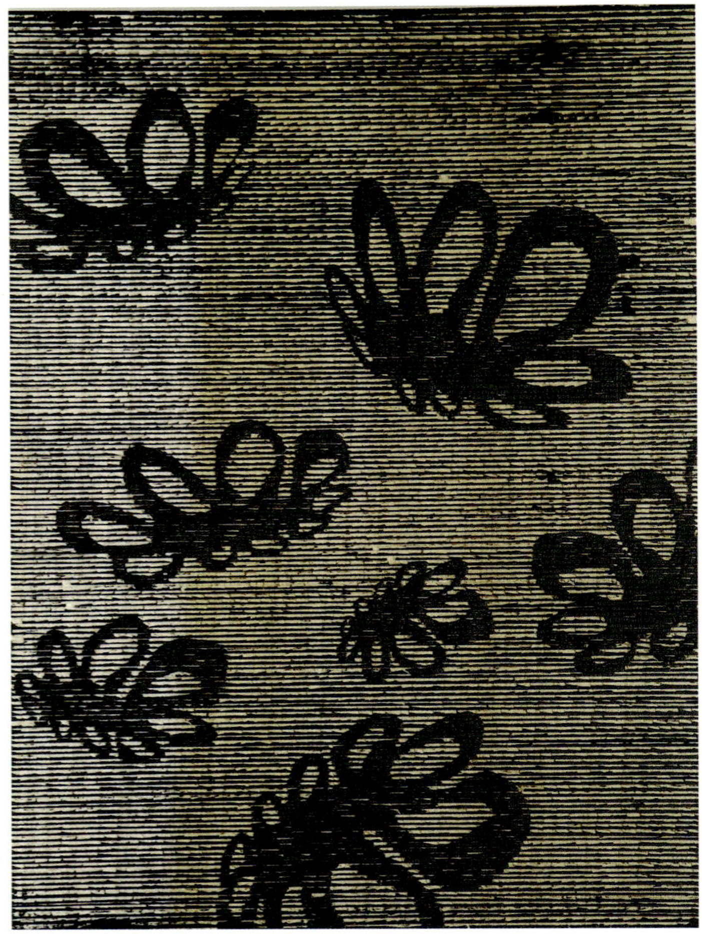

Photo by Mark Sfirri.

Photo by Mark Sfirri.

Mark Sfirri

This sculpture allowed me to pay tribute to two major figures in twentieth century art: Wharton Esherick, who founded the American studio furniture movement and influenced nearly all of the furniture makers who came after him, and Constantin Brancusi, who gets my vote as the most important sculptor of the century. Esherick's homage to Brancusi's work by the same name is a piece that is in the sculpture pit at the Wharton Esherick Museum. My column is a lathe-turned and carved form that repeats, in this case tapering as it ascends.

Continuous Column (2011)
Tulip poplar, ash, and paint
25" h x 5.5" w x 5.5" d

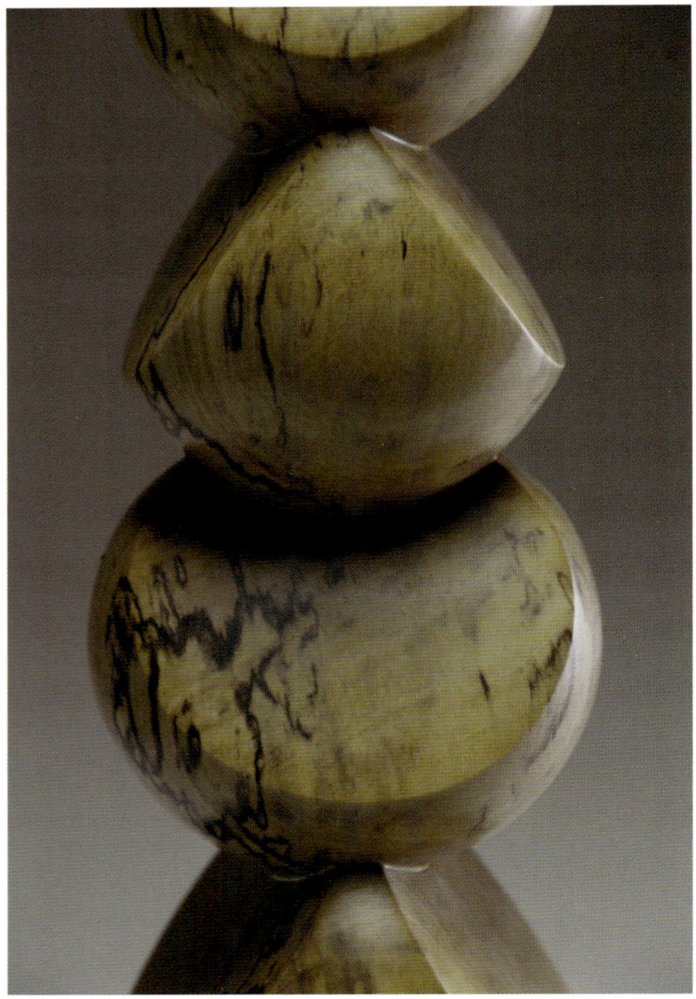

Photo by Mark Sfirri.

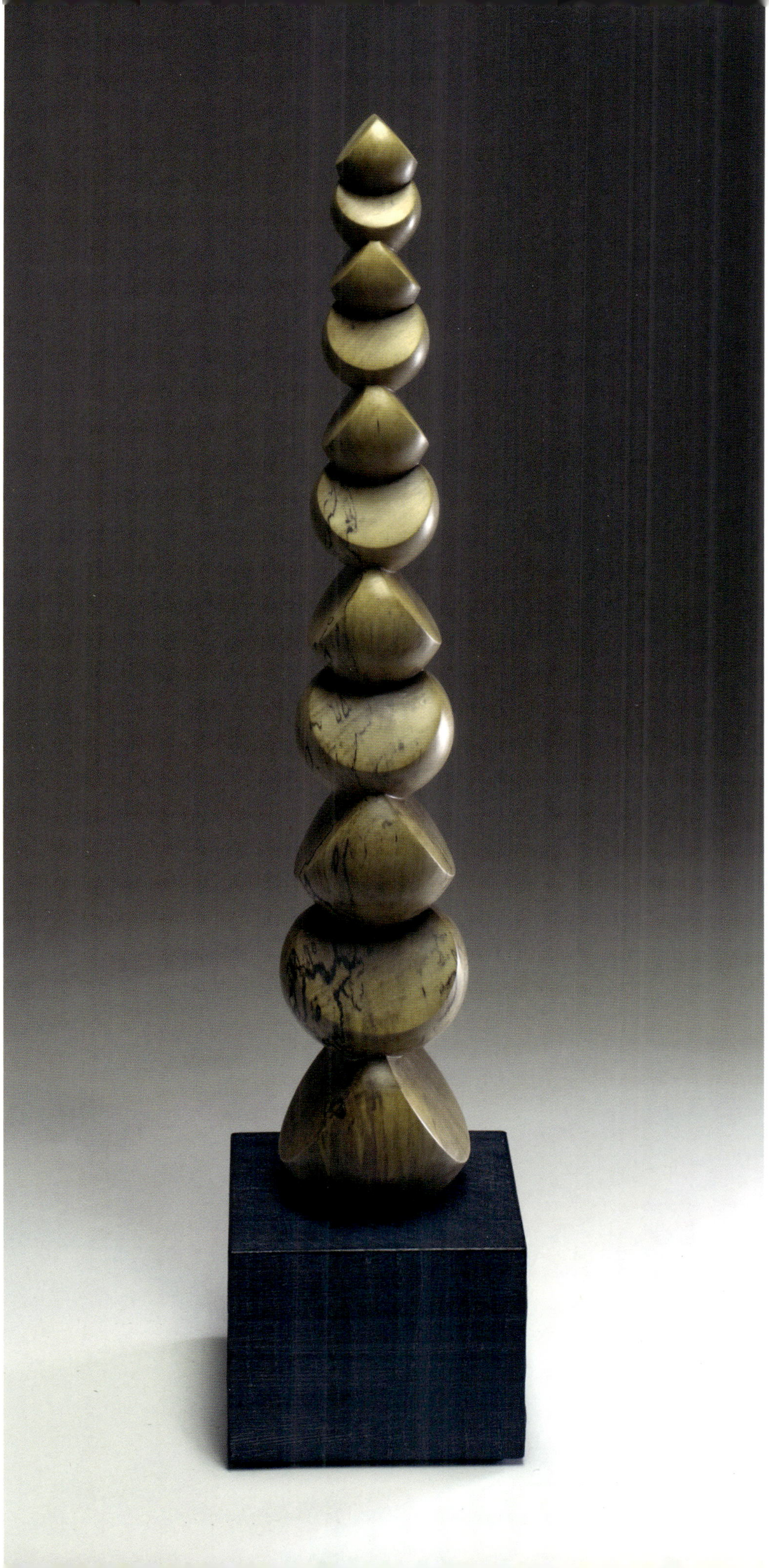

Photo by Mark Sfirri.

The influence for *Dancers* is Wharton Esherick's print, *Rhythms*. In that early woodcut (c. 1923), three twisting abstract figures dance together. About a mile from where I live, there are three trees in a row that appear to be animated and in motion with each other. For several years I have wanted to use them in a print. My first interpretation was more realistic, drawn from observation. When the opportunity to use a piece of poplar from the Wharton Esherick Museum presented itself, I knew that this image would be most appropriate. I chose a more abstract version of this scene, one that plays more on angles, and I used a hatching technique that I saw in another Esherick print, *Moonlight and Meadows*, one of my many favorites.

Dancers (2011)
Woodcut
Rives BFK paper, Gamblin Relief Ink - Portland Intense Black
Image size: 10.5" h x 7.75" w
Paper size: 15.25" h x 11.25" w

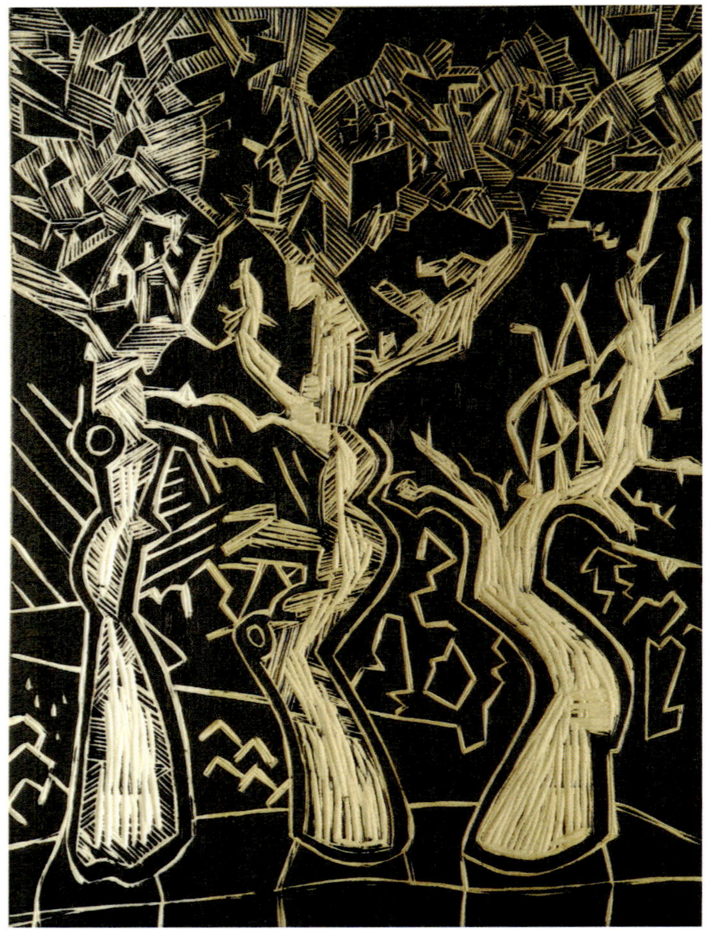

Photo by Mark Sfirri.

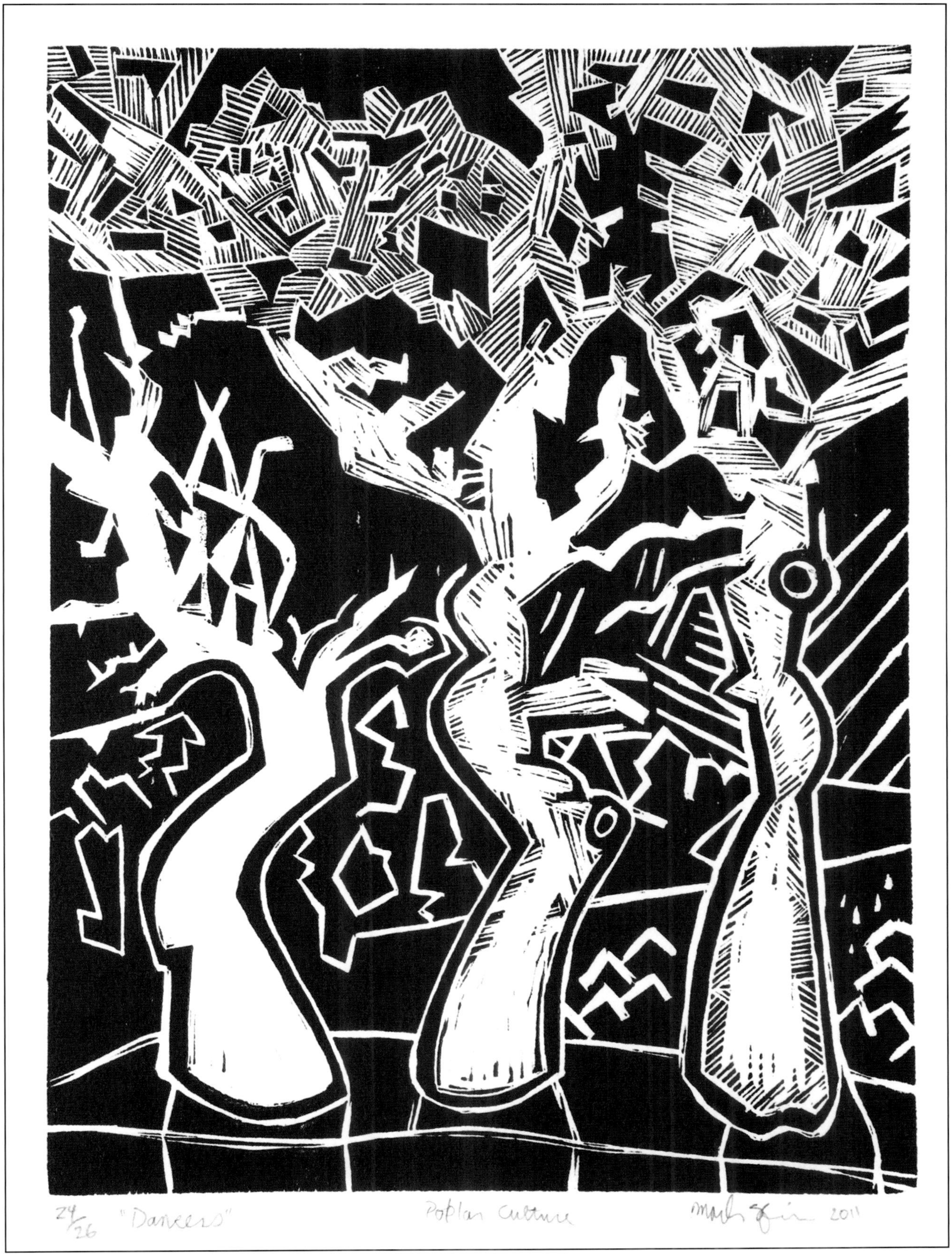

Photo by Mark Sfirri.

Paul Sirofchuck

As Esherick's painterly background is evidenced in his work with wood, my architectural background influences my approach to design with this living material. The *Arch Table*, in particular, reflects my desire to understand the limits of wood's properties and my ability to combine architectural elements for use on a personal scale. The laminated arch, while delicate in appearance, has a structural integrity in its upward movement, providing a pleasing visual tension to the horizontal plane of the top. A single vertical element and thinner aluminum rods provide support, enabling the top to seemingly "float" above the base. The natural "white" of the poplar top contrasting with the blackened poplar base further reinforces this tension, while purpleheart wood and natural aluminum provide a vibrant connection between the dark and light.

Pop Arch Table (2012)
Tulip poplar, purpleheart, aluminum tubes, paint
32" h x 14" d x 60" w

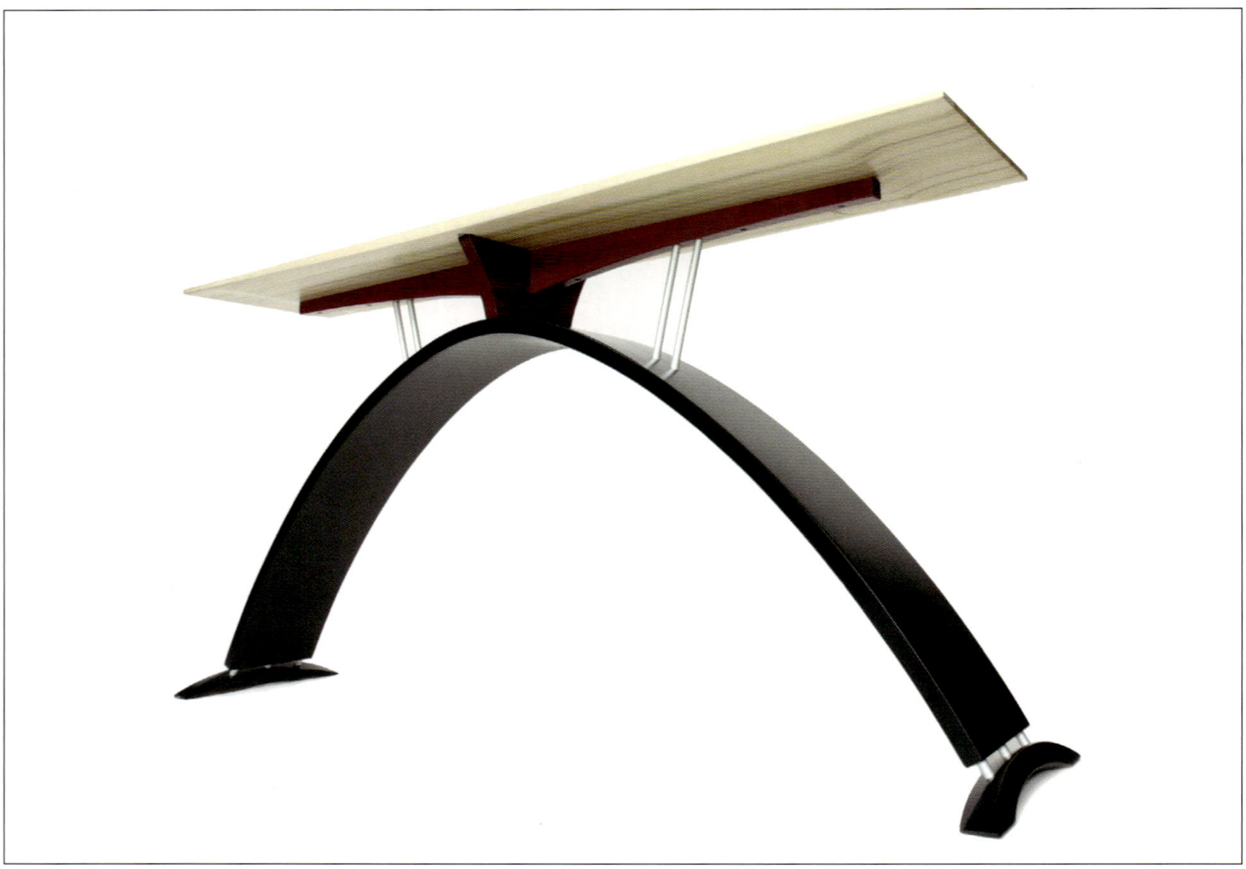

Photo by Paul Sirofchuck.

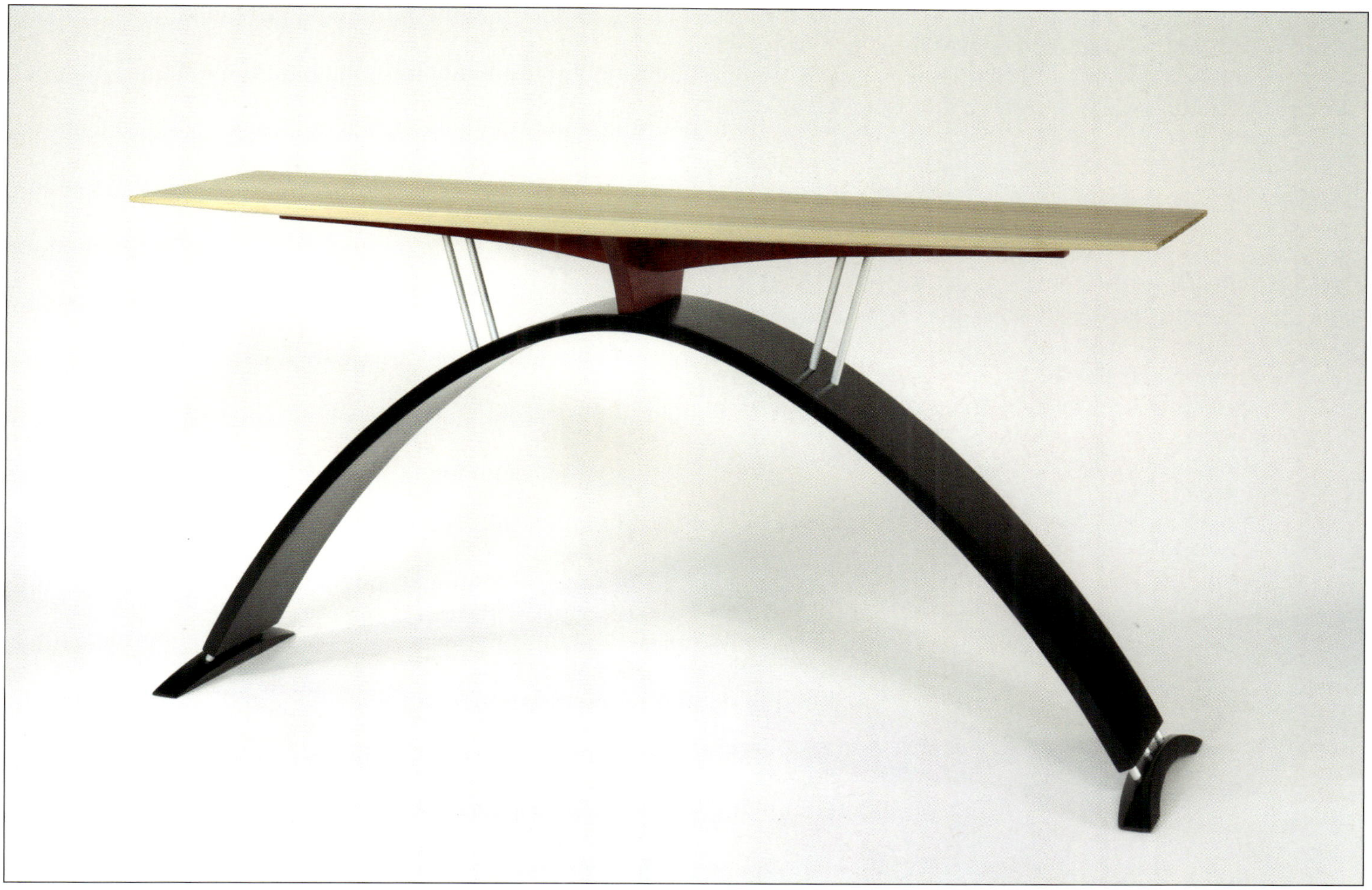

Photo by Paul Sirofchuck.

John Sterling

My work is reflective of what gives me greatest calm. Form and color can change moods, tactile elements can enhance comfort, and natural elements connect us to earths life giving forces. Natural elements add warming touches to our homes.

I am passionate about my materials, craft, and beliefs. I want my furniture to embody the principles of purity, honesty, simplicity, and functionality. I strive to dignify the natural grains and defects of my medium. I believe that things you surround yourself with should connect you to their roots. The naturally occurring defects and organic forms allow you to become in touch with the tree and help to tell its story.

My furniture and philosophy can best be summed up by 20th century architect Irving Gill, "any deviation from simplicity results in a loss of dignity."

Chūrippu 3 tier cabinet (2011)
Tulip poplar, black walnut
28.75" h x 43.62" l x 13" d

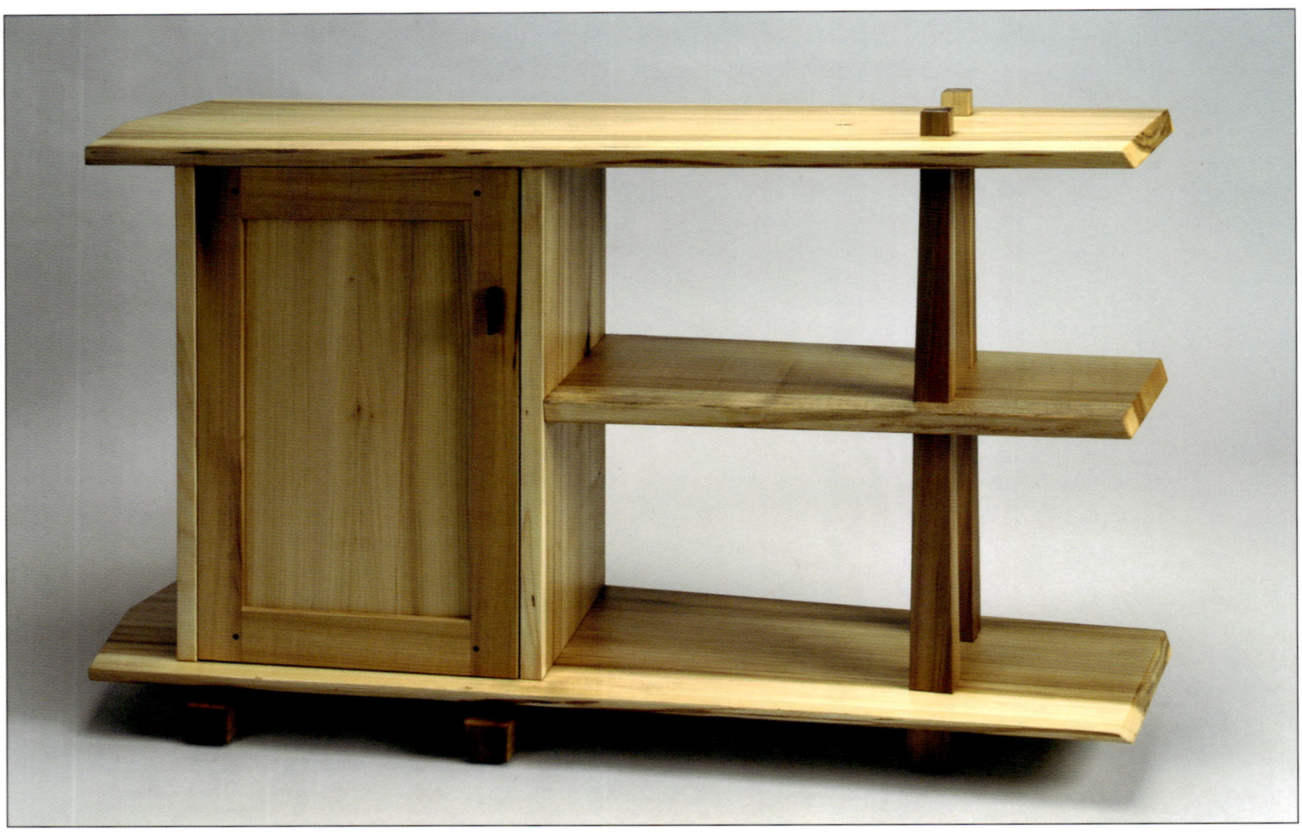

Photo by James Mario.

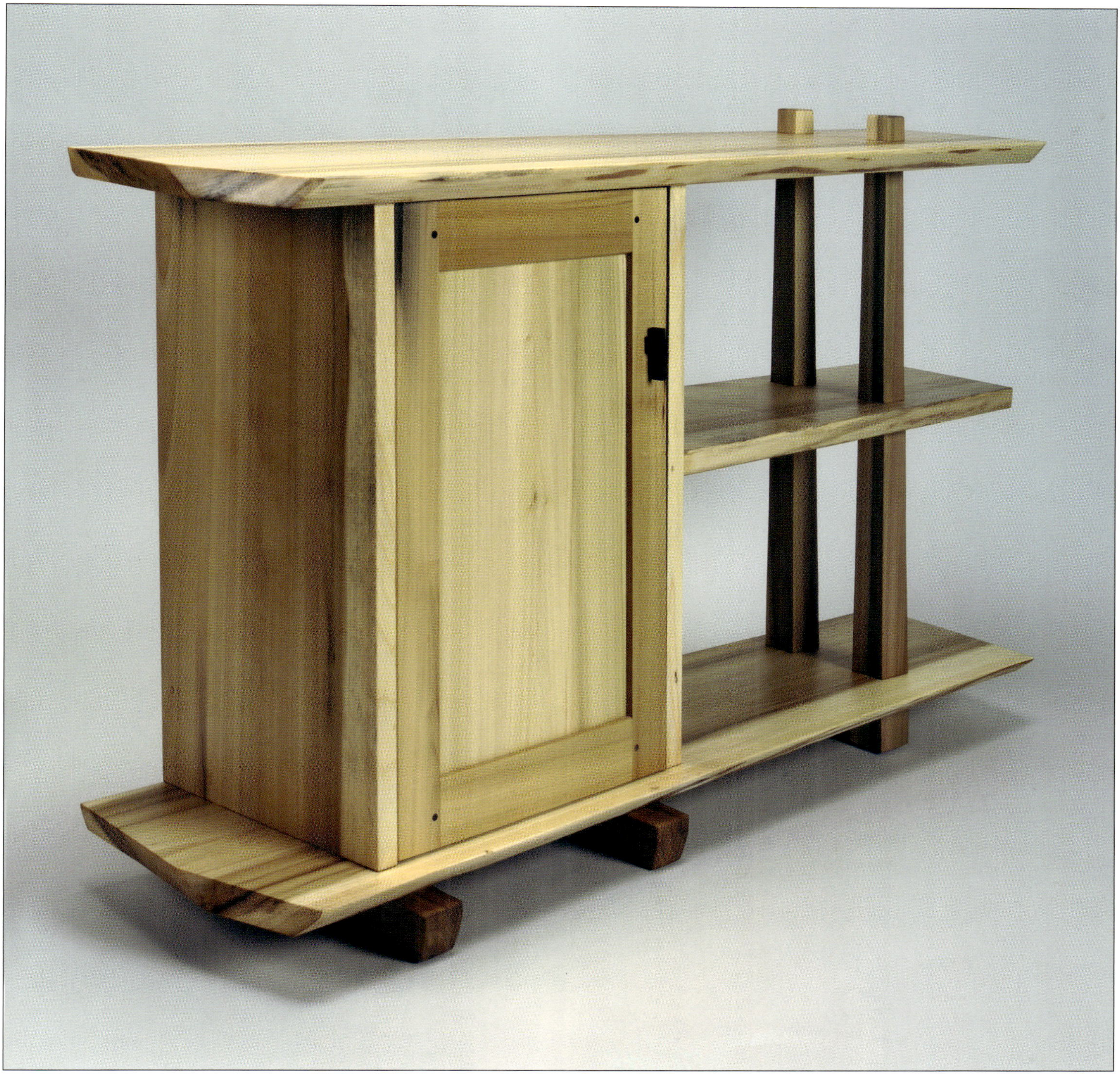

Photo by James Mario.

Ward Stevens

As I started to carve this vessel I couldn't help but think about Esherick's bold smooth sculptures. But as I progressed, it was the repetition of cuts that created another image: Esherick similarly bent over a bench gouging out one of his very vivid naturalistic woodcuts. So, rather than sand away my gouge marks, I left them as a pleasing contrast to the smooth interior of the vessel. There is something about the rhythm of working wood with simple hand tools that gives me a sense of connection to those craftspeople I admire.

Scalloped Vessel (2011)
Tulip Poplar
5.12" h x 4.5" diam.

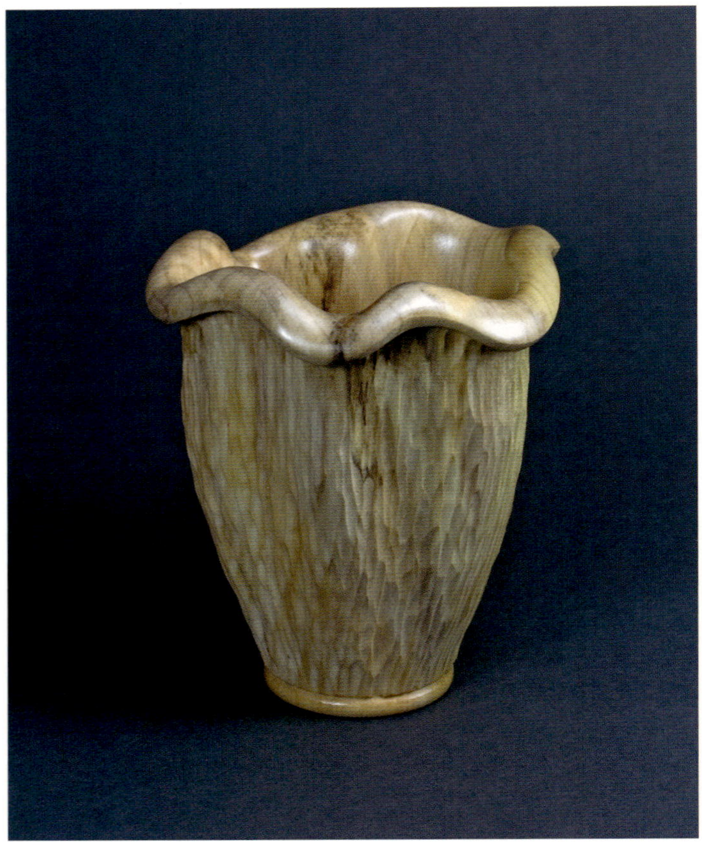

Photo courtesy of Ward Stevens.

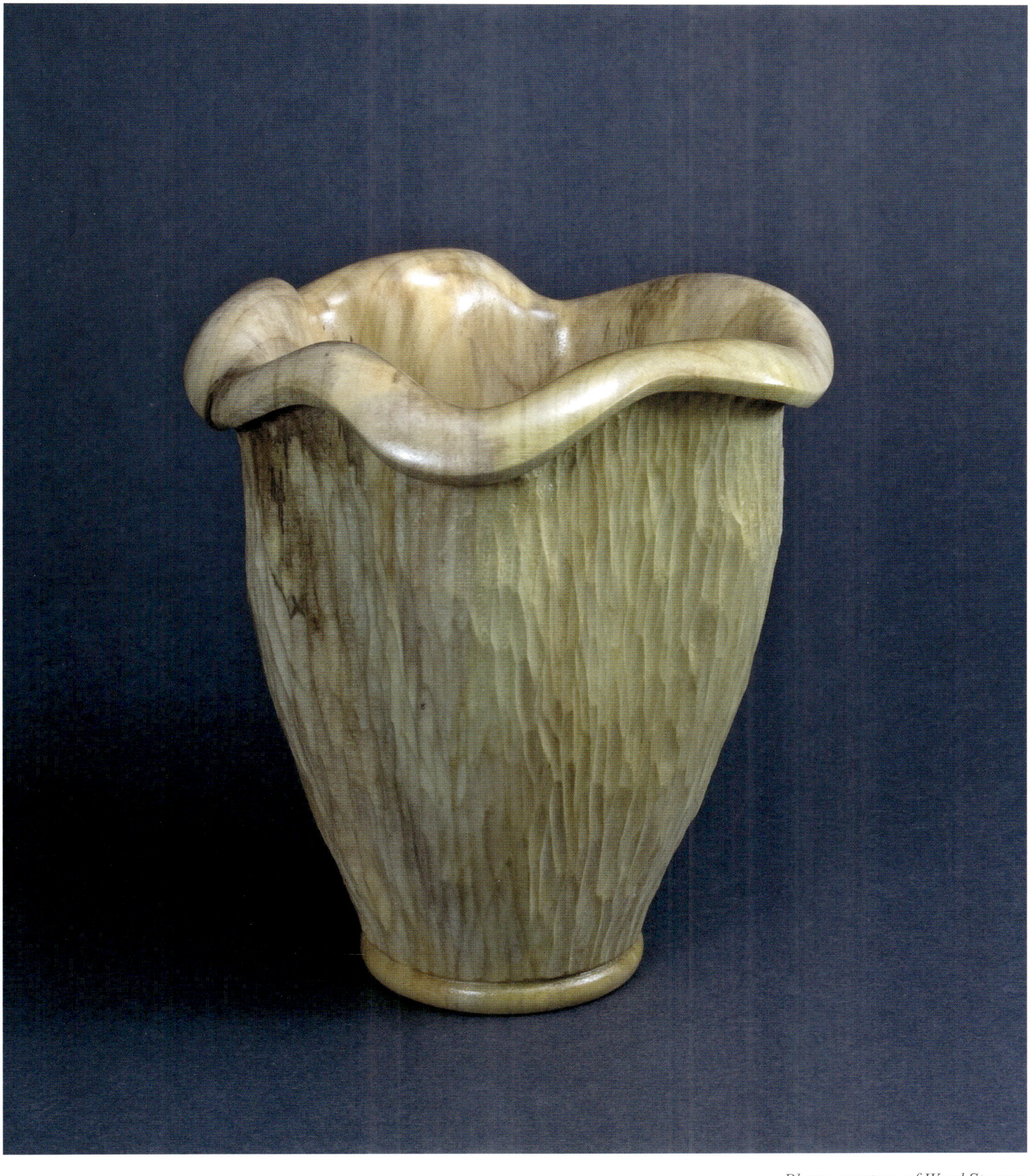

Photo courtesy of Ward Stevens.

Holly Tornheim

I have always enjoyed the daily use of craft – from a laundry basket from Maine to an Erickson rocker to the doors of my home. And so, my first visit to the Wharton Esherick Museum in early September, 2011, filled me with happy memories which returned to help sustain me during the following days spent in Manhattan. In gratitude, I decided to make a functional object for this project. I sought to complement the grain and color of this particular piece of the poplar tree by my design and, in turn, to allow the wood to shape the composition.

Refraction (2012)
Tulip poplar
2" h x 23.5" l x 20" w

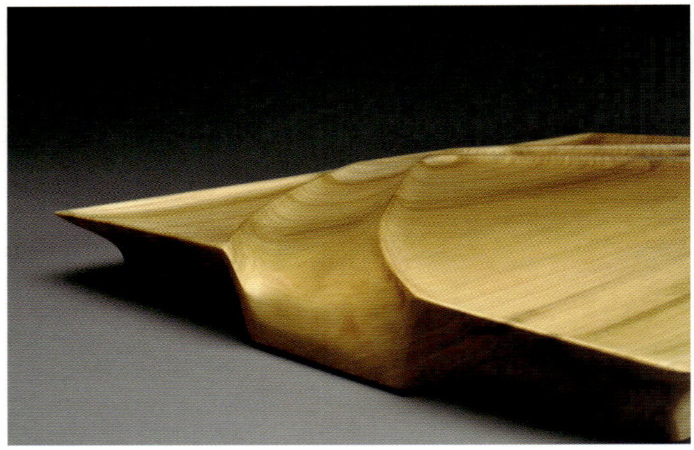

Photo by James Mario.

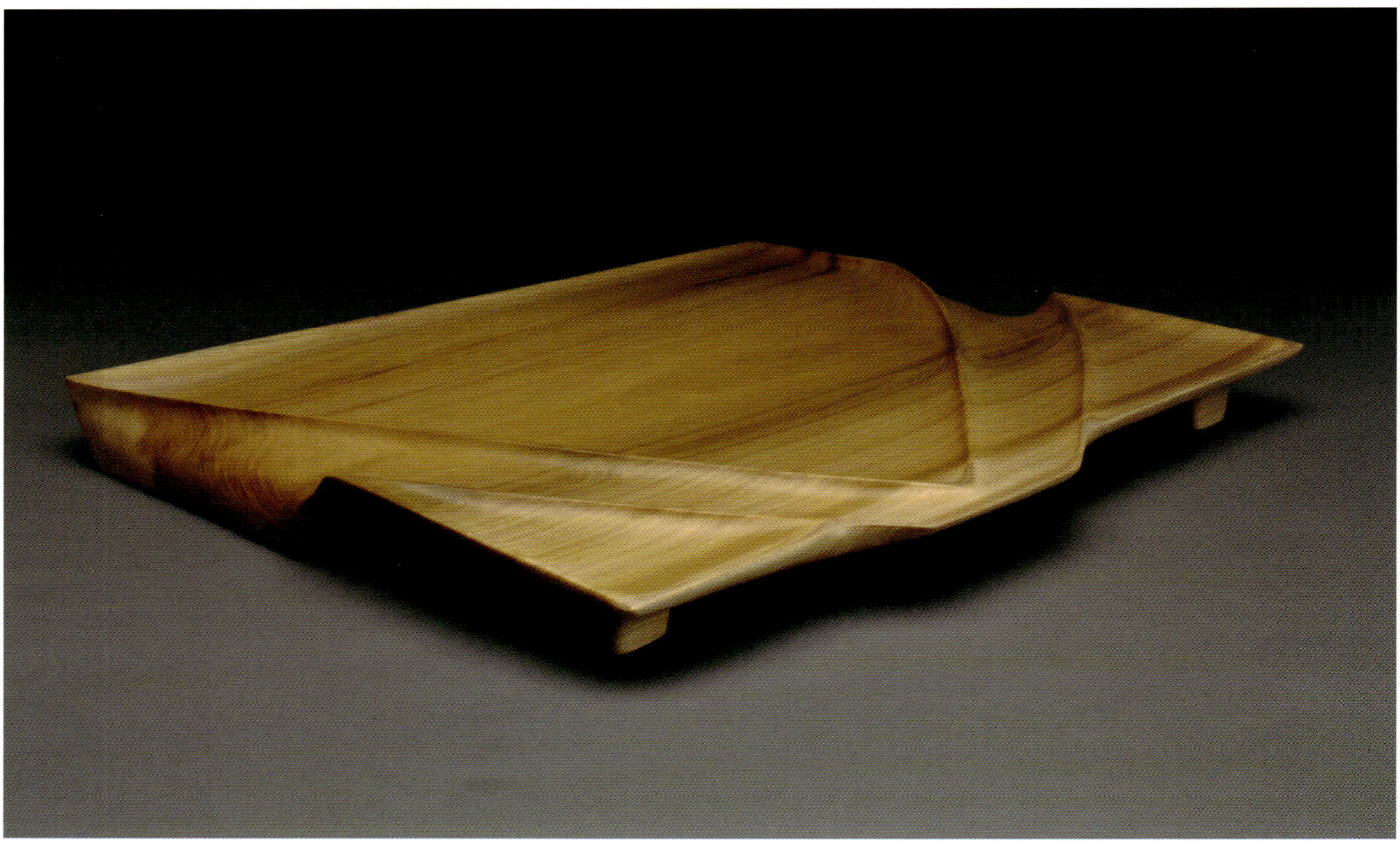

Photo by James Mario.

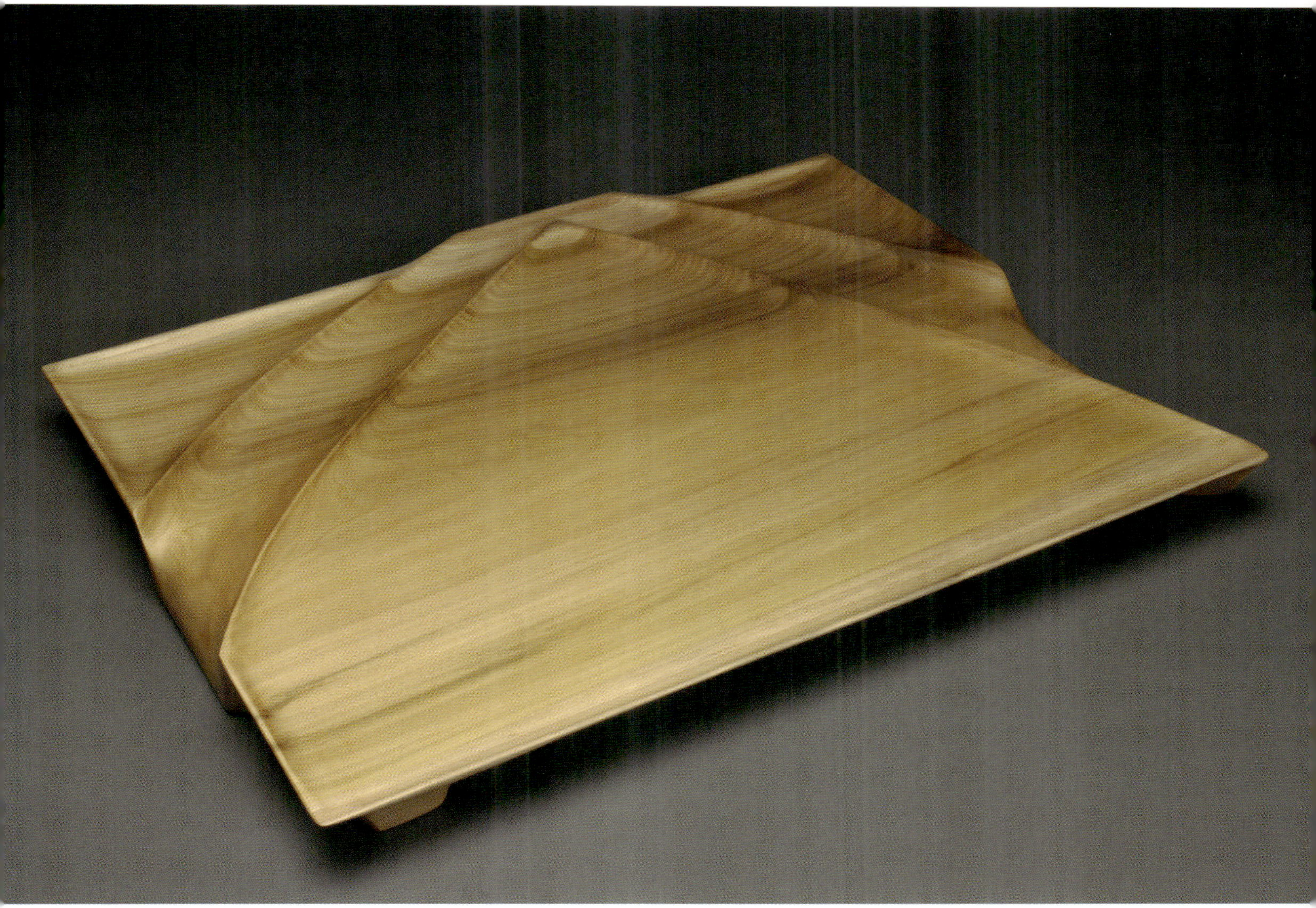

Photo by James Mario.

Daniel Shawn Turley

I enjoy playing with extremes of form and function. This piece challenges the extremes of balance, contrast, and unity, both in its function and symbolic representation. With too much contrast, it is difficult to achieve balance and unity.

The table top perches precariously and pushes the limits of balance, yet it is balanced, stable, and solid. The balance of black and white is not equal in physical surface, but its underlying mass seems to have begun with equal amounts prior to its stretching.

Black and white is in stark contrast to each other. There are no shades of gray. This contrast can be viewed as the ultimate in difference and opposition.

However, "fingers" clasp in the middle of the piece. They are the unifying element that secures the steady balance of the table's weight. They symbolically demonstrate the unity that is so vital in the midst of division.

There can be no balance of contrast without such unity.

Seeking Unity with Extreme Contrast and Balance (2012)
Tulip poplar, enamel paint
34" h x 70" l x 12.5" w

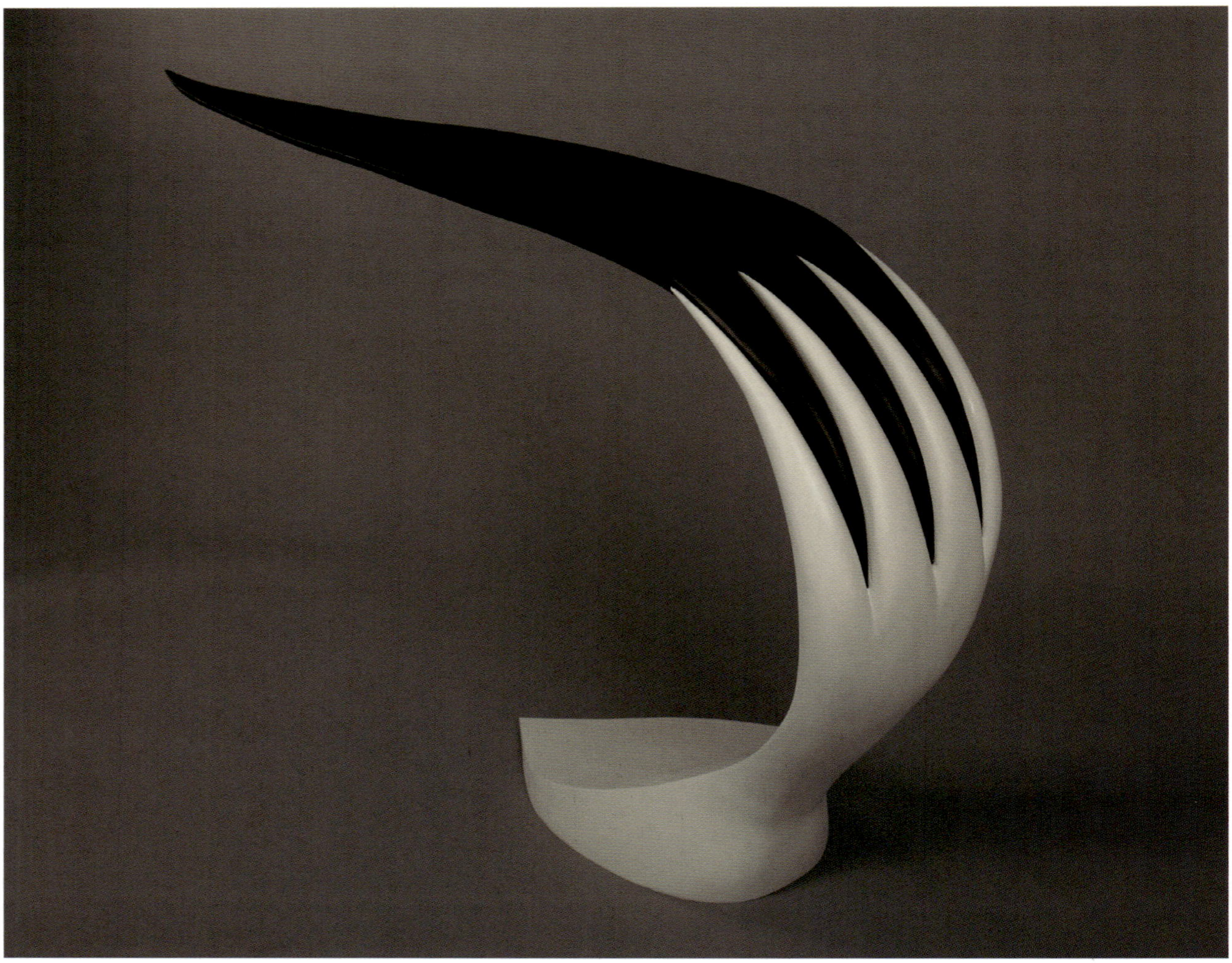

Photo by Bill Mason.

George Wagner

My work as a woodturner derives from two major interests – psychology and segmented turning.

A classic topic in introductory psychology is known as the figure-ground illusion. In this illusion, two facial profile silhouettes are positioned face-to-face against a solid background. The viewer sometimes sees two profiles, but sometimes the image is reversed such that the viewer sees a solid vase. I transformed this illusion into three dimensions by turning two forms – one from the "negative" space of Wharton Esherick's profile as captured in a life mask and one from the corresponding "positive" image (below and following two pages).

Wharton Esherick in Profile: Two Figure-Ground Illusion Vases (2011)
Tulip poplar, walnut
5" h x 4.87" diam.
5.5" h x 4.5" diam.

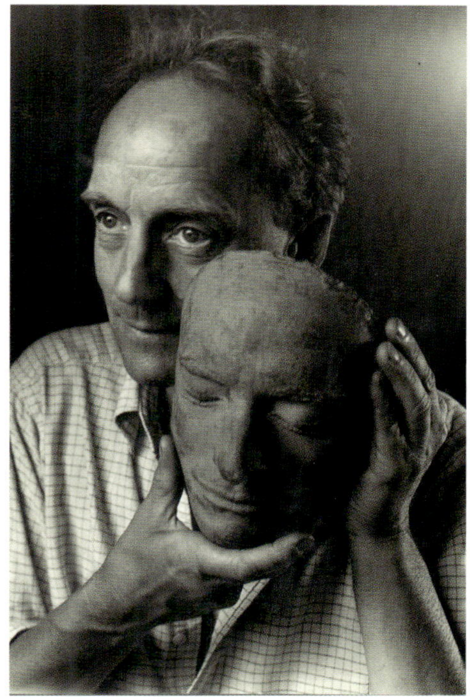

George used this life mask to get Wharton's profile for these pieces. *Photo by Consuelo Kanaga.*

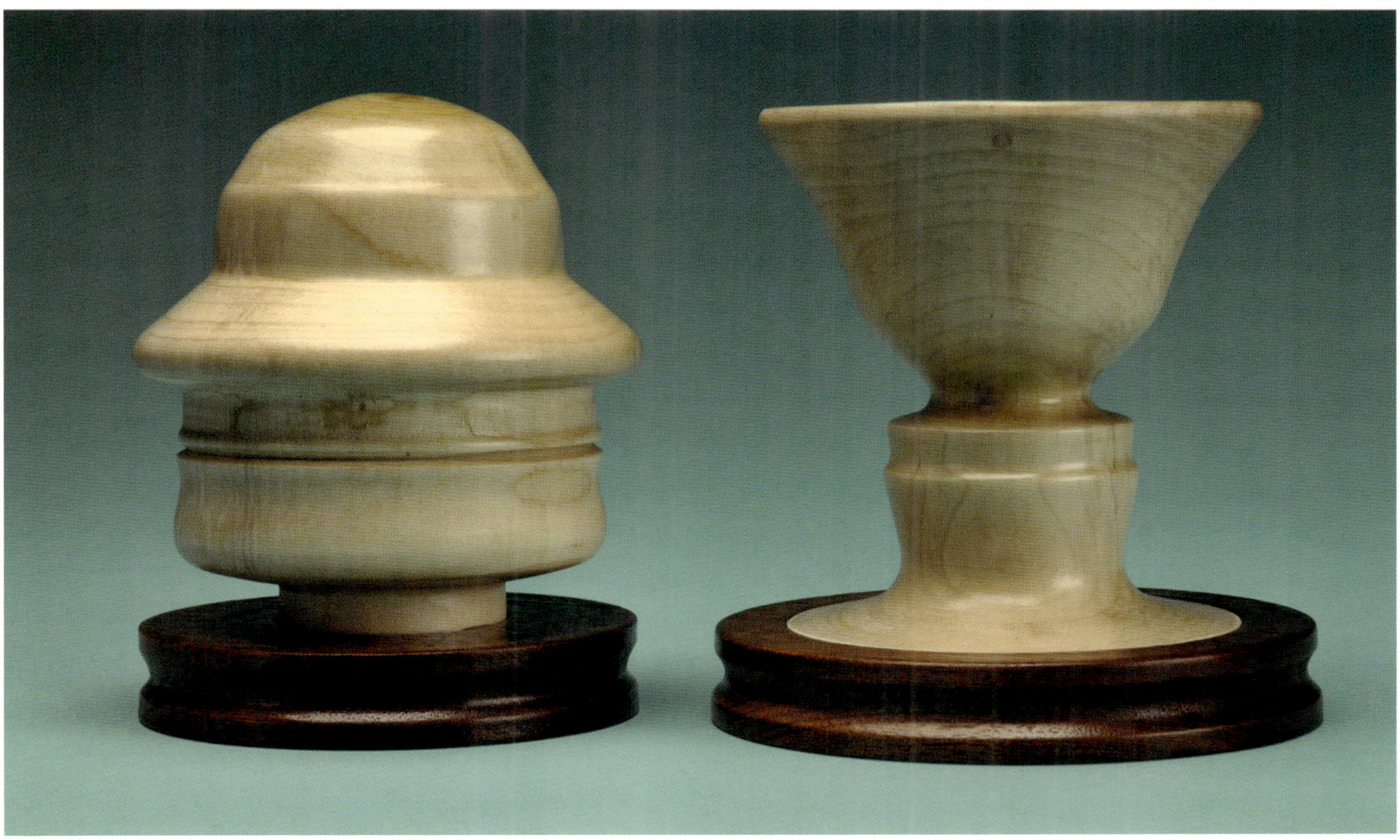

Photo by James Mario.

My third piece is an open segmented vase. This form of turning is most challenging, requiring unparalleled precision in design, calculation, and execution. For each segment, radius, tangent, and angle must be determined for each row and then joined as rough blocks, which are subsequently shaped with a delicacy akin to snipping the corners off of a house of cards without having it collapse. Concentration and confidence are essential, and the vessel must be shaped inside and out. The slightest catch spells disaster; the finished product is a delight. This vase is made of a length of the Esherick poplar, cut into long strips, and then cut into the small blocks. These blocks were then mounted onto the vase one row at a time, allowed to dry, and then turned. The secondary wood is Virginia long-leaf yellow pine salvaged from a New Jersey factory floor built in the mid-nineteenth century and recently demolished.

Open Segmented Vase (2012)
Tulip poplar, Virginia long-leaf yellow pine
15" h x 4.5" diam.

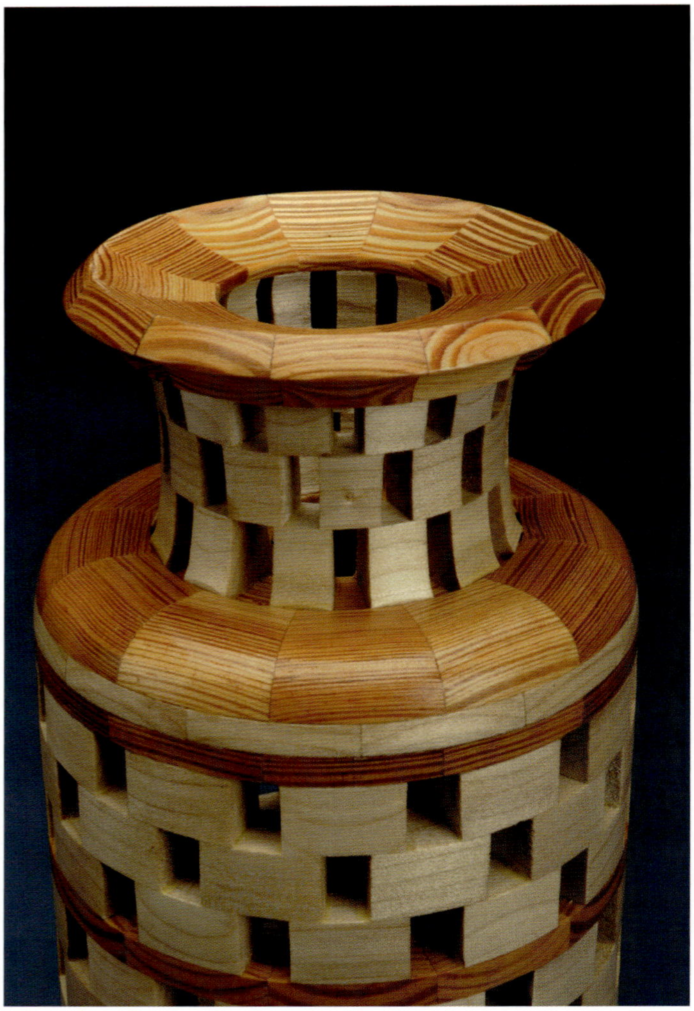

Photo by James Mario.

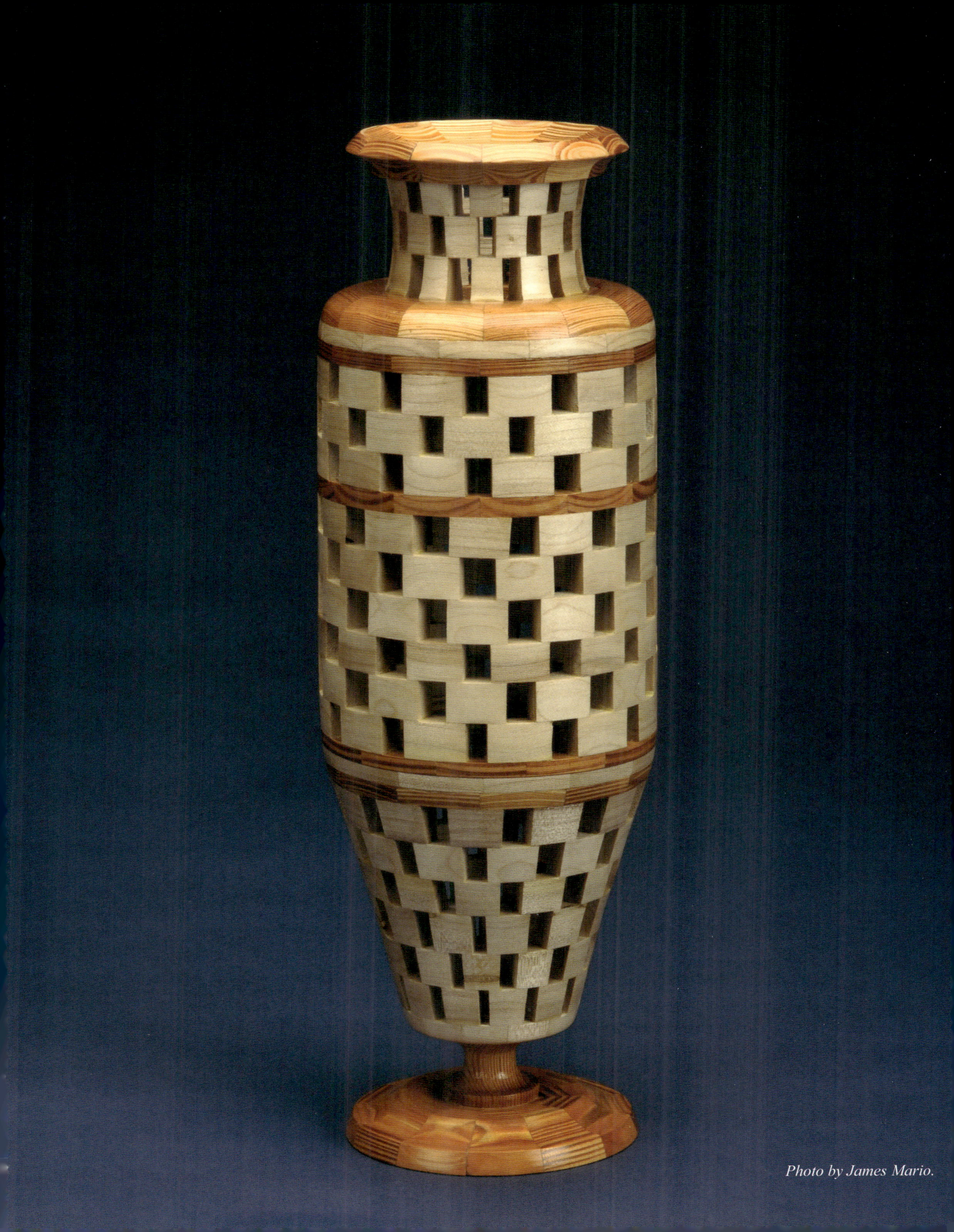

Photo by James Mario.

Abe Warren

A straight clean board has no place in my shop. That exemplifies my craft and the wood with which I choose to work. I select imperfect lumber and accentuate its beauty, creating refined rustic furniture that is functional, sculptural and textural.

This poplar log is different than the wood I normally choose, which presented both a challenge and an opportunity. I was able to pick a piece with a small flaw, thereby allowing me to use my signature natural-shaped butterfly. In addition to the plank, I chose several branches which became the spindles and back of my piece. I was lucky to also obtain mountain laurel from the grounds of Esherick's studio which I used as structural components on the base. The resulting piece is a marriage of rustic and modern.

Settee (2012)
Tulip poplar and mountain laurel
37" h x 26" d x 37" w

Photo by Nicole Priore.

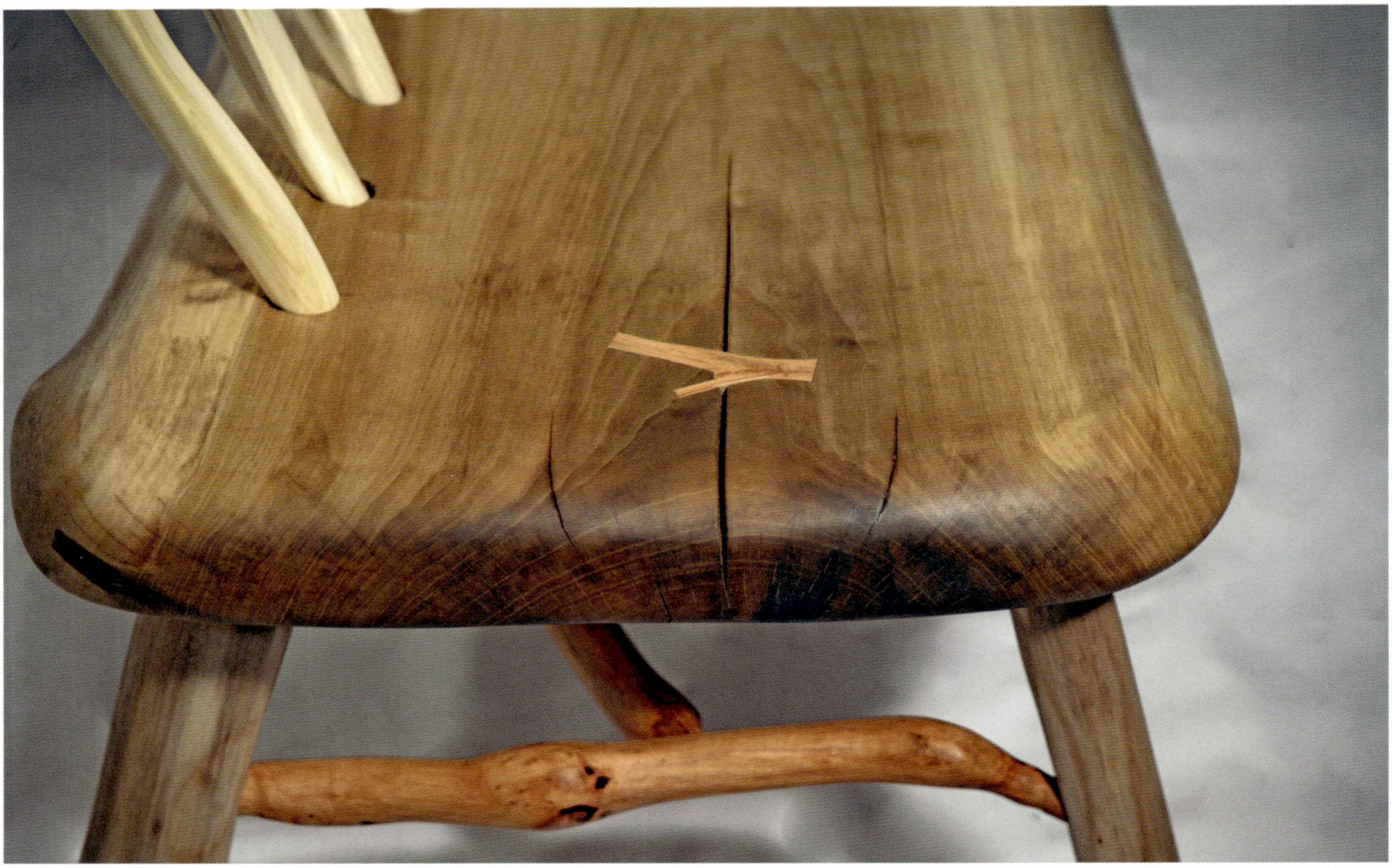

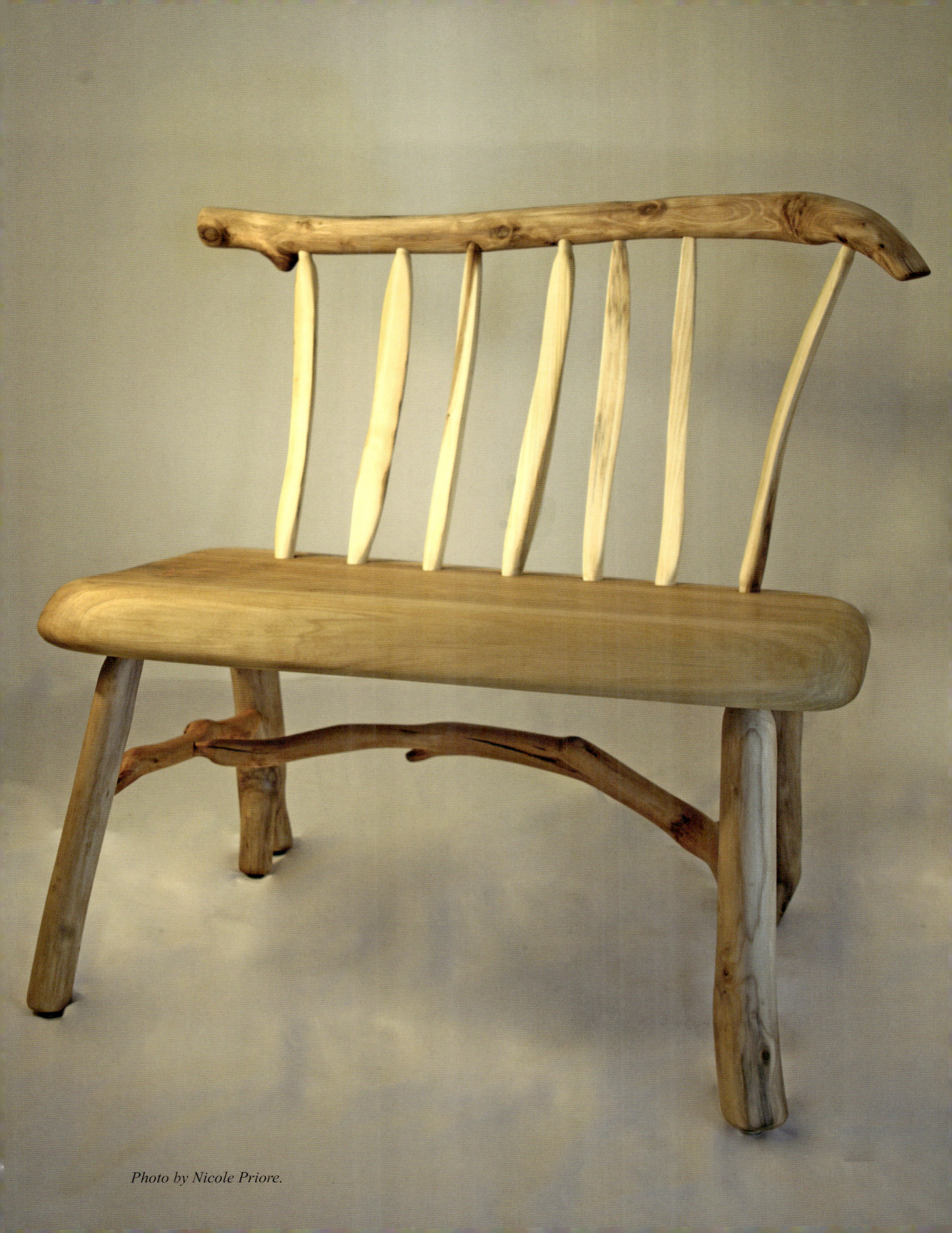

Photo by Nicole Priore.

Derek Weidman

Of all of Esherick's incredible works, his animal-themed pieces had the most powerful impact on me. The abstracted and expressive forms speak to a freedom of line and a beauty of life that I have always found inspiring. To me they are a contemporary link to the styles and sensibilities of Inuit and African tribal art, where the spirit of the subject takes precedence over accuracy, as opposed to more realistic western interpretations. *Smile-Eyed Whitetail* is an attempt to add another voice to this tradition of wood sculpture. I felt it important for this piece, made from a fallen tree from Esherick's estate, to depict an animal local to this part of Pennsylvania. I choose a Whitetail deer for this reason, and hoped to capture the strength and elegance of the animal.

Smile-Eyed Whitetail (2012)
Tulip poplar, holly, ebony, acrylic paint
15" h x 9" l x 9.5" w

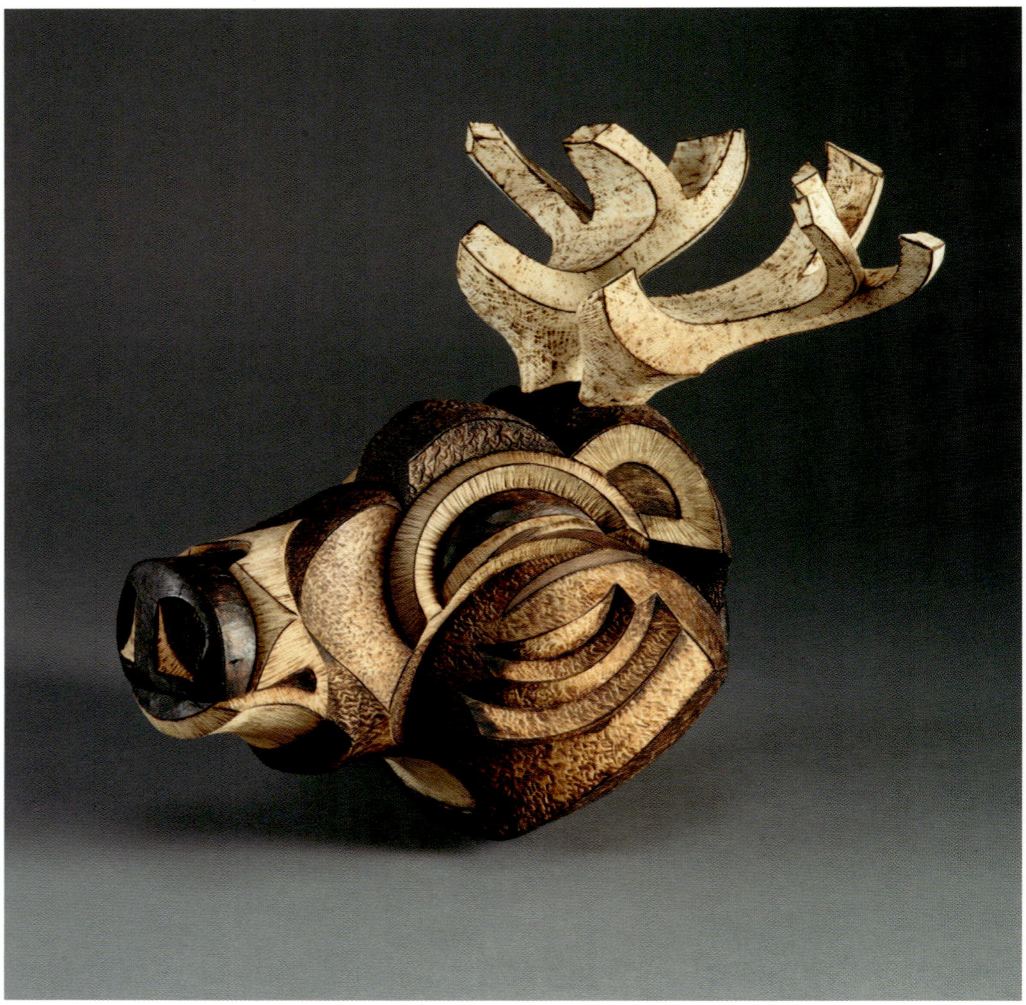

Photo by Karl Seifert.

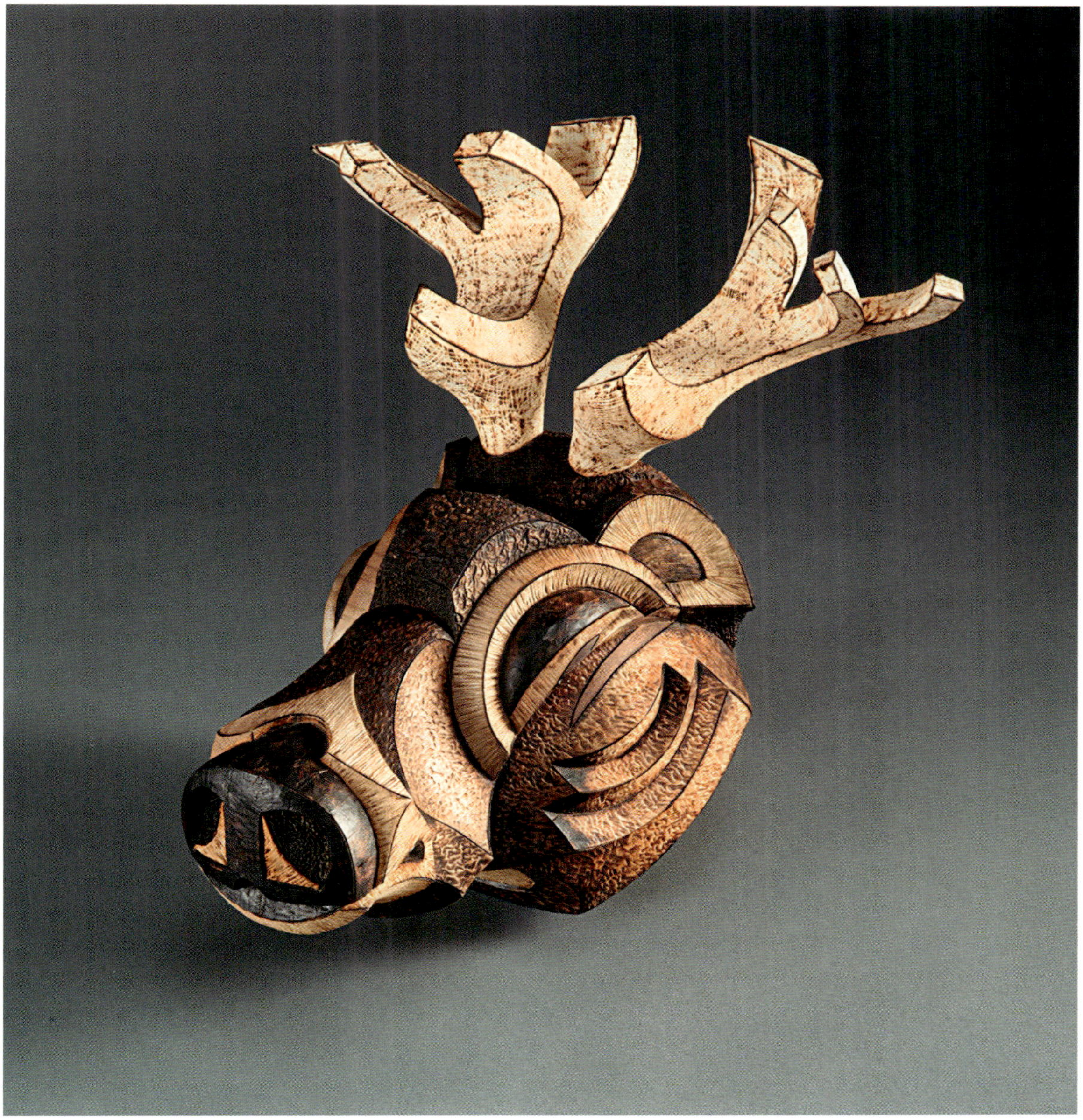

Photo by Karl Seifert.

THE ARTISTS

Ken Bell

Ken and Pat Bell operate the Cedar Knoll Tree Farm in Cumberland County, New Jersey. Ken, a retired K-12 music teacher, began making baskets more than 20 years ago. He produces them primarily from the trees on his farm. The Bells enrolled their farm and forest in the Farmland Preservation Program to prevent development.

Michael Biddison

Chester County artist Michael Biddison has amassed a diverse body of artistic credits, alone and in collaboration with other artists, art consultants, architects, interior designers, performers, and musicians. With a "master's in Making a Silk Purse From A Sows Ear from his Own Private University," he has specialized in using found and discarded materials to create sculpture, functional work, and integrated environments. He has done numerous commissions for both private and corporate clients, from designing and building imaginative store and café spaces and artful elements in homes, to creating the 27 foot lobby centerpiece for AAA headquarters in Wilmington, Delaware. [Web: www.woodsunarts.com]

Jasper Brinton

Jasper Brinton was taught woodworking by a Clydebank shipwright at Gordonstoun, Scotland. Years later, once settled in Chester County, he turned to the challenge – the opportunity – to practice the art of the tree on a serious level. Pennsylvania, blessed with some of the world's finest hardwoods (and of course furniture makers), proved a good place to hang out a shingle. Both George Nakashima and Wharton Esherick and a handful of others had already demonstrated that the times were right – post war – for an acceptance of International Modernism. Brinton first worked at inventing and building domestic utilitarian furniture within this mode and, as his skills and reputation widened, moved into contract work involving the design and execution of multiples for industry. In 1965, he founded Brinton Design, specializing in contemporary furniture and its construction. He has exhibited widely and won several awards over the years. Recently, in 2009, he was awarded Best of Show at the Wharton Esherick Museum Annual Woodworking Competition for a set of library steps.

In 1993, Jasper resumed an interest in clay sculpture and built "Pharillon," a wood firing kiln. He taught glaze chemistry at the Chester Springs Studio and facilitated wood firings with the Pennsylvania Academy of the Fine Arts and Philadelphia College of Art.

Down the years, he has taught fine woodworking, exhibited widely, and consulted overseas. He has always been grateful that Esherick, keeping to essentials, continues to show him the way.

Michael Brolly

Michael Brolly was born in Philadelphia, in 1950, to parents who left Northern Ireland during the Depression so they could make money to send back home. He graduated from Kutztown University with honors in 1981 and started showing nationally the same year. His work is included in many museums and private collections. He graduated with an MFA from UMass Dartmouth in 2007. He had children and started teaching late in life and presently teaches at Moravian Academy in Bethlehem, Pennsylvania. He received the Wharton Esherick Award for Excellence in Wood at the Philadelphia Museum of Art Craft Show in 2011. [Web: www.michaelbrolly.com]

Miriam Carpenter

Miriam Carpenter graduated from Rhode Island School of Design in 2006 with an emphasis on material exploration in furniture and innovations in photovoltaic systems. For the past five years, she has worked alongside Mira Nakashima digging through gigantic logs, sketching slabs of wood, designing furniture, and taking her shoes on and off a ridiculous number of times a day. She is influenced by Japanese and Hindu culture and inspired by indigenous craft and permaculture design. The past two years, she has had the honor of collaborating with talented artists at Echo Lake, and will be trekking to Saskatoon, Saskatchewan, in 2012 to participate in Emma Unplugged.

Andy DiPietro

Andy is a self-taught artist who has worked with wood all his life. He has been featured in several international magazines and won several ribbons for his vessel forms. Andy's more recent work has taken on sculptural forms as an extension of his signature vessel shapes. He has become known as a woodturning instructor and demonstrator who shares his new techniques, finishes and passion for the art form with his students.

Andy's artwork has been exhibited throughout the region and is sold in many galleries in the Delaware Valley as well as around the country. [Web: www.woodartforms.com]

Ron Durr

Ron Durr graduated from Temple with a degree in HVAC design and has worked most of his life in heating and air conditioning. He began woodworking in junior high school, and has been a devotee ever since. He took up woodturning in 2001. He is a member of the Bucks Woodturners, American Association of Woodturners, and the Pennsylvania Guild of Craftsman. He enjoys teaching various phases of woodturning for Bucks Woodturners "Hands-on-Workshops." [Web: www.haguesmillturningsbyrondurr.com]

Chuck Dyke

Chuck Dyke has spent his life in pursuit of Academe. An education at Brandeis University and a PhD from Brown University led to 46 years (and counting) teaching at Temple University in Philadelphia. He has been working with wood ("butchering it" in his words) for most of his life, including "a decent amount of carpentry." As a pipe smoker, his first concerted carving was in the production of pipes. Since then he has turned to some larger pieces in a more serious vein.

David Ebner

David Ebner is an artist/craftsman who works in four modes: classical impressions of furniture, turned objects, sculptural furniture and furniture. He attended the School for American Craftsmen at RIT. There he studied with Wendell Castle, and realized that there could be "an artistic approach" to woodworking. He followed RIT with a two-year stint at the London School of Furniture Design and served two years in the army before deciding to become a full-time studio craftsman.

His inclusion in "Explorations II/The New Furniture" at the American Craft Museum in 1991 signified his place in the forefront of furniture artist-craftsmen. Curator John Perrault wrote, "Through the use of stripped down classic forms, David Ebner has updated and extended the mode of furniture solidified by Wharton Esherick, George Nakashima, Sam Maloof, and the early Wendell Castle."

Since then, he has appeared in many exhibitions in the U.S. and abroad, his work has been featured in publications such as *The New York Times*, *American Craft*, *Fine Woodworking*, etc., and his creations have been added to the collections of many museums and private collectors. [Web: www.davidebner.com]

Craig Edelbrock

Craig Edelbrock was drawn into woodworking only recently by seeing works in which the aesthetics of wood are combined with compelling design to achieve a level of transcendence that defines true art. He sees this rare, perfect union of worldly material on one hand with pure form on the other in the works of Bob Stocksdale, David Ellsworth, and Norm Sartorius, to name a few. His goal is to someday achieve that union in his own work.

Paul Eisenhauer

Paul Eisenhauer is the Executive Director and Curator of the Wharton Esherick Museum. After receiving a PhD, he taught sociology for twenty years before leaving academia for the museum world. Woodworking has been a hobby for many years. He currently carves bowls and spoons.

Jesse Eisenhauer

Jesse Eisenhauer started woodworking at Westtown School, where he received the Craft Award in his senior year. He is currently studying woodworking at Indiana University of Pennsylvania.

David Ellsworth

David Ellsworth's first experience with the lathe was in a woodshop class in 1958. He received a master's degree in fine art from the University of Colorado in 1973. He founded the woodworking program at the Anderson Ranch Arts Center in Snowmass, Colorado, in 1974. During the mid-1970s, David developed a series of bent turning tools and the methods required for making the thin-walled hollow forms for which he is known worldwide. His first article, titled "Hollow Turning," appeared in the May/June 1979 issue of *Fine Woodworking* magazine. His first book, *Ellsworth on Woodturning,* was published by Fox Chapel Publ. in 2008.

David is the founding member of the American Association of Woodturners, of which he was president from 1986-1991, and its first Honorary Lifetime Member. He operates the Ellsworth School of Woodturning at his home and studio in Bucks County, Pennsylvania. His works have been included in the permanent collections of thirty-five museums, including the Metropolitan Museum of Art in New York, the Philadelphia Museum of Art, the Los Angeles County Museum of Art, and the Museum of Fine Arts in Boston. He has taught workshops throughout the world and has received fellowship grants from the National Endowment of Arts, the Pennsylvania Council for the Arts, and the PEW Foundation. In 2009 he was elected the "Master of the Medium" by the James A. Renwick Alliance of the Smithsonian Institution in Washington, D.C. He is an Honorary Lifetime Member of the Collectors of Wood Art, and a Fellow and a former Trustee of the American Craft Council. [Web: www.ellsworthstudios.com]

Philip Hauser

Philip Houser has been a woodturner since 1987. He is a member of several regional woodturning associations and is President of the DelVal Turners in New Jersey. Since 2004 he has been a State Juried member of the Pennsylvania Craft Guild.

He exhibits work at the Wood Turning Center and the SOTA Gallery in Philadelphia, at the Brookfield Craft Center in Brookfield, Connecticut, and the Creative Genius Gallery in Medford, New Jersey. He has been a juried exhibitor at the Perkins Center, New Hope Arts, the Lincoln Center Craft Show, and the Pennsylvania Guild of Craftsmen.

Carolyn Hesse

Since graduating from the Pennsylvania Academy of the Fine Arts, Carolyn Hesse has worked with a local wooden boat builder in Philadelphia, Pennsylvania. Much of what she learned while building boats influenced her approach to making art. Every boat begins with a straight line, and consequently, a drawing. She considers many of her wall pieces to be drawings made with wood, light, shadow, and sometimes a suggestion of color. They are an exploration of the straight line, arguably one of humanity's greatest inventions as there is no such phenomenon that exists naturally. They also reference the horizon, the greatest curve of which we know, disguised as a straight line. [Web:www.carolynhesse.com]

Roger Justice

Roger Justice lives in Doylestown, Pennsylvania. Following retirement in 2003, he found his woodturning passion with an old lathe and hand-me-down tools. Several years later, in order to improve his skills, he studied with Mark Sfirri at Bucks County Community College, and, over the years, he has benefited from tutoring sessions with many other fine artisans of the Bucks Woodturners organization of which he is a member.

Ray Kelso

Ray received his first exposure to studio woodworking in the late 1960s while pursuing a degree in Civil Engineering at Virginia Tech, and "was amazed at and envious of the freedom evident in the work of those students." After trying engineering, he decided "to follow my passion and work with my heart, my head, and my hands."

Ray is a self taught woodworker. His friend Ed Ray first introduced him to the work of Wharton Esherick. A visit to the Wharton Esherick Museum showed him that furniture should be fun.

Ray received "Best in Show" at the 1981 Philadelphia Museum of Art Craft Show and the 24th Contemporary Craft Exposition: Delaware Museum of Art. In 2003 he received the Wharton Esherick Prize for Excellence in Wood at the Philadelphia Museum of Art Craft Show. [Web: www.raykelso.com]

Brian Kolakowski

Brian is a jazz musician from Philadelphia who fell in love with the freedom of woodwork. He says, "If there is an afterlife I hope there are trees and carving tools."

He originally visited the Esherick Museum in 2000 in his first year of studying fine woodworking under Mark Sfirri. He feels Esherick's collective work is "a symbol of love, focus, dedication, dreams, overwhelming and inspiring – a man's beautiful journey still alive." [Web: www.thecapturedsoul.com]

Jack Larimore

Jack Larimore grew up in the cherry orchard region of northeastern Michigan. He attended Michigan State University earning a degree in landscape architecture in 1973. Since 1983, Larimore has been self-employed designing and building furniture and installations. His work has been exhibited internationally and is included in major private and public collections. Additionally, he has served as a professor in the Crafts Department at The University of the Arts in Philadelphia, as an Advisory Board Member of The Furniture Society, and as a Trustee of The Center for Art in Wood and Wheaton Arts and Cultural Center. Jack's work and studio practice is featured in a recently released book, *Furniture With Soul* by David Savage for Kodansha International. Through his work he pursues an intimacy with organic process. His studio is currently on a farm in southern New Jersey. [Web: www.jacklarimore.com]

Stephen Leichner

Steve Leichner's grandfather was a Swedish carpenter, so his love of wood comes naturally. Since retiring from teaching after 34 years in the School District of Philadelphia, Steve has devoted his time to transforming beautiful, locally-harvested wood into vessels of art and function with his lathe. His work has been displayed at New Hope Arts, Perkins Art Center, Rosenbach Museum Shop, and other area galleries.

Steve Loar

Steve Loar is the Director of the Center for Turning and Furniture Design and is an Associate Professor in the Department of Art at Indiana University of Pennsylvania. He is recognized as an innovator in the development of the field of contemporary woodturning and has written and exhibited widely. His artwork is in seven museums and major collections throughout the United States and is featured in over 33 books and texts. In May 2005, after 22 years of teaching and administrative positions, he retired as a professor at the Rochester Institute of Technology (New York).

George Manns

There is a long tradition of woodworking in the Manns family. Over the years woodworking has been a necessity, a hobby, a source of income, and a challenge to four generations of woodworkers. As a custom furniture maker, George continues that tradition with his functional and creative designs.

A self-taught woodworker, George's experiences as a sawyer, lumber grader, and cabinet maker have informed the meticulous way he works. He continues to draw inspiration from his initial visit to the Wharton Esherick Museum and the woods that surround his own shop in northeastern Pennsylvania.

James Mario

James Mario opened his first hair salon at age nineteen, started painting at age twenty-two, and won his first photography award soon after. He designed a line of jewelry and carved his first sculpture "Mother and Child" from a piece of a walnut beam. His second sculpture "Mother and Child II" was carved from a quarter sawn walnut tree, which he notes was "a world of difference from the first." That sculpture won an award at a local art league.

His sculpture "Alvin" won an award at "The Art of the State" in Harrisburg. He has had many solo photo, painting, and sculpture exhibitions including a sculpture exhibit at *Creations in Wood Gallery*, Hockessin, Delaware. James recently won the sculpture award at the Wayne Art Center.

John Matthews

John Matthews is a ceramicist who grew up in Lancaster, Pennsylvania. After his first visit to the Wharton Esherick Museum, his focus shifted to the arts. John received his BA in studio art from Penn State and then an advanced degree at Tyler School of Art. He teaches ceramics at Conestoga High School in Chester County, Pennsylvania, and works in his studio in Yellow Springs, Pennsylvania.

Alphonse Mattia

One of the country's leading furniture makers, Alphonse Mattia dismisses the dichotomy between functional and non-functional objects. He prefers instead the concept of usefulness – something that conveys meaning and emotion along with utility. Mattia has taught in many universities and summer workshops. He is currently teaching at The Center for Turning and Furniture Design at Indiana University of Pennsylvania. He has received fellowships from The Massachusetts Artists Foundation and The National Endowment for the Arts. His work is included in the permanent collections of the Museum of Fine Arts, Boston, the Yale Gallery of Art, the Philadelphia Museum of Fine Arts, the Museum of Art and Design, the Renwick Gallery of the Smithsonian Museum of Art, and the Carnegie Museum of Art. [Web: www.alphonsemattia.com]

Aurora McFee

Aurora McFee, is a printmaker enrolled in her junior year at Rhode Island School of Design. She has worked as a docent for the Wharton Esherick Museum and is a teaching assistant as well as lithography and relief monitor at RISD. McFee received the U.S. Congressional Art Award for the years of 2007, 2008, and 2009. Most recently, her work has been shown in the Print Making Triennial at the Woods Gerry Gallery. She will be traveling to Japan to study traditional Japanese paper making and will intern at Second State Press and the Wharton Esherick Museum this summer.

James McNabb

James McNabb received a bachelor's degree in woodworking and furniture design from the School for American Crafts at Rochester Institute of Technology and is pursuing a master's degree from the Center for Turning and Furniture Design at Indiana University of Pennsylvania. His work has been featured in several local and national exhibitions, and can be seen in several publications including *500 Tables*, by Lark Books. James's work combines traditional craft techniques with contemporary forms, and often utilizes state of the art digital technology.

Mira Nakashima

Mira Nakashima was born in Seattle, Washington, in 1942, was incarcerated in Idaho during the war, but grew up in New Hope, Pennsylvania, where her father, George Nakashima, over time, built his home and studio. Graduating Cum Laude from Harvard University in 1963, she received a master's degree in architecture from Waseda University in Tokyo in 1966. After raising a family in Pittsburgh, she returned to the Nakashima Studio in 1970 and apprenticed to her father until his passing in 1990, when Mira became the creative director of the Nakashima studios.

Mira's designs, named "Keisho" ("continuation" in Japanese) translates to mean preserving the methods and techniques embraced by her father and working from the same wood-pile. She has also continued her father's dream to construct Peace Altars for each of the continents of the world. Mira received a Gold Medal for Excellence in the Decorative Arts from the National Arts Club in New York in 2008.

In addition to her design work, Mira published *Nature Form and Spirit*, a book on the Nakashima legacy which was accompanied by a series of exhibits across the country. [Web: www.nakashimawoodworker.com]

Matt Neff

Matt Neff is a mixed media artist and printmaker who teaches printmaking and manages the Common Press and print shop at the University of Pennsylvania. Selected Exhibitions: *Refugee Reading Room,* Space 1026, Philadelphia, Pennsylvania; *Editions Artist's book fair,* with The Print Center, 548 west 28th Street, Chelsea, New York; *Pulling From History: Letterpress,* The Print Center, Philadelphia, Pennsylvania; *Copy Jam:* Colombia College Center for the book, Chicago, Illinois; *One Theme/Thirty Prints* (*Philagrafika* 2010), Free Library of Philadelphia, Philadelphia, Pennsylvania; *Sweet Spot*, (*Philagrafika* 2010) Center for Emerging Artists gallery, Philadelphia, Pennsylvania; *Works on paper 2009*, curated by João Ribas, Arcadia University Art Gallery, Glenside, Pennsylvania. [Web: www.mattneffonline.com]

Ryan Procsal

Ryan became interested in woodworking because he simply needed to build a stand for his aquarium. After learning the rudiments of the craft by studying books and television shows, Ryan learned to shape and sculpt wood by ambitiously replicating the designs of his Californian neighbor, Sam Maloof . Now, Ryan has developed his own graceful, sculptural furniture by integrating some classic designs with his own, distinct style. His shop, built in 1903, is a block away from his historic home, which he is carefully restoring in historic Pottstown, Pennsylvania. [Web: www.madebyprox.com]

Michael Puryear

Michael Puryear, a self-taught designer/furniture maker, has been practicing his craft for more than 30 years. The Museum of Art and Design, the Mint Museum, and the Peabody Essex are among the museums that have exhibited his work. Puryear's work has been published extensively, most recently in *Furniture with Soul* by David Savage, published by Kodansha. Michael has taught at the top craft schools around the country, including Penland, Haystack, and Anderson Ranch, to name a few. He is currently Associate Professor of Woodwork at the State University of New York, Purchase. [Web: www.michaelpuryear.com]

Norm Sartorius

Born on Maryland's Eastern Shore, Norm received a degree in psychology. Classes with noted wooden object makers, especially woodturners, and an eighteen-month work-study in studio furniture and sculpture provided foundation skills and awareness early in his career. He notes that "making work and sharing it with the public for three decades at retail shows taught me even more."

He adds, "My wife of twenty-nine years, Diane, has contributed greatly with her honest support and criticism."

Norm's spoon carvings can be found in seventeen public collections including the Philadelphia Museum of Art, Carnegie Museum of Art, and the Smithsonian's American Art Museum. [Web: www.normsartorius.com]

Sandra Scicchitani

Sandra earned her master's degree in painting at The Maryland Institute College of Art where she studied under Grace Hartigan. Soon after her graduation she exhibited large-scale paintings both locally and nationally in solo and group shows. When she began teaching at Montgomery and Bucks County Community Colleges she had access to the print studios, which allowed her to pursue her interest in the various methods and techniques of printmaking. As a consequence, her paintings impart the characteristics of a print, and often her prints appear quite painterly. Her work is included in private and permanent collections in New York, Delaware and Pennsylvania.

Mark Sfirri

Mark Sfirri was first exposed to the work of Wharton Esherick upon visiting *Woodenworks*, the inaugural exhibition at the Renwick Gallery of the Smithsonian in 1972, the year that Sfirri began studying woodworking under Tage Frid at Rhode Island School of Design. The concept and execution of Esherick's 1931 *Corner Desk* was inspirational to him and it remains his favorite piece of furniture. He has been researching the life and work of Wharton Esherick since 2006. He has published six articles about Esherick for *Woodwork* and *Journal of Modern Craft*.

Sfirri is a furniture maker and sculptor specializing in multi-axis turning. He has been teaching in the Fine Woodworking Programs at Bucks County Community College in Newtown, Pennsylvania, since 1981. In 2010 he received the Distinguished Educator Award, a national biennial award given by the Renwick Alliance of the Renwick Gallery. His work can be seen in the permanent collections of 16 major museums.

Paul Sirofchuck

Paul Sirofchuck views working with wood as a way of life, not an occupation. Trained as an architect, he has a passion for the exploration of design and construction, finding inspiration in the beauty of nature that surrounds his studio in the woods of western Pennsylvania. Much like Esherick, he continually experiments with organic shapes in a sculptural approach, often using figured slabs and burls as "jewels," creating a setting for them, much as a jeweler does with a diamond or ruby. His goal is to "allow the spirit of each piece of this living material to be recreated through my artistic vision." [Web: www.sirofchuckstudios.com]

John Sterling

John Sterling started building furniture and furnishings in his mid-twenties. He learned his craft gradually, by making mistakes, taking risks, experimenting with different techniques, and getting feedback from others. "I am a kinesthetic learner" he said, "so building pieces and seeing the results reinforced my skills and style slowly over time."

Johns work has changed dramatically over the last 15 years as he found his own style and voice. His work is heavily influenced by the American Arts and Crafts movement and individual craftsmen like George Nakashima and Wharton Esherick.

He regularly exhibits at the Philadelphia Invitational Furniture Show and various juried art shows on the east coast. He just received the award for furniture at the 12th annual works in wood show sponsored by the New Hope arts council. [Web: www.jcsterling.com]

Ward Stevens

Ward Stevens developed his woodworking skills at Bucks County Community College and North Bennet Street School in Boston. His work has been displayed at the Ironwood Gallery in Ridgefield, Connecticut, New Hope Arts, the Wayne Arts Center, and the Woodturning Center in Philadelphia. His turning work was published in the Fall 2007 issue of the *American Woodturner* and in the Winter 2011 issue of *Woodwork* magazine. A piece of his studio furniture was selected by the Furniture Society to appear in their annual journal, *Studio Furniture: Volume 5: The Meaning of Craft* and his reproduction of an 18th century oval stool was chosen for the Furniture Society's Faculty Selects 2008: [Web: www.wardstevens.com]

Holly Tornheim

In 1970 while a student at Antioch College, Holly Tornheim worked on a house building project in the foothills of the Sierra Nevada in Northern California. Modeled after a traditional Japanese farmhouse and a Mandan earth lodge, the house was built using local materials and without electricity. It was her first introduction to working with wood and led to a path through carpentry, door building, and furniture making to her present work. Her first carving was the center pole of a circular staircase. *Topographic Tray* is in the permanent collection of the Smithsonian American Art Museum. [Web: www.hollytornheim.com]

Daniel Shawn Turley

Shawn Turley developed a strong relationship with art growing up in West Virgina trailer parks. He studied interior design at Louisville Institute of Technology before moving on to the University of the Arts' Crafts Department, where he received his bachelor's degree specializing in wood. After working in cabinet shops, he went back to school and completed a master's degree in art education. He is currently working half-time as an elementary art teacher, while working on his career as a furniture maker. His work has been featured in three of the Wharton Esherick Museum's Thematic Woodworking Competitions, where he has twice received the "Members' Choice Award." [Web: www.dststudio.com]

George Wagner

George C. Wagner, a professor of psychology at Rutgers University, has been a serious woodturner for over a decade. His interest began with a pleasurable pastime – the restoration of Victorian-era furniture and the repeated need to reproduce or replace turned ornaments such as finials, pendants, and rosettes. Soon thereafter, he became a member of the Bucks Woodturners at Bucks County Community College in Newtown, Pennsylvania. This woodturning club was one of the very first in the nation, and its early members were founders of the American Woodturners Association. With their guidance and inspiration, George began to turn wood for its own sake, not merely replacing lost or broken parts. He has sold nearly 500 turned vessels in the past decade mostly through craft galleries in New Jersey. His work is currently represented in "Ebb" gallery in Hopewell, New Jersey.

Abe Warren

A self-taught artist, Abe Warren is a lifelong wood enthusiast with sawdust in his blood. Abe's study of wood began with splitting logs, giving him an education in tension and grain. By milling lumber, he developed a keen ability to predict the internal characteristics of a log by studying its external properties.

In addition to studying traditional furniture construction and reading countless books on wood, Abe is a consummate experimenter. He developed a natural-shaped butterfly joinery technique that has become his signature and is featured on the piece included in this exhibit.

Derek Weidman

Derek Weidman, born in 1982, is a sculptor living in rural Pennsylvania. He has dedicated his recent work exploring lathe-based sculpture. His approach involves multi-axis turning as the foundation of each piece, then further refines them with carving, burning, bleaching, and painting. This unique process allows him to create novel representation of a wide range of subjects, from those based on human anatomy to various animal forms. Derek approaches each piece by asking the basic question "What would this look like if rendered through the lens of a wood lathe?" Even with the most rigorous naturalism, an honest abstraction takes place.

Derek has studied with Mark Sfirri and draws inspiration from a wide range of sources – from nature to ancient mythology. [Web: www.weidmanwoodsculpture.com]

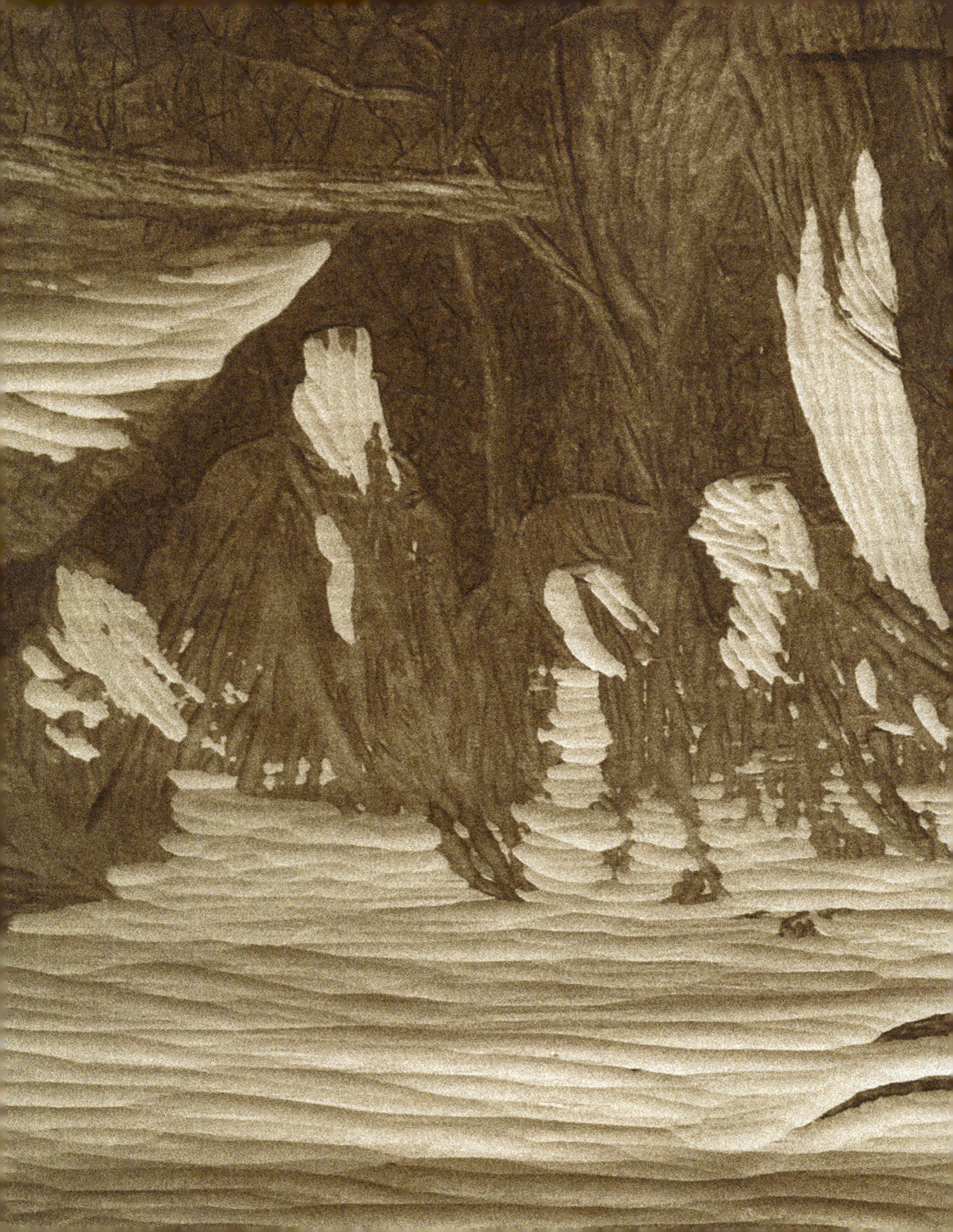